The Entrepreneurial Community College

Edited by
John E. Roueche and Barbara R. Jones

Foreword by George R. Boggs

Community College Press®
A division of the American Association of Community Colleges
Washington, D.C.

The American Association of Community Colleges (AACC) is the primary advocacy organization for the nation's community colleges. The association represents more than 1,100 two-year, associate degree–granting institutions and more than 11 million students. AACC promotes community colleges through six strategic action areas: national and international recognition and advocacy, learning and accountability, leadership development, economic and workforce development, connectedness across AACC membership, and international and intercultural education. Information about AACC and community colleges may be found at www.aacc.nche.edu.

Design: Brian Gallagher Design
Editor: Deanna D'Errico
Printer: Kirby Lithographic

Community College Press
American Association of Community Colleges
One Dupont Circle, NW
Suite 410
Washington, DC 20036

Printed in the United States of America.

ISBN 0-87117-367-0

CONTENTS

Foreword   v

Preface and Acknowledgments   vii

Introduction   ix

Chapter 1   Setting the Stage for Action: Entrepreneurship at Work
Suzanne L. Flannigan, Thomas G. Greene, and Barbara R. Jones   1

Chapter 2   A Wave of Innovation at Florida Community College
Steven R. Wallace   13

Chapter 3   NHMCCD: A Community Partner With Entrepreneurial Spirit
John Pickelman   23

Chapter 4   St. Petersburg College: An E-Spirited Institution
Carl M. Kuttler, Jr.   37

Chapter 5   Entrepreneurial Partnerships
Donald W. Cameron   51

Chapter 6   Embedding Entrepreneurialism: A Canadian Case Study
Robert A. Gordon   63

Chapter 7   A History of Entrepreneurship at Kirkwood Community College
Norm Nielsen   81

Chapter 8   Leveraging Resources: Entrepreneurship at Seminole Community College
E. Ann McGee   93

Chapter 9   Friend Raising and the Entrepreneurial President
David E. Daniel   99

Chapter 10   Education, Enterprise, and Entrepreneurship
Andrew M. Scibelli   109

Chapter 11   Entrepreneurial Leaders
Michael D. Summers and David H. McGilvray   117

Chapter 12   Entrepreneurial Risk Taking
Millicent Valek   125

Chapter 13   The Entrepreneurial College: Focusing on the Future
John E. Roueche and Barbara R. Jones   135

About the Contributors   143

Index   149

FOREWORD

What really determines the long-term quality of an institution? The characteristic that seems to pervade colleges that have a reputation for excellence is that their people have a strong sense of purpose. They share a commitment to the mission and values of the college, and they are not afraid to try something new to meet their objectives. They are proud of their traditions but are not constrained by past practice.

In today's environment of declining public resources and demands to do more with less, it is more important than ever that our community colleges become even more entrepreneurial. Their programs and services must be of high quality, but that is not enough to excel—the best community colleges will be those that are the most flexible and adaptive. The focus of the entrepreneurial college is not merely on making money but also on making things happen and developing resources so that the college can meet the needs of students and communities: Many of the ideas discussed in this book are not about fundraising but about how to expand the capabilities of the institution. It is important that a college's activities are compatible with and contribute to its mission and values.

Strong and creative leadership is, of course, important, but the entrepreneurial culture must pervade the institution. As the contributors indicate, the leaders are not so much creators as they are collaborators, facilitators, consensus makers, and incentive providers—and they must continually acknowledge the accomplishments and contributions of others. Perhaps the most important thing that college presidents and trustees can do is to develop and nurture a culture that rewards risk and innovation while allowing for failure. Although the contributors have highlighted their successes, they would be the first to admit that success would not have been possible had the college's people been afraid to risk failure. Resistance to change and fear of uncertainty are barriers that must be overcome if a college is to be ready for opportunity and successful in an environment of constrained resources.

John Roueche and Barbara Jones have done a great service to community colleges with this timely publication. The contributors discuss the many wonderful things that their colleges are doing in the areas of fundraising and friend raising, building strategic alliances and partnerships, recruiting international students, sharing facilities, providing business and industry training, procuring military contracts, leasing land and facilities, delivering training in other countries, and undertaking legislative lobbying. Many other community college leaders can report significant entrepreneurial activities on their campuses; there are a great many examples of creativity and innovation on community college campuses today. However, the ideas discussed in this book provide some of the best examples of the entrepreneurial spirit that will be ever more necessary for our colleges to thrive in the future. *The Entrepreneurial Community College* is an important book for all who are involved in community colleges.

George R. Boggs
President and CEO
American Association of Community Colleges

PREFACE AND
ACKNOWLEDGMENTS

Environmental factors currently affecting today's community colleges either will cause irreparable damage to their fiscal health and organizational structure or contribute to their rebirth—transforming systems and processes to meet current and future challenges successfully. In our effort to understand the circumstances in which we find ourselves in this special community college world, we discovered multiple emerging realities.

- During the 2003 academic year, North Carolina's 58 community colleges estimate that they turned away 56,000 students.
- College enrollments at most institutions are projected to increase by 13% in the next decade.
- Community college budgets are not growing at a rate commensurate with enrollment growth.
- In 2003, state appropriations for community colleges in some states decreased by 13.6%.
- Most community colleges anticipate the retirement of almost half their faculty and administrative staff.
- Since Oregon's financial crisis began, its community colleges have lost $35.3 million and stand to lose approximately $19 million more in 2004 and again in 2005.
- Community college campuses, buildings, and infrastructures are deteriorating quickly, jeopardizing the safety and effectiveness of their learning environments. (Jamilah, 2004; Sliverman, 2003)

Although community colleges have always faced challenges, ongoing community support and inherent resiliency have helped them conquer many of their diverse problems. However, research suggests that resting on reputation and traditional ways of doing business will not deal sufficiently with the problems we highlight here. In *Bowling Alone*, Putnam (2000) observed

> The final false debate to be avoided is whether what is needed to restore trust and community bonds in America is individual change or institutional change. Again, the honest answer is "both." America's major civic institutions, both public and private, are somewhat antiquated a century after most of them were created and they need to be reformed in ways that invite more active participation. (p. 413)

Change may be polemic for many; for others, it is a chance to explore new opportunities, to reshape and reinvent the organization. We agree that it is a serious and special gift. The contributions in this book, by some of the most successful community college leaders in the country, convince us further that it is time for reform and innovation and for community colleges to embrace entrepreneurship in new ways and to new degrees.

The Entrepreneurial Community College showcases best practices and introduces effective strategies for increasing revenue and reducing costs. It is a work born from our passion for community colleges and their ability to transform lives daily. In essence, this book is an anthology of hope.

We appreciate and acknowledge the contributions made by an extraordinary group of authors, who, in some chapters, combined messages from their leadership teams. We offer our profound gratitude to these community college entrepreneurial leaders for the extraordinary time and effort they invested in sharing their colleges' experiences.

We also appreciate the generous contribution of Suanne Davis Roueche, Senior Lecturer, Community College Leadership Program, at The University of Texas at Austin, and editor of publications at National Institute for Staff & Organizational Development. Her insights, sincerity, sense of humor, and phenomenal editing abilities contributed to the successful completion of this project.

Finally, we dedicate this book to current community college leaders and others aspiring to become entrepreneurial leaders. Peter Drucker observed, "Successful entrepreneurs do not wait until 'the Muse kisses them' and gives them a 'bright idea'; they go to work" (p. 34). The best practices presented in these chapters offer engaging strategies for becoming entrepreneurial in these unsettling times. With genuine enthusiasm for all that is possible in the entrepreneurial college, we hope this book represents a valuable guide and a first step toward transformation.

REFERENCES

Drucker, P. (1985). *Innovation and entrepreneurship: Practices and principles.* New York: HarperCollins.

Jamilah, E. (2004, September). Tuition is up 11.5% at community colleges, survey finds: State budget cuts are blamed. *The Chronicle of Higher Education, 50*(5), 43.

Putnam, R. D. (2000). *Bowling alone.* New York: Simon & Schuster.

Silverman, J. (2003, March). Battered by budget blows, Oregon colleges shut down to the bone. *Community College Week, 15*(16).

INTRODUCTION

John E. Roueche and Barbara R. Jones
—The University of Texas at Austin

If we are to smooth the transition between the old, dying civilization, and the new one that is taking form, if we are to maintain a sense of self and the ability to manage our own lives through the intensifying crises that lie ahead, we must be able to recognize—and create—Third Wave innovations.

—*Toffler (1981, p. 124)*

Speaking to the American Association of Community Colleges assembly on April 26, 2004, President Bush shared these thoughts:

> I've come today to talk about practical ways to make sure we lead the world when it comes to innovation and change. And by leading the world…we'll make America a hopeful place for those who want to work, and those who want to dream, and those who want to start their own business. And the community college system is an integral part of that strategy. That's what I'm here to tell you. It's an integral part so long as you're willing to listen to the needs of those who are looking for workers. It's an integral part so long as you continue to be entrepreneurial in the delivery of education. The community college system is a cornerstone of good economic policy. It's a cornerstone of sound educational policy. And it's one of the reasons why I'm optimistic that America will lead—continue to lead the world when it comes to innovation and change. And that will be good for our people. That will be good for the revitalization of what I call the American spirit and the American dream.

The American spirit and dream are more alive in community colleges than anywhere. In responding to the forces in society that are reshaping the world and the immediacy with which workers will require retraining or updating of job skills to maintain a vital economy, community colleges must act quickly, effectively, and decisively. They must reconsider operational strategies and become engineers of innovation and transformation—applying equal and positive pressure to the external forces that are driving change. And, as President Bush made clear, community colleges will need to be "entrepreneurial in the delivery of education."

Changes in the world of higher education are occurring at a dizzying pace. As a college community turns to address a challenge in one direction, a new and unexpected challenge propels it in another. Technology, globalization, accountability, recruitment and retention, workforce development, diversity, and accreditation each represent full-time and compelling work. All are challenged by funding issues.

> We see declines in traditional funding sources as demands for services increase, competition in the educational marketplace [becomes] more intense and competitors more sophisticated, current trends in workforce development bringing new meaning to collaboration and articulation, expanding classroom and workplace technologies, and impending retirements and diverse hiring strategies changing the teaching and leadership landscape. Taken together, they will continue to create fundamental change for community colleges and will affect dramatically the way we work. (Roueche, Roueche, & Johnson, 2002, p. 10)

Uncertainty is not new to the private sector. Business and industry are accustomed to overcoming challenges by seeking innovative strategies that ensure competitiveness and cutting-edge technology while meeting the needs of demanding customers—and doing so with less. In fact, doing more with less is a constant reality in the 21st century. To those who have been around long enough to witness the growth in the 1960s and 1970s of community colleges and their bumpy financial journey through the 1980s and 1990s, it is clear that today's funding crises are different. As was indicated by the National Association of State Budget Officers in its 2004 report, *Budgeting Amid Fiscal Uncertainty*, "Nearly every state was in fiscal crisis…during 2003" (p. 5).

Although we do not intend to minimize the importance of the challenges facing community colleges, this book is not about catastrophe. On the contrary, this book is about hope, potential, and an honest examination of the community college environment and how creative ideas and people are shedding the past to transform organizations for the future. As Drucker observed in *Managing in Turbulent Times*, "An enterprise that has sailed in calm waters for a long time similarly needs to cleanse itself of the products, services, ventures that only absorb resources; the products, services, ventures that have become 'yesterday'" (2002, p. 43).

Unfortunately, higher education professionals as a whole have never been fond of change. In fact, over the past 50 years, most colleges have not witnessed significant change in their missions. It is interesting to note that more than a decade ago, The Wingspread Group on Higher Education indicated that "Education is in trouble, and with it our nation's hopes for the future. America's ability to compete in a global economy is threatened" (1993). Such an ominous forecast ought to have inspired college personnel to rally and refocus. Sadly, at many community colleges, this did not happen. Some merely hit the snooze button on the national wake-up call and now are less prepared for turbulent times and the subsequent changes that must be made. However, such has not been the experience and behavior at all colleges.

There are many powerful examples of community colleges that have responded to the wake-up call by taking more than a casual glance at their mission and organizational structure.

These colleges have confronted their long-term traditions and habits and decided to try something new. In the true sense of entrepreneurship, they have elected an alternative course to program and service delivery as they reinvent themselves almost daily.

In *The Third Wave*, Toffler observed that as society constructs a new "infosphere" for a third wave civilization, "we are imparting to the dead environment around us not life but intelligence" (p. 168). For a community college, becoming entrepreneurial represents a new way of thinking, using acquired intelligence about the world surrounding the college. New waves of invention are born of imagination, creativity, and courage to change. In the 1960s, pioneers of the community college recognized that its mission was incongruent with societal demands and therefore ill-prepared to help colleges face the challenges of the future. These leaders had the courage and fortitude to suggest a better way of doing business, to radically and undeniably alter the focus, mission, and future of 2-year colleges.

At the 1963 UCLA Conference on Establishing Junior Colleges, Edmund Gleazer, president of the American Association of Junior Colleges (as AACC was then called), shared his perspectives of opportunities for the 20 to 30 new colleges that were opening each year. He suggested prospects for innovation and interpretations of the college to the community. These same opportunities exist today. At present, an equally entrepreneurial, innovative breed of leaders is forging a new identity for community colleges. They are recognizing the potential of change and are proactively, if not aggressively, seeking to transform their colleges. They recognize that the entrepreneurial college must think differently about how it is organized and about the roles and responsibilities of its employees. They understand that, as entrepreneurial leaders, they must engage in responsible risk taking, seek partnerships with a variety of constituents, reexamine their college's mission, and transform the college's culture.

Their focus is not on activities that the college pursues, but on how it pursues them. They fit in the new innovation regime of the 21st century: dream, explore, invent, pioneer, and imagine (Kuratko, 2003). The leaders who share their stories in this book are dreamers, explorers, inventors, and pioneers with exceptional imaginations. They have transformed their colleges into entrepreneurial enterprises successfully and are disarming the formidable challenges of the day.

This book is about these transformations. It is a testament and authentication of courageous and innovative college leaders and their teams who decided to take charge of their destinies. These entrepreneurial leaders enthusiastically embrace change and innovation. Their stories represent a new voice in community college administration and an entrepreneurial way of doing business in turbulent times. The following are synopses of stories told in the chapters of this book.

- Florida Community College at Jacksonville (FCCJ) moves to the steady rhythm of growth and development in the region, a driving force in entrepreneurial activities. An award-winning and nationally recognized college, FCCJ is the largest provider of education and training for the U.S. Navy, providing extensive training to other branches of the military as well. President Steven R. Wallace identifies for the reader strategies that FCCJ used to secure multimillion dollar contracts and introduces the concept of revenue-generating institutes.
- For John Pickelman, chancellor of North Harris Montgomery Community College District (TX), entrepreneurship is all about relationships. Pickelman demonstrates how shared values, interests, and goals can produce unique, cost-effective, successful,

and long-lasting partnerships and how decentralization, risk taking, and innovation helped foster an entrepreneurial culture. Among other collaborations, the district engineered the building of a joint library (Cy-Fair College and Harris County Public Library) and a fire station on the Cy-Fair campus.

- St. Petersburg College (SPC) in Florida has a rich history of entrepreneurial activity. With a beautiful location, low cost-of-living index, and plenty of room for growth, SPC is situated perfectly for practicing and perfecting innovation. And it has done just that. Under the leadership of SPC President Carl M. Kuttler, Jr., the college has embraced entrepreneurship enthusiastically and successfully. Entrepreneurship, or the e-spirit, as it is referred to at SPC, is alive and well. Kuttler presents four case studies of particular importance demonstrating the college's innovative resource development and successful strategic alliances.

- Jamestown, North Carolina, is far from Wall Street and Silicon Valley, but Guilford Technical and Community College (GTCC) reaches beyond the boundaries of the city to offer programs and services to the citizens of Guilford County in extraordinary ways. GTCC's President Donald W. Cameron has been facilitating innovation and invention for 14 years. Among other efforts, he has applied entrepreneurial tactics to create a state-of-the-art culinary technology facility, the Larry Gatlin School of Music, and the Quick Jobs With a Future program.

- Entrepreneurship in the community college system is not just an American ideal. Humber College Institute of Technology and Advanced Learning in Toronto, Canada, serves a city of more than 12 million ethnically diverse citizens and has not allowed itself to be limited by legislative restrictions that prevent the college from gaining revenue through local taxation or capital improvement campaigns. Rather, it has built a portfolio of entrepreneurial programs that can be packaged and delivered to students in Canada and throughout the world. Humber President Robert A. Gordon illustrates how the college's view of global education has expanded and the community has responded by creating a resilient and inventive entrepreneurial culture that secures sufficient revenues to be independent of government support.

- According to Kirkwood Community College (IA) President Emeritus Norm Nielsen, the vision of the college is to invent, develop, and deliver learning solutions for the 21st century. And the college has more than succeeded in this endeavor. At Kirkwood, entrepreneurship begins with an innovative board and is strengthened by partnerships with local business and industry. One obvious example was Kirkwood's response to the tragedy of September 11, 2001, when, through innovation and ingenuity, the college created the National Mass Fatalities Institute, providing national leadership in terrorism-response training and other services and training in emergency preparation.

- It is difficult not to be an entrepreneurial college when everyone in the college is responsible for fundraising. Such is the philosophy of E. Ann McGee, president of Florida's Seminole Community College (SCC). McGee employs her "45-second elevator speeches" and her "120 days, 120 speeches" plans as focused marketing strategies to enhance college fundraising and minimize competition from successful community colleges in the region. Leveraging resources, most often of the human kind, SCC raised millions of dollars to build and expand facilities.

- Midland, Texas, represents more than just the hometown of George Bush or the location where baby Jessica fell into a well. It is a place where strong community life thrives and the citizens care about the resources provided by their college. The town is a virtual testament to the boom of the oil business, and Midland College has been the benefactor of its riches. In a true Texas way, President David E. Daniel weaves a tale of how friend raising ensures a steady flow of revenue and support. Daniel has successfully created an entrepreneurial momentum that has proved contagious and profitable in a small Texas town.
- Technical colleges, in general, have a history of entrepreneurial activity. Dependent on partnerships with local businesses and industry, these colleges are accomplished at developing and implementing programs and services that meet the needs of students and employers. However, in Massachusetts, under the leadership of Andrew M. Scibelli, president emeritus of Springfield Technical Community College (STCC), the college has gone well beyond the typical expectations of a technical college—adding transfer courses and expanding noncredit offerings over the years. STCC promotes entrepreneurial activity and is known nationally for entrepreneurship education and the creation of the National Association for Community College Entrepreneurship. With the successful development of entrepreneurial programs and partnerships, the college has made a significant impact on the economy of its community.
- The success of an entrepreneurial college is dependent on the quality of its leadership. Thomas Barton, president of Greenville Technical College (GTC) in South Carolina, epitomizes the entrepreneurial leader. For 42 years, Barton has led GTC, building approximately 1,000 partnerships with entities outside the college. As Michael D. Summers and David H. McGilvray describe, he is optimistic and fair, modeling his approach on coaching. And at GTC, winning is the name of the game. Whether the college is converting an abandoned shopping mall into a profit center or building partnerships with local universities to share resources and improve services, GTC is an entrepreneurial college and Barton a courageous leader.
- Lake Jackson, Texas, is known as the city of enchantment—perhaps because of its close proximity to the Gulf of Mexico and its bounty of resources, many of which are the benefits of being hometown to Dow Chemical Company. Brazosport College (BC), under the leadership of President Millicent Valek, is one of the recipients of this company's generosity. According to Valek, BC's entrepreneurial spirit is built on its long-lasting relationship with local industry, including Dow.

Although colleges may approach entrepreneurship differently, each telling a unique and compelling story, the impetus for change and innovation is the same. It is unlikely that state support will return to the same level community colleges enjoyed 20 or 30 years ago. But it is more likely that students will continue to enroll, seeking an affordable and accessible education.

In *Dateline 2000*, Dale Parnell predicted, "The 1990s will introduce us to the new age of technology, the new learning age, and it will bring rich possibilities as well as challenges for colleges and universities" (1990, p. 3). He pointed to the resiliency required of colleges to bounce back from setbacks and maneuver around obstacles. Although there were signs in the 1990s of the challenges ahead, no one in community colleges predicted the extent to which reductions in state support and increases in student enrollment would affect colleges nationally. For community colleges, the Y2K crisis was more than a computer glitch; it was a prophetic tap on the shoulder. How colleges respond to this tap is key to advancing the future of their missions.

The Entrepreneurial Community College, conceived and written with the intent of defining a new way of doing business, boldly suggests that all organizations can transform themselves to be flexible and responsive. The colleges and leaders profiled have made significant strides in cultivating the entrepreneurial ethos at all levels within their organizations. Recognizing the uncertainties of the future and appreciating the realities of the past, these colleges are seeking invention and innovation as they advance the mission of the community college through the entrepreneurial spirit.

We know of other colleges and other leaders whose stories could have been told here. We sought to capture a sample of the community college system by including both small and large colleges from rural and urban settings. The colleges featured here have made significant progress in organizational transformation and serve well as best practices for others just beginning or further developing their own journeys toward entrepreneurship. Their stories testify that community colleges are the wave of the future and the hope for a better tomorrow for all who pass through their open doors.

In Toffler's words, community colleges are creating third wave innovations. They are the institutions integral to President Bush's strategy to lead the world in innovation and change. For this reason, they can respond uniquely to environmental challenges more quickly than any of their counterparts in higher education. They are poised to reenergize the American spirit and revitalize the American dream.

REFERENCES

Bush, G. W. (2004). *Remarks by President Bush at the American Association of Community Colleges annual convention.* Retrieved August 6, 2004, from http://www.whitehouse.gov/news/releases/2004/04/20040426-6.html.

Drucker, P. (2002). *Managing in turbulent times.* New York: HarperCollins.

Kuratko, D. (2003). *Entrepreneurship education: Emerging trends and challenges for the 21st century* (2003 Coleman Foundation White Paper Series for the U.S. Association of Small Businesses & Entrepreneurship). Retrieved August 5, 2004, from http://www.usasbe.org/pdf/CWP-2003-kuratko.pdf

National Association of State Budget Officers. (2004). *Budgeting amid fiscal uncertainty.* Washington, DC: Author.

Parnell, D. (1990). *Dateline 2000.* Washington, DC: Community College Press.

Roueche, J. E., Roueche, S. D., & Johnson, R. A. (2002, April–May). At our best: Facing the challenges. *Community College Journal, 72*(5), 10–14.

Toffler, A. (1981). The third wave. New York: Bantam Books.

Wingspread Group on Higher Education. (1993). *An American imperative: Higher expectations for higher education.* Racine, WI: Johnson Foundation, Inc.

Chapter 1

Setting the Stage for Action: Entrepreneurship at Work

Suzanne L. Flannigan, Thomas G. Greene, and Barbara R. Jones

—The University of Texas at Austin

When Omid Kordestani showed up for his new job as head of sales at Google in May 1999, the place was a mess. Founders Sergey Brin and Larry Page . . . were working out of a cramped, disheveled office in Palo Alto. Their "business plan" wasn't much more than a series of notes scribbled on a whiteboard. Nearly all 12 employees had Ph.D.s in engineering or computer science, but nobody had a clue how the sophisticated search engine technology they were building was supposed to generate any money…"Sergey and Larry never really wanted to start a company," explains Jeff Ullman, former computer science professor at Stanford University and member of Google's advisory board. "They had hoped to sell Google to Yahoo for $1 million, but Yahoo wasn't willing to pay that much. So they launched the company as a last resort." Funny how things turn out. (Warner, 2004, paras. 1 & 2).

There is an axiomatic link between Google's story and the evolution of the entrepreneurial college. In its recent history, in responding to myriad challenges, the comprehensive community college has realized tremendous untapped potential. Change is imminent. Opportunities abound for generating revenue to offset declining state support. The leaders who have chosen to ignore the status quo are harnessing innovation and embracing change in ways that strengthen and expand their missions and transform their institutions.

INTRODUCTION

The dawning of the 21st century has coincided with enormous shockwaves that have and will continue to reverberate throughout the entire community college system. Converging forces have set the stage for what should be a momentous, illimitable, perhaps even radical rebirth of the comprehensive community college within this decade. Rapid innovation, societal change, and an uncertain world are reshaping the environment within which these institutions have functioned historically. Now more than ever, community colleges are realizing that business as usual is untenable. Traditional structures and systems, established when these colleges first opened, today limit their capacity to be productive. Colleges are looking instead toward innovative methods to transform themselves into flexible, adaptive, responsive, and financially secure entrepreneurial organizations.

The overarching challenge in this transformative process is starting on the journey; for those community colleges seeking to become entrepreneurial, the first step involves a giant leap of faith. Entrepreneurial organizations must choose risk taking, trust, and passion. They must cultivate an insatiable appetite for change, thrive on creative problem solving, and rely on courageous leadership. They will be shaped by people who have unique talents and abilities for identifying inventive responses to environmental challenges and who possess a sense of purpose and an unwavering commitment to achieving the college's mission. Leaders will set the pace for change, infusing the organization with a contagious entrepreneurial spirit.

At Springfield Technical Community College, President Andrew Scibelli believes that trusting in employees, putting them first, and building confidence and pride in performance ensure shared faith in the direction the leader sets for the college. "To be successful, one must encourage freedom of thought, innovation, and risk taking, and discourage run of the mill 'caretaker' mentality." Florida Community College President Steven Wallace adds, "entrepreneurial ventures are most successful when built on a compatible and nurturing foundation… the organizational synergies that result can be exceedingly important and beneficial to college performance."

Throughout the case studies in this book, similar views present innovative and creative solutions to current mounting challenges facing community colleges. The reader is introduced to the concept of the entrepreneurial college and its leader, to examples of innovative activities that generate revenue and enhance resources, to a picture of the future, and to how the entrepreneurial leader ultimately will transform the college.

CHANGES DRIVING ENTREPRENEURSHIP

From its idyllic beginnings to its most troubled immediacies, the community college has embraced challenges openly, responding to all who walk through its doors. The end of the depression, the GI Bill, and the Truman Commission set the stage for the emergence of the comprehensive community college. This new kid on the block offered hope for affordable and accessible education across this country. Business, government, and communities embraced the purpose of these colleges and were willing to provide the resources to support growth and development, resulting in an abundance of resources and state support.

Like an upstart new business with grandiose ideas, community colleges were busy fulfilling their emerging missions and coping with their burgeoning enrollments. Opening at a rate of one a week in the 1960s (Brint & Karabel, 1989), a more moderate growth continued through the 1970s and 1980s as the doors to the colleges opened widely to accommodate diversity, technology, and the changing needs of business and industry. People had faith that the colleges were doing the right thing, at the right time, in the right way.

In this 21st century, colleges find themselves in challenging circumstances. Declining state support and increased enrollments represent converging forces, driving change in the system. Leaders are facing a future of increased enrollments, advancing technologies, deteriorating buildings, and an impending mass retirement of faculty and administrators.

Money is one of the primary drivers of activity in any system. Traditional sources of funding are disappearing rapidly while needs are steadily increasing. In 2003, when 37 states made mid-year cuts to higher education totaling approximately $1.2 billion (Selingo, 2003), colleges recognized a trend indicating that other avenues of support would be needed. The 2003 cuts were not an anomaly; since 1980 the share of state funds used for higher education has dropped from 44% to 32% nationwide (Selingo, 2003).

State funding cuts have resulted in drastic cost-cutting measures. However, with increased enrollments, institutions can no longer afford to restrict programs and services, especially because half of all students in higher education are enrolled currently in community colleges. Thus, responding to enrollment growth and other serious challenges requires embracing change, accepting current realities, and being willing to do things differently—entrepreneurially. Colleges that choose to ignore the implications of change risk jeopardizing their missions. This need not happen. Colleges can reinvent themselves, draw on their innate entrepreneurial resiliency to respond creatively, and take advantage of this need to change. The stories of colleges and leaders featured in these chapters demonstrate genuine talents for shaping environments and navigating teams toward more entrepreneurial ways of doing business.

One example is Seminole Community College's new construction trades facility in Florida. Through a partnership with industry representatives, the college and key industry leaders raised approximately $6 million, including in-kind services of labor and materials, to fund the state-of-the-art Center for Building Construction. The center has enhanced enrollment in construction technology and met the training needs of the industry.

DEFINING ENTREPRENEURSHIP

Unfortunately, there is no common conceptual framework for discussing the basic principles—the essence—of entrepreneurship (Bygrave & Hofer, 1991). As one definition of many, this one from Humber College Institute of Technology and Advanced Learning, in Toronto, Canada, describes entrepreneurship as "the constant pursuit to initiate, establish and sustain ventures, relationships and/or partnerships." A reknowned economist, Joseph Schumpeter, defined entrepreneurship as the engine of economic development (McGraw, 1991). Knight (1921/1971) highlighted the importance of managerial activities as a key component.

Most dictionaries define entrepreneurship as the assumption of risk and responsibility in initiating business strategies or creating a new business. Other definitions include characteristics such as "responsible risk taking," "proactive responsiveness," and "high ambiguity tolerance." In education, definitions of entrepreneurship share common threads of "taking and creating opportunities within an institutional context that leads toward the generation of monetary profit for the institution and its participants" (Faris, 1998, p. 3). Although accurate for the community college, this definition captures only part of a multidimensional response to today's challenges.

Community college entrepreneurship involves a variety of initiatives. It represents creative routes to leveraging resources and generating revenue. At Seminole Community College, successful entrepreneurship is linked directly to leveraging resources. The college established the expectation that fundraising is everyone's responsibility. Foundation board members function under the edict, "give, get, or get off."

Most successful entrepreneurial initiatives described in this book involve unique cost-sharing partnerships, profit-generating initiatives, and other innovative ways to use resources and generate additional funds, including strategic alliances, business and industry training, programming, foundations, fundraising and friend raising, outsourcing, and legislative lobbying.

Strategic Alliances

Community colleges have a long history of forming partnerships with business, industry, community, and government organizations. Most have reorganized their technical occupational programs into a comprehensive workforce development department, with programs built from and around relationships with area businesses. Partnerships may lead to advisory committees or opportunities for student internships or jobs. They may lead to new initiatives that generate revenue or leverage resources.

Robert Gordon, president of Humber College Institute of Technology and Advanced Learning, defines partnerships as "cooperative relationships where parties have specified joint rights and responsibilities in common enterprises. When fully operational, these partnerships can become the catalysts for collaboration, providing the synergy for empowering people and creating new and entrepreneurial opportunities."

In addition to serving as catalysts for collaboration, as suggested by Gordon, partnerships contribute to the social and economic health of the community and the nation. Some community colleges have expanded the definition further by developing innovative partnerships with external constituencies to offset declining state support or reduce internal expenses through shared resources. National attention has turned toward the community college's role in promoting growth in American industries and changes in the country's economy, especially since President Bush established a $250 million community college initiative for workforce professionals to create partnerships and to train individuals for high-growth industries.

Business and Industry Training

Another entrepreneurial strategy is developing programs for business and industry training. As most community colleges' business and industry training services concentrate on noncredit offerings, colleges are free to pursue competitive pricing, charging fees consistent with the market demands and needs. These profit-generating units operate in a similar fashion to for-profit businesses: They do not receive state reimbursements and, therefore, must be self-sufficient.

Many colleges featured here have created training centers for business and industry. Brazosport College's Center for Business/Industry Training provides customized training classes, workshops, and seminars for business clients. Revenue from the center enables the college to maintain a balance in its reserves and support its base operations. Similarly, Kirkwood College's Training and Outreach Services Center offers business and industry a variety of modern facilities for training seminars and programs. The center, owned by AEGON USA, represents a partnership with the college in which both entities use the facilities.

Programming

Other than generating revenue, entrepreneurship leads to a fundamental shift in the way a college does business. Organizational synergy is required for entrepreneurship, transforming programs and services to respond better to students and residents in the community. Redesign of course offerings, instructional modalities, and semester lengths are a few of the programming changes indicative of an entrepreneurial college. Florida Community College embraces a 24/7 operational philosophy; classes are offered whenever and wherever needed.

Instructional programming at Humber College is entrepreneurial in its capacity to bring national attention to the institution. The Comedy College is built on a partnership with professionals in the comedy industry. Courses are structured such that students can take advantage of creative programming and hands-on experiences.

Foundations

Many community colleges have established foundations that seek private donations and keep private funds separate from tax dollars, accomplished by filing for a Section 501(c)(3) of the Internal Revenue Code. This classification allows a college foundation to receive and administer funds and gifts from private sources. Foundations serve as the recipients and holders of gifts and endowments. Because philanthropic activity is linked directly to relationships internal and external to the college, foundations must cultivate close relationships with the college president and college community, as well as community residents and stakeholders.

A foundation allows the college flexibility in fundraising and contributes to entrepreneurial activities. For example, under the leadership of President Thomas Barton, the Greenville Technical College foundation purchased a deserted shopping mall, with approval from the State Budget and Control Board. The college created a University Center where a number of 4-year universities could rent space for extension services. The remaining space is available for lease to local business organizations. The projected annual revenue for the college from this venture is $400,000.

Fundraising and Friend Raising

The foundation and college play key roles in fundraising. In some states, colleges are reluctant to engage in a bond election, because state dollars cannot be used for expanding or enhancing facilities. These colleges often turn to fundraising via a capital campaign as a means of generating additional dollars.

Another aspect of fundraising, friend raising, as identified by Midland College President David Daniel, is a philosophical shift, recognizing that friends made today contribute to funds needed tomorrow. Even when the college is not faced with an immediate financial need, seeking potential donors is still a priority. Daniel has generated millions of dollars for the college through his friend-raising activities. According to the chancellor of North Harris Montgomery Community College, John Pickelman, "Competence in relationships remains most important in making organizations places of realized potential." The financial level of gifts and endowments provided for any college depends largely on the extent to which donor relationships have been cultivated.

Outsourcing

Outsourcing, another entrepreneurial strategy, is often the most expedient way to offset costs and save money. Many community colleges outsource services such as grounds keeping and maintenance. Personnel costs, especially insurance and benefits, represent the largest percentage of the college's budget. Some colleges are moving to outsource technology services, faced with the realities of increased salaries necessary to maintain qualified technical employees. Other colleges outsource auxiliary services such as the bookstore and cafeteria. These contracts not only save dollars, but also they offer the college some percentage of operating profits.

Legislative Lobbying

During a lecture to a graduate class at The University of Texas at Austin, professor Wilhelmina Delco declared that the problem with community colleges is their inability to tell their story effectively. As a former representative in the State of Texas House, Delco explained that there is a lack of expertise among community college administrators in lobbying and getting external groups to buy into and provide support for the institution's mission. As if learning from that lecture, many entrepreneurial community colleges are finding that the ability to form long-term relationships with political figures and lobby successfully for funding plays a significant role in generating revenue and advancing the college mission.

THE ENTREPRENEURIAL LEADER

Although academic entrepreneurship and terms related to it have emerged only recently within the context of higher education, community colleges have a long history of academic entrepreneurial leadership. The pioneers of the community college movement had an inventive spirit and a creative vision. Their success seemed more dependent on who they were rather than on the leadership skills they possessed. Are entrepreneurs made or born? Is entrepreneurship an innate talent or an acquired skill? Do social and environmental changes drive entrepreneurial activities, or are entrepreneurs the drivers? According to a recent article in *USA Today*, entrepreneurs are born, and the real question is whether entrepreneurial characteristics can be taught. As CEO Richard Branson of Virgin Group observed, "There are definitely (entrepreneurial) traits which I inherited." Characteristics such as "creativity, drive and a willingness to take risks" are viewed as inherited traits; however, they are traits that can be taught" (Hopkins, 2004, para. 2).

This presupposition is supported by Bird (1988), who credited family history, previous entrepreneurial experiences, and a drive toward realizing a vision as variables associated with an entrepreneurial leader. Bird further suggested that entrepreneurs are now-oriented people; they focus on the present while planning for the future. They have a keen sense of what will be and are able to visualize how to navigate successfully from point A to point B. As flexible learners, they are able to adjust quickly as they respond to the changing environment, taking their entrepreneurial ideas from concept to practice.

Cartwright (2002, p. 6) identified seven traits representative of an entrepreneur:

- Vision
- Commitment
- Self-belief
- Discipline
- Risk taking
- Concern for the customer
- Creativity

Cartwright suggested that entrepreneurs are motivated by recognition and achievement and that entrepreneurship "is about moving forward and innovation" (2002, p. 10). As recognized by the dean of Howard's Business School, Barron Harvey, entrepreneurship is not limited to business but can develop anywhere (Hopkins, 2004). Freiberg and Freiberg (2004, p. 17) have identified some of the more common qualities of entrepreneurial leaders:

- They are all pioneers, not followers in their industries.
- They have a record of long-term success and extraordinary business results.

- Whether they are flamboyant or low-key, they are deeply dedicated to inspiring their people to higher levels of engagement and performance.
- They care about their people as individuals, not just assets or resources.
- They are all doing things radical enough to make people say, "That takes guts!"
- What they are doing can be replicated to help other businesses succeed.
- They all run organizations people would want to work in themselves.

Leaders of entrepreneurial organizations are unique, possessing qualities that set them apart from traditional CEOs. They take risks, creatively generate new sources of revenue, and innovatively and proactively respond to the uncertainties and challenges in changing times. In this book, we provide examples of successful community colleges and leaders who have used their entrepreneurial skills to respond to challenges facing their systems. Examples herein include Greenville Technical College's President Thomas Barton using the lessons he learned from the legendary Clemson football coach, Frank Howard, to instill a passion for winning, and President Ann McGee converting the lessons she learned as a vice president of marketing and fundraising into Seminole Community College's institutional philosophy that fundraising is everyone's responsibility. Such leaders demonstrate a genuine talent for shaping their environments and navigating their teams toward entrepreneurial ways of doing business. It is from this new ethos, this entrepreneurial culture, that creative, proactive approaches to generating alternative sources of revenue are born and that new leaders emerge to facilitate needed change.

In *Management Challenges for the 21st Century,* Drucker (1999) observed that people are living in a period of "profound transition." Drucker believed there are no more quick fixes or trendy techniques that will ensure a leader's success in a technologically advanced, global society. Neither individuals nor organizations can realize success if they continue with old assumptions. Results are mostly achieved by groups of individuals and do not depend solely on the leader. Drucker suggested that a key to effectiveness resides in a leader's ability to understand the people with whom he or she works—recognizing strengths and weaknesses. In addition, the leader should take responsibility for communications. This means determining what needs to be shared and how to disseminate information in a manner that matches the worker's ability to receive and understand the message.

Can the CEO of a college do it alone? Is one entrepreneur enough? A common theme that emerges at each of the colleges featured in the following chapters is the role that the board of trustees plays in ensuring the success of innovative practices. Guildford Technical College president Don Cameron attributes the entrepreneurial spirit of the board to much of the college's success. Management guru Warren Bennis (1976) observed more than 25 years ago that leaders are conceptualists. Possessing entrepreneurial visions, leaders of organizations can alter or affect the destinies of their institutions. Bennis suggested that educating board members about the differences between leadership and management contributes to minimum involvement in routine and mundane tasks for leaders.

Management theorists have speculated that an entrepreneurial approach to leading a company might prove to be the best strategy for ultimate organizational success. The vision of entrepreneurial leaders drives change, determining the strategic directions of any new organizational venture. Entrepreneurial ideas are seen as intentions and suggest that "intentionality is a state of mind, directing a person's attention (and, therefore, experiences and action) toward a specific object goal" (Bird, 1988, p. 442). These goals tend to focus primarily on the development of a new initiative or on reshaping existing ventures.

Entrepreneurs are one thing; leaders of entrepreneurial organizations are another. The latter serve as architects of change. Peck, who researched entrepreneurship as a significant factor in leadership adaptation, observed

> presidents are not the primary sources of the new ideas and creative efforts that characterize their colleges…Presidents in successful (entrepreneurial) colleges appear to perform more as collaborators, facilitators, consensus makers, and incentive providers than as creators. They work through and with the influential people on campus as well as through the organizational structure. They provide a context for change and are the primary formers of opinion on the campus. This means that creative response and innovation take place in a collaborative setting. (1984, p. 274)

As president of Kirkwood Community College, Norm Nielsen considered himself a facilitator whose primary objective was to motivate people to do their best. "If leaders acknowledge accomplishments, employees stay motivated. I strongly believe in the saying, 'There is no limit to what can be accomplished if it doesn't matter who gets the credit.'" Creating this culture requires leaders to embed values, beliefs, and norms of entrepreneurship throughout the institution. The role of leaders is to ignite the culture, making it come alive. First, these leaders must possess a genuine, unwavering commitment and concern for all employees.

> Executives who lead by creating a transformational or visionary paradigm build organizations, systems and cultures that respect, develop and truly appreciate employees who share their vision. The result is an organization that allows individuals to achieve reasonable dreams by fulfilling the organization's mission. (Eggers, 1999)

Second, these leaders must nurture and sustain culture; provide flexible, unwavering support; encourage innovation; instill creativity; facilitate change; trust, transform, inspire, and provide purpose; and truly care.

LOOKING TO THE FUTURE

Colleges and universities throughout America, including the community colleges presented here, are making great strides toward change—none perhaps more important than those initiatives that reduce reliance on state support. Establishing strategic alliances, endowments, and profit centers; leasing underutilized resources; and creatively sharing facilities are successful examples of innovative responses to diminishing taxpayer support. Some leaders realize that as state support continues its precipitous decline, creative endeavors alone may not be enough to ensure continued vitality. The time may come to take the next step courageously—to move beyond behavior—to cultivate an entrepreneurial spirit or ethos across and at all levels of the institution. This action creates hope that the autonomy and financial independence necessary to ensure the future vitality of this country's community colleges will be secured.

Transformation represents a profound undertaking, setting aside traditional organizational theory. Entrepreneurial community colleges represent a new paradigm that embraces the notion that these institutions are social entities, influenced largely by their people. Organizational design theorists Jelinek and Litterer suggested, "To understand how an entrepreneurial organization functions, we must first understand how the people in the organization choose to act on its behalf" (1995). On the surface, this perceptual shift appears simple; yet, the implications are profound. Flexibility and innovation must replace traditional, bureaucratic structures and insular cultures; people must be positioned at the center of the organization. Within entrepreneurial colleges, creativity sets the tone: A flexible, organic, supportive culture of healthy fanaticism provides a foundation for growth.

Employees connect to the inherent nobility within their individual college's mission—a connection that transcends self-interest for the common good. Pursuing a heroic cause inspires zeal, a personal commitment, and a sense of responsibility to important work. In *Guts! Companies That Blow the Doors Off Business-as-Usual*, Freiberg and Freiberg (2004) pointed to this zeal as a distinguishing characteristic of those who work in outstanding, entrepreneurial organizations: "Heroes are ordinary people who make the routine extraordinary, regardless of their job descriptions or where they sit on the organizational chart. People who bring the best of who they are to work every day inspire others to do the same" (2004, p. 218).

A responsive culture is only one characteristic of an entrepreneurial community college. Support systems and operational structures are realigned to mirror the autonomous, agile nature of entrepreneurship, freeing employees from restrictive rules and red tape so that they can creatively and collaboratively act in the best interests of their colleges. Does this imply that the institutions' policies, procedures, and operational systems can or should be ignored or abandoned? Hardly. It means that the planning and budgetary cycles, decision-making processes, and information and communication systems—a college's infrastructure—are streamlined and well run. In entrepreneurial organizations, these systems are efficient and flexible and support the creative efforts of the employees.

In entrepreneurial community colleges, influence and leadership follow expertise rather than a formal organizational flow chart. Those who demonstrate leadership and initiative are those who lead; those who identify a problem are those who are authorized to solve it creatively. Employees are empowered. They are entrusted to accomplish goals in their own ways. This trust engenders a resilient, unwavering commitment by employees to their college and mission. Specific roles and responsibilities are not absent. Rather, they remain flexible and open enough to incorporate the whole individual. Members' roles are built around their unique strengths, talents, and interests, as much as they are based on needs to accomplish specific, often repetitive tasks.

Rules and regulations no longer dictate actions; they serve only to provide guidance to individuals who possess a clear understanding of what they must and should do. This follows a strong commitment to the missions of their organizations. In entrepreneurial institutions, people, not policy, drive progress and change. Employees develop the ability to tolerate ambiguity and the grit and bravura to use it as a source of renewal.

Entrepreneurial community colleges thrive on uncertainty. Institutional planning exists but on a much shorter, more responsive cycle that is intended to prepare for, not predict, the future. Employees feel grounded in intuition, able to step outside of their comfort zones and exercise the initiative, creativity, and chutzpah to overcome obstacles, recognize opportunities, and pursue new, untested solutions. Risk taking serves as the wellspring of innovation and is the defining characteristic of entrepreneurial organizations. For enterprises seeking to become entrepreneurial, responsible risks must be taken. But risk taking occurs only when the fear of failure is reduced or eliminated. In entrepreneurial organizations, failure is interpreted as an opportunity to learn. The extraordinary amounts of energy that typically go into establishing policies and enforcing rules are no longer necessary. Trust and an unwavering commitment to the mission of the college ensure integrity. Sanford Shugart, president of Valencia Community College, summarizes the challenge: "Institutions do not render authentic human service; only people do." This is the challenge for all entrepreneurial colleges.

CONCLUSION

Community colleges become entrepreneurial only when they position themselves strategically to take advantage of rapidly changing times and when critical behaviors are at work throughout all levels of the institution. It is this infusion—this ethos—that creates synergy, resulting in flexible, highly responsive, self-sustaining organizations that are less reliant on outside support for survival. The task for community colleges is to develop this entrepreneurial spirit in every person, department, and process.

Many community colleges are embracing the challenges before them. Although forces are daunting and hard work lies ahead, the colleges and their leaders profiled here have accepted the task of reinventing their colleges in preparation for the uncertain times to come. All of these community colleges are becoming entrepreneurial colleges.

Entrepreneurship is not an individual act, but a collaborative endeavor. Individuals may be entrepreneurs, but no one can create an entrepreneurial organization alone. The leader is a source of creativity and change, but true transformation requires the dedication of many to build this special culture of innovation. It is a mindset rather than a skill set. It is a transformation, not a technique. We invite the reader to share in the journeys that follow here, to learn firsthand how these leaders have led their colleges to extraordinary achievements and to remarkable levels of entrepreneurial success.

REFERENCES

Bennis, W. (1976). *The unconscious conspiracy: Why leaders can't lead.* New York: Amacom.

Bird, B. (1988). Implementing entrepreneurial ideas: The case for intention. *Academy of Management Review, 13*(3), 442–453.

Brint, S., & Karabel, J. (1989). *The diverted dream.* New York: Oxford University Press.

Bygrave, W. D., & Hofer, C. W. (1991). Theorizing about entrepreneurship. *Entrepreneurship Theory and Practice, 16*(2), 13–22.

Cartwright, R. (2002). *Creating the entrepreneurial organization.* Oxford, UK: Capstone.

Drucker, P. (1999). *Management challenges for the 21st century.* New York: HarperBusiness.

Eggers, J. H. (1999, May–June). Developing entrepreneurial growth. *Ivey Business Journal, 63*(4), 76–82.

Faris, S. K. (1998). *Community colleges: Innovators of entrepreneurial spirit.* (Digest No. 98-4). Kansas City, MO: CELCEE Kauffman Center for Entrepreneurial Leadership. (ERIC No. ED 433 886).

Freiberg, K., & Freiberg, J. (2004). *Guts! Companies that blow the doors off business-as-usual.* New York: Doubleday.

Hopkins, J. (2004, April 7). Entrepreneurs are born, but can they be taught? *USA Today*, p. B1.

Jelinek, M., & Litterer, J. (1995). Toward entrepreneurial organizations: Meeting ambiguity with engagement. *Entrepreneurship: Theory and Practice, 19*(3).

Knight, F. H. (1971). *Risk, uncertainty and profit.* Chicago: University of Chicago Press (Original work published 1921).

McGraw, T. K. (1991). Schumpeter ascending (re-emerging intellectual interest in entrepreneurship, innovation, and economic development). *The American Scholar, 60,* 371–392.

Peck, R. D. (1984). Entrepreneurship as a significant factor in successful adaptation. *The Journal of Higher Education, 55*(2), 269–285.

Selingo, J. (2003). The disappearing state in public higher education. *The Chronicle of Higher Education, 49*(25), 3.

Warner, M. (2004). What your company can learn from Google. *Business 2.0.* Retrieved August 10, 2004, from www.business2.com/b2/web/articles/0,17863,634420,00.html

CHAPTER 2

A WAVE OF INNOVATION AT FLORIDA COMMUNITY COLLEGE

Steven R. Wallace
—Florida Community College at Jacksonville

> The challenge isn't to keep your eye on big competitors.
> It's to pay attention to the innovators.
> —*Dave Duffield, president and CEO, PeopleSoft, Inc.*

Innovation is the definitive essence of individual and organizational entrepreneurship. Although there are many striking examples of extraordinary innovation in America's community colleges, institutions of higher education continue, in the main, to be highly tradition bound. Consequently, ubiquitous innovation is not a cultural norm or an urgent imperative in contemporary postsecondary education. Although not explicitly required, innovation and entrepreneurial behavior may provide highly effective solutions to many of the challenges community colleges face.

In the absence of a mandate to innovate, college officials have an important choice to make as they determine how to respond most effectively to the needs of their students and community. In some situations, traditional modalities of institutional conduct are sufficient (and, sometimes, politically necessary). In other instances, a compelling need may exist to advance the services and capabilities of the college faster and more aggressively. Such is the case for Florida Community College at Jacksonville (FCCJ), given the significant growth and development of the region the college serves. The leadership of the college is convinced that significantly high levels of innovation are essential to the realization of the college's full potential.

FCCJ serves a population of approximately 1.3 million people on Florida's northeast coast. Founded in 1965, the college is the second largest of the state's 28 community colleges. The five campuses and five major education centers collectively enroll about 60,000 students each year. Consistent with the character of the large and diverse service area, the college features urban, rural, virtual, global, and military elements.

FCCJ represents one of America's most comprehensive transfer colleges. In addition to traditional credit courses, the college offers workforce development, adult and continuing education, and cultural programs. It offers preparation in almost every academic and career area imaginable, including 215 degree and certificate programs. FCCJ's recent emphasis on distance learning courses and programs has resulted in a significant and rapidly growing online education program enrolling in excess of 20,000 students each year. The college's technology capabilities and services were ranked first in the nation by the Center for Digital Education in 2003 and again in 2004, following a number two ranking by the Yahoo Internet Group in 2002. Contributing to that recognition is a strong professional development program, named best in the country in 2002 by the National Council for Staff and Program Development.

The college takes particular pride in its service to the U.S. military. Through its successful Military Education Institute, FCCJ has become one of the largest providers of education and training services for the U.S. Navy. Programs range from the highly specialized, such as nuclear power and weapons of mass destruction security, to traditional degree programs. With similar programs for other branches of the military, FCCJ enrolls students in every time zone on the planet continuously. To provide these programs at the requisite level of quality, a learner support center offers technical assistance, student services, and academic support to remote students around the clock.

I view the college and, arguably, all community colleges as being in the early stages of the second major of wave of innovation. The first wave was driven by powerful and urgent demographic forces that demanded extraordinary and unprecedented access to higher education. While access remains central in the second wave, economic drivers have become more prevalent as the country moves into a knowledge-based, global economy. The fact that nearly all employees need to be prepared as knowledge workers makes FCCJ's mission more relevant and vital than ever before. Although many challenges will be encountered in the second wave, at FCCJ we are confident that we are more than equal to the task. Rapid and responsive adaptation has always been a hallmark of community colleges. This opportunity, however, will not be realized without significant innovation in nearly every dimension of the college. FCCJ welcomes this challenge and is fully invested in the requisite transformative processes.

Jack Welch, former CEO of General Electric, has been known to say that if the outside of the organization is changing faster than the inside, the end is near. Although this observation aptly describes the current situation of higher education, it provides no guidance regarding the changes colleges need to make. Even more significantly, it provides no answer as to how to finance the innovations in an era of insufficient funding. College leaders are responsible for finding effective solutions to these difficult challenges; at FCCJ, my colleagues and I have made some real progress in that regard. Our analysis suggests that an organizing scheme for the development and funding of innovation is driven by three significant types of opportunity: strategic alliances, contracting, and business development. Each type is described here, with examples of current applications at FCCJ.

STRATEGIC ALLIANCE WITH XEROX

Historically, partnerships between colleges and businesses too often have been largely rhetorical in substance and unsustainable economically. Such relationships lacked the essential ingredient: long-term, significant mutual gains (most important, in business terms). Educators have not always understood well the profitability requirements of the private sector and often have failed to perceive the incredible collaborative opportunities.

The college's motivation to partner with Xerox was essentially the result of the failure of our offset printing program. With the emergence of digital printing technology, our program had become obsolete, despite considerable support through our College Program Revitalization process. Although it was clear that the program needed to be replaced by a contemporary digital printing program, the college did not have the required in-house expertise, or the funds, to make this change. At the same time, Xerox was finding its customers reluctant to purchase large digital reprographic systems without the assurance that the necessary technicians would be available.

Xerox was struggling financially in the post–September 11, 2001, economic recession and needed to reduce operating costs. Discussions between the South Campus president and the regional Xerox manager led to a creative and mutually advantageous solution. Xerox agreed to support a new digital printing technology program at the campus, pledging curriculum development assistance, staff support, and top-of-the-line products. The campus committed to converting the printing program to a digital focus and to renovating appropriate facilities in a visible, accessible location. The partners then collaborated in the development of the new curriculum as facilities were prepared and equipment was installed. Program marketing and student recruitment began shortly thereafter.

The new program provided significant benefits to both parties immediately upon opening. Students found the digital technology program to be far more attractive than the previous program. The continuous presence of the Xerox technical staff offered essential expertise and added an exceedingly valuable real-world connection. Because the Xerox Center is an authentic production operation with extraordinary capabilities, and because the college needs actual project work for students to do, most of the college's printing projects were shifted to the new program.

Substantial cost savings have been realized since the creation of this program, along with significant gains in the quality and delivery time of printing services. Unanticipated academic benefits have been discovered as well. For example, faculty can develop materials on their own computers and send them via Internet for immediate printing and binding. College employees have been thrilled by the quality and fast turnaround time of many types of print projects. Correspondingly, students in the new program benefit substantially from the opportunity to apply the full range of digital printing processes in a simulated employment setting.

Shortly after the opening of the new program and facility, there was a surprising and positive development. Xerox Corporation decided to close its Jacksonville office and use the new college facility as its regional showroom and demonstration center. All of the Xerox employees in the area became remote workers, using the new Xerox Center at South Campus as a home base. This development strengthened the relationship between the college and the company, added considerable economic value to the partnership, and strengthened the sustainability of the collaboration. Exceeding the expectations of both parties, this partnership serves as an excellent illustration of a strategic alliance, affirmed by the campus president, Norman Will, who noted,

> Florida Community College's partnership with Xerox Corporation has produced multiple benefits. First, our students in the digital printing program have the daily opportunity to watch a high-volume, full-service digital print shop in operation. They see and hear the customer service issues, observe the ebb and flow of job volume, watch the response to technical problems or to

emergency demands, and generally get first-hand experience of what the career field is really like. Second, the students interact with digital print professionals at various skill levels, from a part-time college employee, to a more experienced full-time employee, to the highly skilled Xerox associate who is on staff as part of the contract between Xerox Corporation and the college. They see in these individuals the base-line skills required for entry-level employment and the advanced skills (both hard and soft) that will open doors to career advancement. Finally, students get to work on state-of-the art, industry-standard equipment, running real jobs for real customers. They learn to use the front-end software and to run the production print machine and the finishing equipment. The college could not afford to provide such high-end equipment in a typical instructional lab, but when it serves as the college's actual production equipment, the synergy makes it possible to give students the best possible experience.

Another level of benefit to the partnership has been its impact on the quality of instructional materials produced by faculty. A Xerox associate serves as an in-house sales representative for the services of the Digital Print Shop, and his outreach has educated faculty to the ease of producing custom course packs, lab manuals, and other print materials, as well as the conveniences of electronic file transmission and archiving. Color print volume has far exceeded initial estimates, as faculty discovered the value of including color graphics in their supplemental teaching materials. With print-on-demand capabilities and 24-hour turnaround, faculty will never run out of copies, or waste resources through overestimating demand. These services and capabilities have proven so successful that faculty in some disciplines are now exploring how to produce their own custom textbooks, which will result in more targeted instructional materials, cost savings to students, and a more energized and engaged faculty.

CONTRACTING WITH THE NAVY

Jacksonville is a Navy town, and the college has a long history of providing classes at local bases and on board ships. Because a comfortable relationship had been achieved, college staff could have maintained the status quo indefinitely. Leaders of the Open Campus saw, however, the potentially enormous opportunity to respond to the education and training needs of all branches of the military worldwide. The challenge was immense. Clearly, the existing staff of the campus had neither the time nor expertise to pursue programs on such a grand scale. After vetting the opportunity through the college's Continuous Dynamic Strategic Planning process, a new Military Education Institute (MEI) was formed to pursue training and education contracts aggressively with the U.S. military. Integral to this decision was the clear understanding that this was to be a high-risk, high-cost initiative with extraordinarily high-performance aspirations. The risk and cost were deemed acceptable because of the great potential rewards and because the new institute would be built on the substantial foundation of the college's long history of success with the Navy. In other words, we were certain that we could do this well.

Several essential foundations were laid from the start. One key strategic decision in the development of the MEI was that the new institute must be led by recently retired senior military officers who also possessed the requisite academic credentials. A former navy commander with a doctorate and MBA. was selected to lead the development of the institute. He proceeded to build an exceptional leadership team quickly. Because the development of the institute was underwritten by short-term risk capital, both the leadership team and the college understood how important it was for the MEI to become profitable as quickly as possible. In fact, one of the reasons the MEI was created was to generate residual revenue (profit) to support other programs and initiatives.

As a result of how it was launched, the MEI quickly became a remarkable success. The leaders of the MEI took extraordinarily wise steps at the outset. They began, for example, with an open mind, and they listened closely to the needs and concerns of the constituents. It was immediately apparent that although many tremendous opportunities existed, there was significant complexity in deployment that required responses outside of the range of traditional community college operations. That, in fact, was actually the genesis of the opportunities— colleges and universities were simply not responding to many of the military's greatest needs.

The creativity and responsiveness of the MEI leadership were rewarded quickly. Millions of dollars worth of contracts began to flow in so rapidly that the college's human resources systems were overwhelmed, and employment agencies had to be engaged to assist with the large hiring bursts. This occurred, however, because the MEI team had succeeded in another critical part of the equation—they had built the necessary relationships with military decision makers. They were able to do this because they came in as insiders with the credibility possible only when providers understand a client's needs, interests, and perspectives at a deep professional level.

The scope of MEI programs expanded exponentially as the success of projects opened doors to entirely new opportunities. Carol Spalding, the Open Campus president and chief administrator of the MEI described the evolution as follows:

> In 1999, Florida Community College capitalized on its 35-year tradition of providing onsite education to the military at Jacksonville's Naval bases. When the Navy began to emphasize both contracted and distance education, the college's Open Campus leveraged its Virtual College, contracted training unit, and Military Education Institute (MEI) to compete for the national military market.

The first successful proposal yielded a 5-year, $10 million contract to provide home-port training for four military occupational specialties in the local area. Based on the success of this contract, the college further pursued inclusion in the Navy College Program Distance Learning Partnership. As 1 of 4 community colleges and 10 universities selected by the Navy, the college expanded and accelerated its online credit offerings to meet the growing need for degree completion programs and became the Navy's designated provider for three AA degree programs and an AS in information systems. As a result of this contract, the college created a learner-support center to advise sailors pursuing degrees.

Increased concern regarding terrorist activities after September 11, 2001, created a unique military training challenge and presented the Navy with the task of finding additional resources to train its sailors in antiterrorism. The college, through a competitive bid process, was awarded a contract for antiterrorist training. Within a month, the college had hired trainers, contracted with shooting ranges, and graduated its first of many classes. As enrollment grew, the college realized it could not respond quickly enough with its normal hiring processes to meet the Navy's needs. The college developed a contract with a staffing agency to hire trainers more rapidly, solve the problems, and position MEI to react even more expeditiously to entrepreneurial opportunities.

MEI's executive director, a retired Naval officer and Naval Academy alumnus, networked through military professional meetings within the state and region to inform its members of the college's capabilities in responding to the military's training needs. These presentations generated an interest that led the U.S. Coast Guard, the U.S. Army, the U.S. Army National Guard, and the U.S. Marine Corps to sign memoranda of understanding with the college. An additional specific memorandum was signed with the Ft. Bragg army installation to articulate army CISCO training into FCCJ's AS degree in computer engineering technology. This outstanding partnership was recognized with a statewide Florida's Best award for exemplary educational partnership with employers.

By 2003, the college was serving 4,800 military students in distance learning, 2,342 military students in contracted Homeport Training, and 2,600 students a year at its military bases. The MEI has served as a catalyst in pushing the development of distance learning courses and services and in creating seven articulation agreements with 4-year universities. The income from the contracts has supported the new enrollment and the development of the degree and training programs. Also, the MEI contracts with the armed services have generated a relationship with soldiers and sailors, resulting in education road maps and transcripts that will serve them well as they work to complete their degrees and military training.

The success and growth rates of the MEI continue to stun observers. A consortium of similar programs across the country has been formed to enhance the capability to respond to the military's needs any place, any time. The MEI has completed an ongoing series of contracts in areas such as search and seizure, shipboard security, armed sentry, force protection, and Navy law enforcement. The success of these programs has allowed the college to become a favored provider in ongoing educational programs such as the Navy College program and the Coast Guard's Servicemembers Opportunity College program.

MEI proves that contracting can produce far more benefits than are achieved traditionally in community colleges if opportunities are identified that build on the college's major strengths, the administration is willing to take significant financial risks, and leaders are selected more in terms of who is best qualified to succeed as opposed to best qualified by traditional academic credentials. The MEI has been remarkably successful from an economic standpoint, and the good feelings associated with serving the people who are defending the nation cannot be overstated.

New Business Development Via the Institute Model

Public community colleges have operated historically under a de facto philosophy of academic altruism. Colleges take justifiable pride in optimizing access by maintaining the lowest possible tuition rates. Although low-cost tuition will continue to be an essential attribute for most community college programs, dramatic changes in the environment require colleges to be alert and receptive to special opportunities to generate revenue in ways that do not have an adverse impact on student access.

The pricing of goods and services is almost always a highly complex endeavor. Typically, the goal is to set prices as high as possible without being exploitive and adversely affecting demand. The pricing of education services by public institutions is particularly challenging because profit is usually not the prime consideration and the tolerance for charges is often low. Consequently, colleges have tended not to optimize the elasticity of price demand and, in some cases, have charged less than the ideal amount for courses and programs. In fact, college administrators sometimes subvert their own interests by attaching such a low price to what the college offers that consumers assume, incorrectly, that the programs are of a different type or quality than those offered by private sector competitors that charge much more for essentially the same thing. Accordingly, the ultimate lose–lose situation is created when consumers choose the higher-cost offerings under these circumstances.

The pricing consideration, when approached aggressively, can lead to a matter of some controversy—the issue of profit making through the programs of public community colleges. Aggressive profit-making strategies rarely are found, perhaps because significant profit making is not in the organizational DNA. This is an area that college leaders should seriously reconsider. As the economy becomes increasingly knowledge based, the economic value of the expertise and capabilities of colleges increases substantially. Provided that administrators stay within the applicable laws and public policy guidelines of the state, elevating prices to market rates such that there will be no adverse effect in doing so may be a smart move, given the limitations on the public funding available.

A team of FCCJ administrators has committed considerable time to developing effective pricing strategies and related marketing efforts. We have identified several major opportunities wherein business happily would pay far more than we normally charge for quality programs directly responsive to significant needs. The economic market for these high-demand continuing workforce education programs is separate from our mainstream programs for traditional students. Businesses often are willing to invest at costs above our regular tuition rates in the development of their employees and people they would like to bring into their organization. This type of investment does not make an adverse impact on student access, whereas it does generate substantial revenue for the college. In other words, profit need not be a dirty word when pursued in an appropriate manner.

Considering this opportunity, FCCJ has chosen to create an array of carefully selected, thoughtfully crafted revenue-generating entities called institutes. Institutes offer conventional low-cost preservice education to people in a particular career area, and they are designed to offer customized programs for employers at market cost. Institutes currently operational include the Technology Institute of the South, the Institute for Financial Studies, the Florida Construction Institute, the Culinary Institute of the South, the Florida Security Institute, and the Military Education Institute.

The business model and operating style of these institutes are different from those of the usual customized training programs found in many community colleges. Accordingly, FCCJ's institutes have the following characteristics:

- High demand—Institutes are created only in areas where very substantial enrollment volume is expected. Boutique or niche programs are not allowed.

- Responsive design—The design of each institute is driven by extensive focus group research in the applicable business sector.
- Leadership—Institutes are always led by current practitioners in the relevant field or professionals with recent and successful professional experience.
- Agility—As an essential requirement, institutes are designed and operated to evolve constantly and adapt quickly in alignment with the sector they serve.
- Pricing—Pricing is based on constant market research with care taken to maximize both enrollment levels and revenue.
- Faculty—Institute faculty must be current practitioners who are respected in their field and who possess a gift for teaching.

Institutes develop formal business models and are required to do the same continuous business planning that one would find in a successful private sector enterprise. Pricing and cost management decisions are supported by a unique analytical computer application created by the staff. It is important to note that institutes are freed by the college from as many bureaucratic constraints as is legally and practically possible. Special policies and procedures governing human resources and financial operations have been developed to provide the institutes with the maximum degree of flexibility. Most institute employees, for example, serve on performance-based term appointments, and venture capital is available from several sources to underwrite new initiatives. Finally, agreements are in place to share residual revenue (profits) with the institutes and with their campus of affiliation.

Although not a model for traditional collegiate programs, the institutes have proven to be highly successful and beneficial to FCCJ. The response of students, employers, and professional organizations has been positive, and the institutes consistently achieve their intended purposes. New institutes currently in development include the Institute for Successful Small Business, the Institute for Teacher Preparation, and the Institute for Staff and Organizational Development. Additional institutes are likely to be developed over the next few years.

The executive vice president for instruction and student success described our approach in this area:

> The institute model is an organizing structure that optimizes use of related college resources. The institute model connects disjointed but related aspects of the institution, creating synergies that otherwise would fail to materialize. The implementation of the model can serve as a catalyst for significant cultural change, internally and externally to the college.

Four major internal aspects of the college will realize immediate change as a result of instituting the model:

1. Disparate but related programs of the college will benefit from programmatic coordination and communication, a structure that makes ongoing communication an expectation. An example would be an education institute, an organizing structure that brings together programs such as pre-K education, adult basic education (noncredit), GED, high school, dual enrollment, credit education, and continuing education for teachers.

2. The college will engage in resource optimization that represents the efficiencies realized as staff from the different areas share activities that cross over various programs. Replication of efforts will become apparent immediately when program managers meet to discuss the implementation of goals.
3. The new structure will represent a creative environment and will lead to new ideas, interactions, and relationships, both internal and external to the college.
4. Communication will include a mix of people involved in sharing initiatives. Benefits will be realized in equipment standardization, software standardization, and expansion of functionality and procedural enhancements.

External benefits to the institute model derive from brand extension program packaging, communication, and relationship development with niche-market segments targeted through institute programming. Brand extension through institute packaging will enable markets to develop a brand perception of the institute that transcends the traditionally held low-prestige perception of community colleges in general. Coordinated communications with niche markets will focus the institute's value proposition and eliminate the confusion that occurs among customers when disparate college entities compete for the same share of a market. College clients, especially employers, are best served with a single point-of-contact strategy. A single point-of-contact through a college will represent one account executive who is accountable for the client's total interaction with the college and who understands the outcomes expected, delivering meaningful data on the accomplishment of those outcomes.

The improved relationship between colleges and corporations resulting from the institute model will produce multiple by-products for the entire college. Opportunities for cross-selling and up-selling will emerge. For instance, an automotive institute responsible for the continuing education of technicians may capitalize on an opportunity to provide sales and customer service training to a car dealership's nontechnical staff. Other opportunities for student internships, job placement, philanthropic development, and faculty or staff development may emerge as a relationship-oriented consequence of the institute model. As a college involves more faculty, administrators, and staff in the institute model, words such as *performance, deliverables, data,* and *profit* will become more common.

Expanding on the market-based value of institutes, both corporate and individual consumers should expect to realize the following benefits from an institute model:

*   A higher quality product or program line, which is flexible to specific client needs in content, delivery modality, and delivery timing
*   A stronger relationship to the college facilitated through a single point-of-contact service model
*   An improved perception of the product's quality and improved confidence in the college derived from quantitative return on training dollars and achieved learning outcomes
*   A partner in achieving the client's business goals through education and training innovation and beneficially assertive account management

The institute model represents a dramatic departure from the more traditional product or production-marketing concept of higher education. Market-driven and market-responsive institutes define the college from the perspective of clients rather than defining the college to the client. The resource management synergies and relationship management rewards from successful institutes will deliver tangible economic and intangible good will returns that ultimately benefit the entire college.

It is important to note that the innovative programs described in this chapter exist and succeed because of an extremely supportive (and somewhat unique) organizational structure and attitude. We have learned from experience that entrepreneurial ventures are most successful when built on a compatible and nurturing foundation and that the organizational synergies that result can be important and beneficial to the college's performance. FCCJ's approach to innovation has enabled the success of several collegewide contextual initiatives such as the following:

- Lifetime membership—All students are given a lifetime membership at the college. Members receive benefits such as free Internet services, e-mail, and Web site hosting. The college communicates constantly with active and inactive members, encouraging them to swirl back into the college whenever they have a need for more education or career assistance.
- Modular trimesters—The college operates year-round with three full 16-week semesters, each subdivided into 4-week instructional modules. Consequently, the college is able to offer students the choice of 8-, 12-, and 16-week versions of many courses. This model also allows nine admissions and registration entry points per year. Responses from students and faculty have been phenomenal.
- Innovation fund—The college's Strategic Planning Council administers an innovation fund with a continuing available balance of at least $1 million (usually closer to $2 million). Innovative initiatives that will enhance the achievement of collegewide goals are funded and authorized on the spot through the use of this extremely responsive resource.
- Internal articulation—A large noncredit program has been transformed into an even larger workforce credit program, consistent with the philosophy that all learning is valuable. Knowledge and skills obtained in non–college-credit career and technical programs can be articulated through the organized conversion of workforce credit and applied to the completion of related degrees and credit certificates.

The pride that the FCCJ community takes in these innovative programs and services is paralleled by the many benefits they bring to the college. The more entrepreneurial the college becomes, the more the culture of the college becomes increasingly receptive to and supportive of innovation on a broad scale. Accordingly, we cannot envision a future in which innovation and entrepreneurial endeavors are not significant and distinctive qualities of Florida Community College.

CHAPTER 3

NHMCCD: A COMMUNITY PARTNER WITH ENTREPRENEURIAL SPIRIT

John Pickelman

—North Harris Montgomery Community College District, Houston, Texas

Promise only what you can deliver. Then deliver more than you promise.

—*Unknown*

Entrepreneurship is described as the ability to recognize, create, and act on opportunities. The history of the North Harris Montgomery Community College District (NHMCCD) reflects such entrepreneurship, from its establishment in the early 1970s to its remarkable growth over 30 years, highlighted by unique and innovative partnerships and programs. Table 3.1 illustrates the tremendous growth of NHMCCD's service area and student population since the first school opened in 1973. Clearly, the good partnerships established by the district have contributed to NHMCCD's growth. The district now includes 11 school districts, nearly 40,000 students enrolled in the five colleges, and a tax base of $70 billion. The growth and success of the college district are attributed to the development and cultivation of good partnerships and the support and opportunities they bring.

Table 3.1	The Evolution of North Harris Montgomery County College District
Date	**Event**
October 1972	The North Harris County College District was established to meet the higher education needs of the growing greater Houston area. The district encompassed 256 square miles and served a population of approximately 160,000 with a tax base of $264 million.
Fall 1973	The district's faculty and staff of 15 welcomed 613 students to night classes at Aldine High School while construction began on the permanent North Harris County College campus.
Fall 1975	The North Harris County College campus officially opened.

Table 3.1	The Evolution of North Harris Montgomery County College District (cont'd)
1982	The district was serving a population of 713,000, within a boundary of 466 square miles.
1984	A smaller east campus in the Humble area was constructed and eventually named Kingwood College, moving the district toward a multi-college system.
1985	District enrollment swelled to 10,000.
1988	Construction on a third campus, Tomball College, was complete. Now serving the western region, the total district enrollment reached 13,000.
1991	Voters in the Conroe Independent School District in Montgomery County voted to join the district. The district adopted a new name, North Harris Montgomery Community College District (NHMCCD), to better reflect the district's entire service area.
August 1995	Then-Governor George W. Bush provided the keynote remarks at the opening of the fourth college in the district, Montgomery College.
1995	Montgomery College added another 3,000 students to increase districtwide enrollment to 19,000 students.
1996	Largely through the efforts of a Willis High School math teacher, voters in Willis and Splendora Independent School districts elected to join the district.
January 1998	The University Center building, home to a partnership with six public universities and next to Montgomery College, was officially dedicated in honor of George Mitchell. Designed to include state-of-the art telecommunications technology to offer interactive video broadcasts in classrooms from the home university, the University Center allowed local citizens to pursue bachelor's and master's degrees.
1998	The North Houston Economic Development Alliance brought together the district with 11 local chambers of commerce. The alliance agreed that the vast college district should function as a key partner in economic development efforts.
August 1998	Citizens in the Klein Independent School District voted to join the college district.
2000	Magnolia Independent School District voters joined the district, and the Cy-Fair Houston Chamber of Commerce began a process to select a college district to serve the Cypress-Fairbanks Independent School District.
Fall 2003	The Cy-Fair Houston campus opened with an enrollment of almost 7,000 new students, bringing total district enrollment to nearly 40,000 on five college campuses.

LEADERSHIP AND AN ENTREPRENEURIAL ENVIRONMENT: ORGANIZING TO EMPOWER

Until 1991, NHMCCD was highly centralized in its organizational structure and decision-making processes. As the district's enrollment quickly grew, it became clear that its organizational structure was not as effective as needed to deliver basic services to students and provide support for faculty and staff. As a result, the district underwent a comprehensive reorganization to place decision making at the most appropriate level within the organization, preferably as close to the point of implementation as possible. In developing this organizational plan, three issues were addressed:

- Would the proposed organizational change affect students favorably?
- Would the proposed change help create a culture of risk takers, once employees are given the authority and responsibility to make responsive decisions?
- Were the institution's resources sufficient to accommodate this new culture, especially ventures that projected some risk?

The highly successful department store, Nordstrom, is renowned for its customer-driven culture, empowering sales personnel to make floor decisions in the best interests of customers. These decisions do not require a supervisor's approval. NHMCCD has embraced a similar model by promoting a style of management that allows individual employees to experience greater freedom in the conduct of their duties. Authority and accountability to evaluate decisions encourage risk taking and entrepreneurship. Walter B. Wriston, former chairman and CEO of Citicorp, wrote in *Risk and Other Four Letter Words*, "Without innovation, companies die over time. One of the central tasks of management, therefore, is to overcome or thin out the underbrush, and to keep alive and well the spirit of entrepreneurship" (1986, pp. 224–225). By loosening the decision-making process and by placing it at the most appropriate level in the organization, the underbrush is thinned out; risk taking is not only permitted but also encouraged and rewarded.

One of the critical changes in the district's organizational processes was the decentralization of hiring decisions, especially appointments of faculty and administrative personnel. Heretofore, decisions related to hiring and salary placement had to be approved by the district's CEO. Hiring authority was given to immediate supervisors with appropriate review by second-level supervisors and the human resources division. Such reviews were important to verify credentials and ensure that salary placement was consistent throughout the district. The district benefits from decentralizing hiring decisions: Authority and accountability are placed where the action is. Faculty and staff are empowered to try new and different things, knowing that their performance will be judged by the person who hired them, rather than by a district executive several levels removed.

EFFECTIVE RELATIONSHIP BUILDING

As chancellor of NHMCCD, I have the unique opportunity to interact with internal and external constituents, and these positive relationships contribute to the overall success of the organization. In *Leading Without Power*, Max de Pree, former chairman and CEO of the Herman Miller Company, stated

The longer I live and the more I see of organizations, the more I am forced to the conclusion that at the heart of our organizations is always the matter of competence in relationships. While technical skills and life-time learning are essential, I'm convinced that competence in relationships remains most important in making organizations places of realized potential. (1997, pp. 166–167)

I have been fascinated for most of my professional life with how and to what or to whom people attribute success. At one end of the spectrum is the person who claims all credit; at the other is the person who avoids all recognition to the point of near anonymity. The comfort zone for most others lies somewhere in between. One does not achieve success without help of one kind or another. This is especially true in organizations. Effective leaders recognize the importance of establishing positive relationships throughout the organization and with external constituents. But how are effective relationships established? How does one learn competence in relationships?

There must be a mutual recognition of shared interests, goals, and values. People associate themselves with others who tend to believe in similar principles, whether social or professional. In effective organizations, leaders hire people who have common ideals and goals. High-performing teams are established when this principle of hiring is implemented. That is not to infer that team members must be clones of one another. In fact, diversity within a team contributes to the effectiveness of the organization by producing a variety of perspectives on how to reach a common goal. For community colleges like those in NHMCCD, that means serving students better. Therefore, the first principle in establishing competence in relationships is looking for partners who share primary interests, goals, and values.

The second essential principal in developing competence in relationships is credibility. If an organization is to operate at optimal levels, its members must be committed to being truthful. Those who trust their colleagues are able to develop teams that can take their effectiveness to higher levels of performance. But trust does not come easily and, unfortunately, can be lost. A commitment to trust others and to be trusted by others affords opportunities for unlimited achievements.

This is true not only within organizations, but also externally. I am not aware of any optimally performing community college that has not developed strong relationships in the community it serves. Administrators often say that their college district has great relationships with community organizations such as chambers of commerce, school districts, and municipal governments. But solid organizational relationships are the results of well-established personal relationships. A good example here is the mutually cultivated relationship between a progressive-minded school superintendent and me.

ANNEXATION: WHY WOULD I WANT TO PAY MORE TAXES?

In Texas, community college districts are political subdivisions whose boundaries can be defined by school districts, counties, or other municipalities. NHMCCD is a union of school districts. When I joined NHMCCD in 1991, as chancellor, the district consisted of five school districts whose residents had voted to pay property taxes primarily for the construction and maintenance of facilities to support the college. Unlike many other states, Texas prohibits the use of state funds for facilities, including salaries and benefits for physical plant employees.

In 1991, the state's share of the NHMCCD operating budget was 65%. The remaining revenue sources were tuition, fees, and ad valorem taxes. As demands on the state budget increased from other sectors of government, the level of state appropriations for community colleges declined steadily to a low point of 3% in FY 2004. Faced with skyrocketing enrollments, colleges were forced to look locally to find additional revenue. The two primary sources were property owners and students. Raising taxes and tuition rates are not attractive options to governing boards faced with already overburdened taxpayers and the commitment to keep community college doors open to all who seek to improve the quality of their lives.

However, there was another option for increasing revenues without increasing costs to students and taxpayers: expanding the value of the local tax base. There are two means by which the tax base can increase in value. One is by adding value to the existing base through economic expansion, such as land development, or by increases in appraised value of properties currently on the tax rolls. The other means is by expanding the district's geographical boundaries through the process of annexation, a process that is arduous and fraught with numerous pitfalls.

Powers of annexation, according to Texas statutes, are so limiting that, from a practical perspective, there is no real power given to community colleges to annex. What the law does provide, however, are certain conditions under which a school district's voters could decide to join an existing college district, provided the college's governing board would accept the petition for annexation. The conditions under which annexation may occur include the following:

- The school district's boundary must be contiguous with the college district's boundary.
- A minimum of 5% of the registered voters in the school district must sign a petition calling for an election.
- An election solely within the school district must be held to determine voters' choice of whether to join the district.

Although the procedure appears to be straightforward, the obstacles to a successful election are formidable, the most difficult obstacle being the understanding that a successful annexation election means that local taxpayers will assume the college district's tax rate. NHMCCD's tax rate is relatively low, nearly $0.1145 per $100 valuation. Nonetheless, property owners are overburdened with school tax rates averaging $1.50 and county taxes near $.60. NHMCCD might be a small part of the pie, but as concerned taxpayers are quick to point out, the district is nonetheless a part of the problem.

A related concern about increasing taxes within the school district to be annexed is the school district's leadership. It is uncommon for school superintendents and their boards of trustees to support another taxing entity entering their district. Whereas some welcome the community college's presence, especially to partner in projects that expand or enhance students' public education experience, they fear that college taxes and school taxes will be combined from the tax payer's perspective. There is a concern that this will hamper the school district's efforts to increase its own tax rate or to pass elections granting authority to issue tax-supported bonds.

Since 1991, six additional school districts have voted to join NHMCCD. Cypress-Fairbanks (Cy-Fair) Independent School District was one of the six; it voted to join in August

2000. At the time, Cy-Fair was the largest school district in the nation not to have an institution of higher education within its boundaries. With a residential population in excess of 600,000, a school population of 60,000, an area of 186 square miles, and a tax base in excess of $16 billion, the school district exceeded the minimum state standards of a $2.5 billion tax base and 10,000 students to establish its own community college. The superintendent was Rick Berry, a community college product, who came to Cy-Fair from a superintendency in Arlington, Texas, where he had established a good working relationship with Tarrant County Junior College. My initial meeting with Rick established the first condition of relationship building. We found that we shared common values and goals.

As I explained that my first commitment was to serve students, he echoed the same sentiment. I heard him repeat many times, "It has to be good for the kids." Our conversation was not about tax rates or fund balances; it was about how we could cooperate to serve students better. Of great interest to him was concurrent enrollment in classes in the high school. He and I believed that education offerings should complement the competencies of the students. If high school students could handle college-level work, why not make it possible for them to enroll in college while still in high school? We agreed to pursue the idea aggressively, and, within a short period of time, Cy-Fair high schools had the highest participation in concurrent credit classes of any school district we served, despite its not yet being part of the college district.

Rick believed that Cy-Fair should join NHMCCD. As a man of conviction, he was unafraid to get out front to support the proposition. He convinced the Cy-Fair Board of Trustees that it was the right thing to do for their students and that a college would bring opportunities to adult learners and the business community. Rick became a champion for the cause and played a big role, along with the chamber of commerce, in making the election a 2–1 success.

The relationship Rick and I established was founded on a common value of service. We trusted each other because we both dealt in the truth. As a result, NHMCCD expanded through the vote of Cy-Fair residents to join the district. Revenues were increased by $18 million, and a new $100 million campus was built and opened to an initial enrollment of 7,000 students.

THE ENTREPRENEURIAL COLLEGE DISTRICT: OPPORTUNITIES AND CHALLENGES

Since the district's founding, growth has been both the greatest opportunity and the biggest challenge. When the founders envisioned their community college, they were surrounded by a landscape of farms, forests, and small towns. But they were also aware of powerful economic forces in play that would transform the entire region.

Energy entrepreneur George Mitchell drew national attention in the 1970s with his development of The Woodlands—an innovative, planned community where the district services and training center are located. Mitchell's vision included fostering synergy between Houston's academic and industrial leaders. Today, major corporate facilities are appearing on the landscape, along with the retailers, restaurants, and hospitals.

This rapid transformation created a huge demand for expanded education facilities. Public school construction has boomed over the past three decades, with school districts adding new campuses and expanding their existing buildings. The voter registration rolls of

North Houston have been adding more new residents who demonstrate a strong commitment to education and a keen awareness of the role the district can play to build the local economy and the community.

New growth is projected to come from an unexpected direction: In 2003, the Texas legislature enabled state universities to set their own tuition rates. This action, combined with the deep cuts in state funding, has resulted in dramatic tuition increases at these institutions. The high costs of attending a 4-year university are driving more students to community colleges. NHMCCD must prepare for the challenges to its resources and the opportunities this expected growth will bring.

The district's successful management of past and future growth has been cited by two top bond rating companies, Moody's and Standard & Poor's, as one of the top reasons why the college district's credit rating has been raised seven times in 7 years. Managing double-digit growth over the last 5 years and anticipating future growth have been two of the greatest challenges for NHMCCD, requiring the district to look at new and more efficient ways to leverage its limited resources so that students may be served. By far, the most effective and entrepreneurial method has been forming partnerships with public schools, universities, businesses, economic development organizations, and local government.

The district has partnered with public schools and universities to share facilities and staff. For instance, the district participates in a unique shared counselor program that calls for the local school district and the college district to share the cost equally of the salary for a college and career counselor who works with juniors and seniors at designated high schools. NHMCCD shares a Career and Technology Training Center with Humble Independent School District. It offers a host of technology training programs in a facility owned by the East Montgomery County Improvement District, an economic development organization serving the Splendora and New Caney area of the college district. Additionally, the district built the North Harris College Carver Center on school district property adjacent to George Washington Carver High School in the historically Black neighborhood of Acres Homes in the Aldine school district.

A change in demographics has occurred that brought many more minority families to the area. As in most of Texas, the Hispanic population is the fastest-growing demographic within the district's boundaries. This shift in demographics has presented a need for new and better programs that ensure that all students receive the required support and services. NHMCCD faculty and staff have developed a comprehensive student success initiative to help students achieve their academic and career goals. In addition, the colleges have seized the opportunity to enrich campus life with events that celebrate the many cultures represented in the student population.

Another challenge for NHMCCD is responding to the needs of local businesses and industries so that district workforce programs reflect the current technology and training needed by employers and so that graduates are prepared to enter the workplace. Through advisory councils whose memberships include local business and industry leaders, NHMCCD has formed partnerships with Nissan, Compaq, City of Houston Airport System, Tomball Regional Hospital, St. Luke's Hospital, and other local companies. These partnerships have spawned new programs and expanded existing programs. Several companies have provided the expensive equipment or software needed to start a new program or provided the funds to pay for a much-needed faculty member in order to expand an existing program. NHMCCD is also home to the Small Business Development Center, which helps the district keep up with issues faced by small businesses in the region. The Center for Business and Economic Development was created to serve the larger companies within the district and to work to develop programs and services that encourage the economic development of the region.

A challenge NHMCCD faces along with all sectors of education is securing adequate funding. The bulk of the district's revenue comes from state funding, local property taxes, and student tuition and fees. State funding has fallen from 65% of district revenues in 1991, to only 32% in 2004. Property tax is 39%, and tuition is 27%, whereas 2% comes from other sources such as grants and auxiliary functions including the college bookstores. While the state struggles with budget woes of its own, the district has cultivated strong relationships with its legislative delegation, ensuring that the district's need for adequate funding has been heard at the capitol. In addition, the district is focused on finding other sources of funding to support programs through the District Office of Institutional and Resource Development department and the NHMCCD Foundation.

ENTREPRENEURIAL ACTIVITIES

Two excellent examples of entrepreneurship at the NHMCCD are The University Center and the purchase of buildings and land from the Houston Area Research Center, including the subsequent development of the NHMCCD District Services and Training Center. These initiatives have used the concept of entrepreneurship to expand services and opportunities at NHMCCD, developed community partnerships that have strengthened the position and standing of NHMCCD, and leveraged facilities and relationships to support operations through other sources of revenue. In addition, two entrepreneurial projects at the district's newest campus, Cy-Fair College, have brought increased revenue, realized savings in capital and operating budgets, and improved services to students and the community.

The University Center
The University Center (TUC) was developed by NHMCCD through a partnership with universities to provide unduplicated bachelor's degrees, master's degrees, and continuing professional studies to the district service area. Seamless articulated programs, collaborative governance, shared facilities, interactive telecommunications, and first-stop student services provide the basis for TUC to serve as the critical link for community development. TUC serves more than 1 million residents of North Houston, North Harris, and Montgomery counties.

The district was responsible for funding, constructing, and equipping a permanent facility to house TUC, located in The Woodlands. The construction was financed with approximately $9.5 million of tax funds, a gift of $2 million, and 10 acres of land from the Woodlands Corporation and George P. Mitchell. In 1995, voters of the district approved the $77.87 million bond issue by a 3–1 margin. The $9.5 million for TUC was one of the listed projects.

Construction of the facility was completed in late 1997. NHMCCD, as the owner, operator, and landlord of the facility, is responsible for providing the basic support services such as custodial, utilities, security, maintenance, duplication, and telephone. The district office also offers an interactive telecommunications system to support distance learning, instructional, and other needs. The equipment includes the telecommunications system to support two-way interactive video, voice, and data for distance education, as well as the computers, software, and networking systems necessary to support the on-site instructional program. TUC university partners are responsible for the operating budget that is divided among them, based on a pro rata share of annual student credit-hour generation at TUC. It is worth noting that NHMCCD provides no direct financial support to the operating budget of TUC.

NHMCCD's local taxpayers and private sector partners built the facility and telecommunications infrastructure at no cost to the state. Universities are responsible for their degrees and support the instructional facilities used, sharing support services costs. NHMCCD is responsible for the instruction and student services at the freshman and sophomore levels.

The spirit of entrepreneurship is evident in a number of partnerships and agreements housed by TUC. These partnerships provide direct and indirect benefits to NHMCCD. Direct benefits include increased visibility and awareness and actual funding of operating costs at the building. Citizens who use the facility for college classes provide indirect benefits. These citizens view the college district as an integral part of the community, perceiving it as a viable option for education and seeing that their tax dollars are at work. All these factors contribute to strong community support for NHMCCD.

TUC is also used extensively by local businesses and companies as a meeting place. The fees for these meetings are reasonable and based on actual expenses. Revenues generated are applied directly to the operating costs of the facility. Other civic, charitable, and professional organizations such as school districts, chambers of commerce, and community associations use the facility at no charge. The benefits in terms of support and image for the college district are manifested in the overwhelming support the district has received in tax support for operating and capital budgets. Surrounding cities, government organizations, and state and federal legislators use the facility as a site to bring together diverse groups and hold private meetings. NHMCCD relies heavily on support from state legislators for adequate funding and, most recently, for start-up operating funds for the two newest colleges.

The most recent entrepreneurial partnership at NHMCCD is an agreement with three Texas universities to house the Center for Research, Evaluation, and Advancement of Teacher Education at TUC. This collaborative partnership among NHMCCD, The University of Texas, Texas A&M, and the Texas State University System focuses on the enhancement of teacher education programs. In addition to providing direct revenue to the district, this partnership benefits NHMCCD by providing additional sources of federal funding from grants and by strengthening seamless transitions in teacher education programs. TUC is not only a model for educational partnerships, but also it is an excellent example of how community colleges can use their assets in an entrepreneurial manner to foster financial support and visibility among the college's stakeholders.

The NHMCCD Services and Training Center

In 2003, NHMCCD made the decision to move its district offices from the southern part of the service area to a more centrally located site. Because of its reputation and financial resources, NHMCCD was approached by the Houston Advanced Research Center (HARC) about the purchase of approximately 100,000 square feet of office buildings and more than 100 acres of prime real estate in The Woodlands. HARC is a nonprofit organization that works with a number of state universities, industry, and government agencies to address issues relating to how people interact with ecosystems on a regional scale. In more recent years, the focus has been on sustainability.

After lengthy negotiations, NHMCCD purchased the land and buildings, valued at approximately $23 million, for $11.5 million, and a long-term lease agreement was signed with HARC to ensure the continuance of its noteworthy work. NHMCCD renamed the facility the NHMCCD Services and Training Center and added another 40,000 square-foot office building and the 20,000 square-foot District Training and Development Center. The training center has become the hub of meetings both internally and externally. The facility features 12 state-of-the art meeting rooms with a full complement of technology support and a large board room for more formal meetings. A director was hired to coordinate activities at the center and to ensure high-quality service.

NHMCCD envisions that the training center will become a regional training facility for area businesses and will provide overnight accommodations and comprehensive food service eventually. In addition to having a premier meeting facility, the center's operating budget is based on an entrepreneurial model. Rates for facility use have been established, and it is anticipated that meeting and usage fees will generate more than $150,000 each year. Although these revenues will not cover the entire operating budget of the center, the benefits to the college system are significant. The visibility, the sound financial operations, and the variety of programming develop support for NHMCCD, directly and indirectly. For example, it generates revenue to support internal professional development programs for faculty and staff. NHMCCD is considered a community partner because of its entrepreneurial spirit. The development of two highly successful centers is strong evidence of that spirit.

ENTREPRENEURIAL COMMUNITY COLLABORATION: CY-FAIR COLLEGE

As the nation's first fully comprehensive college to open in the 21st century, Cy-Fair College had the unique opportunity to break new ground via innovation and entrepreneurship. As the fifth college in NHMCCD, Cy-Fair College began meeting the critical unmet need for higher education in the northwest region of suburban Houston in August 2003, with an opening enrollment of almost 7,000 credit students. Facing the same resource challenges being faced by other colleges, it was important that Cy-Fair College maximize its ability to serve the community, as well as find new sources of support and resource enhancement.

To make sure that it met the expectations and needs of the local community, the college was planned with extensive community involvement. As plans for the college got underway, two exceptional opportunities for community collaboration arose that have altered significantly the resources available to the college to serve the community. In both cases, the community partner and the college were able to multiply the resources and level of service available to the public significantly.

Joint College and County Library Partnerships

Several joint library partnerships have been developed across the country. These vary widely in the extent of integrations of services and collaboration between the partners. The Cy-Fair College and Harris County Public Library Joint Library is one of the most seamless and successful integrations of a library partnership yet developed. The key to the success of this collaborative project lies in the initial agreement by both the college and the county on a clear joint vision and on service values.

Construction of Cy-Fair College was well under way when the local county commissioner brought forward the idea of a joint library. Immediately, a planning team began to determine the advantages, as well as barriers, to accomplishing the goal of a joint facility. Clearly, the advantages to the county would be the savings on land, construction, parking, security, utilities, and collection. With no library in the region and demand growing daily, the gap in public library services was enormous. For the college, the advantages included extensive enhancements to the collection, a children's library, a teen library, an expanded periodicals collection, exposure to the college of many new potential students, and technology advances such as self-checkout. For both it would mean a library and learning resource center open 7 days a week. Also, it would mean significant cost savings and services—reaching populations not possible to reach by either entity alone. The resulting joint library is a 109,000 square-foot space, with a cybercafé and 300 computers that are fully integrated with college tutoring, counseling, and technology assistance, available to students and the community.

In terms of added resources to the college, the county contributed $4,291,000 to expand the original building plan by 28,000 square feet and invested $1.3 million as compared with the college's collection budget contribution of $290,000. Annually, the county contributes more than $1,030,000 to the support of the staff, including 11 professional librarians and administrators and 13 full-time staff. An additional $175,000 annually goes toward the support of infrastructure. But beyond the financial and resource enhancements to the college, the number of nonstudent patrons who other than visiting the library may not ever have come to the campus is significant. In the first 9 months of operation, the library issued more than 6,000 new public library cards.

Two key factors account for the high level of success of this entrepreneurial collaboration. First, both partners fully embraced a joint vision for the project. That agreement allowed difficult decisions and compromises to be made without jeopardizing the project. Because both partners were committed to providing seamless service to the public, it was critical that there be only one employer. The college assumed that role. Similarly, it was important that there be only one book classification system.

The overall goals of the project offset any individual barriers because of the extent to which both partners would see cost savings and increased service to the community. An entrepreneurial partnership such as this involves risk on both sides, particularly in the diffusion of mission by either party. Because of the strong commitment to access and service by the county and the college, the financial savings and service capabilities of both entities were enhanced significantly.

EMERGENCY SERVICES TRAINING CENTER AND COMMUNITY FIRE STATION PARTNERSHIP

An important aspect of the planning of Cy-Fair College was determining critical workforce training needs. As the planning proceeded, it was clear that there were many more needs for specialized training facilities than the construction and equipment budget would allow. One of the needs identified by the community was fire science and emergency technician training. The local volunteer fire department (Cy-Fair Volunteer Fire Department) was hampered severely in recruiting new firefighters and maintaining currency in the staff's skill sets because of the long commutes necessary to access the closest fire science programs in the region. But the construction budget would not allow for the training facilities and technology that would be necessary to provide a credible program.

What the college had was land, an undeveloped 200-acre site of which only two thirds would be needed for the construction of the five major buildings that make up the campus. In exploring possible solutions, Emergency Services District (ESD) #9, the taxing entity providing funds for emergency services in the community, along with the fire department, identified a need for a new fire station close to where the college was being built. The innovative proposal brought forward by the local emergency services partners was to build both the fire station they needed and the training center the college and fire department both needed on a 5-acre portion of undeveloped college land. Plans began immediately to lease the unused land to the ESD for a nominal fee. The result was a three-way partnership between the Cy-Fair Volunteer Fire Department, the ESD #9, and Cy-Fair College, for a complex that has become a center for service and training in all emergency services in the region.

The ESD funded the construction of a 25,000 square-foot complex, including a three-bay fire station, fully equipped as a local community fire station. The fire station is connected to a state-of-the-art emergency services training center with classrooms, laboratories, a mock emergency room, media room, life-flight helicopter pad, and four-story burn building and tower. The total investment by the ESD was approximately $4.4 million. The college significantly enhanced that investment by providing access to the entire campus, including a public library, conferencing facilities, computer labs, and other resources that would not have been possible in a stand-alone training facility.

The fire department operates the fire station, which provides service to the local community. The college manages the training center, providing training for the local fire department with reduced tuition via guaranteed scholarships for local fire department personnel. The college's training center includes overnight rooms so that students can intern with the fire department on 24-hour rotation for experience in responding to community emergency calls. The center has been in operation for less than a year and has enrolled more than 1,100 students in EMT, paramedic, and fire academy classes. This spring, 50 students graduated from the first fire academy with a 100% pass rate on the state examination. Very few of those students would have been able to attend another program; as a result, the college has had a major impact on emergency personnel resources for the community.

As the contractual arrangements were developed, there was extensive discussion about what the college would owe the local emergency partners for the construction of the $4.4 million facility. As the partnership relationship deepened, it became clear that what the college should pay in return for the facility was nothing more than to provide responsive, accessible, and credible emergency services training to meet the local emergency partners' needs.

As in the example of the joint county and college library, the success of this collaboration was attributed to the existence of a firm agreement, based on a common vision, by caring individuals who shared the same goals and values and who trusted each other. Not only has the college gained facilities worth millions of dollars, but also it has provided the community access to a fire station with fire trucks and ambulances. This would not have been possible with college resources alone. Beyond the financial benefits, the collaborative team is now in a position to plan emergency and homeland security services for the entire community, knowing that providing the skilled personnel necessary to carry the vision will never be in question.

Conclusion

The successes NHMCCD has enjoyed are the results of collaborative partnerships established at personal levels. The realization of shared values and goals opens doors to real partnerships, providing real benefits that are shared mutually. Continuation and expansion of partnerships rely on the most important value: truth. Credibility among partners serves as the foundation on which additional ventures may be explored.

In December 2000, NHMCCD residents were asked to approve a $184 million bond referendum to construct not only the Cy-Fair campus but also projects at other campuses, including libraries, classroom buildings, tech centers, and theaters. Several days before the election, an editorial appeared in a local newspaper, taking a position on the proposed referendum. Interestingly, the editorial made no mention of the specific construction projects to be supported. Rather, it highlighted the district's long-time contributions to the community and the importance of supporting this initiative. It was an advocacy piece on the entire district and its performance. The headline read "Promises Made, Promises Kept." No further testimony was needed about the district's credibility. The election passed by a 9–1 margin.

References

De Pree, M. (1997). *Leading without power.* San Francisco: Jossey-Bass.
Wriston, W. B. (1986). *Risk and other four-letter words.* New York: Harper & Row.

CHAPTER 4

ST. PETERSBURG COLLEGE: AN E-SPIRITED INSTITUTION

Carl M. Kuttler, Jr.
—St. Petersburg College, Florida

Lord, grant that I may always desire more than I can accomplish.

—*Michelangelo*

Key words to describe the entrepreneurial movement include *imagination, possibilities, dreams, creativity, parlaying, innovations, future, synergy, pioneers,* and *explorers.* These words help define an entrepreneurial enterprise and suggest that such an organization is not just entrepreneurially fueled or motivated, but spirited. St. Petersburg College (SPC) is entrepreneurially spirited: e-spirited. An e-spirited institution thrives on inspiration and energy (see, e.g., Farrel, 2001). In fact, as enrollments continue to increase and traditional funding sources diminish, SPC's e-spirit ensures SPC's survival and success. In this chapter, I provide a summary of SPC and its communities, a discussion of the meaning of entrepreneurship and its implications for community colleges, a review of smaller projects or initiatives that provided a platform for SPC to take greater risks, and four examples of larger initiatives that have provided opportunities for thousands of citizens.

ST. PETERSBURG COLLEGE AND ITS COMMUNITIES

SPC is located in Pinellas County on Florida's west coast—a large metropolitan area of approximately 1 million people. Between 1995 and 2000, according to the U.S. Census Bureau, the Tampa Bay area had a net gain of more than 100,000 residents. Tampa Bay is a renowned tourist destination noted for its climate, scenic beauty, progressiveness, friendliness, and all-around charm. The area is home to several professional sports teams, including the 2003 Super Bowl Champion Tampa Bay Buccaneers, the Devil Rays baseball team, and the 2004 Stanley Cup champion Tampa Bay Lightning hockey team. Two of the top five beaches in the United States are located within Pinellas County, according to *America's Best Beaches* (Leatherman, 2003), as well as 1 of the 15 largest U.S. media markets. The ACCRA Cost of

Living Index cites Pinellas County as the most economical place to live in the southeastern United States, with the cost of living 91% of the national average.

Founded in 1927, St. Petersburg Junior College began as a 2-year private college. Fluctuating from a 3-year private college, to a 2-year private college, it became a 2-year public college in 1948. In 2001, St. Petersburg Junior College became the first 2-year community college in Florida to be awarded 4-year degree status; it was renamed St. Petersburg College.

SPC employs more than 1,000 people full time and has educated more than 1 million people in its 75-year history. Located on approximately 385 acres of land, the facility comprises 11 learning sites and 66 permanent buildings with 179 learning labs. About 65,000 students enroll annually. The typical SPC student is 30 years old, female, works, and goes to school part time. More than 85% of SPC's students live in Pinellas County, and approximately 3% are international students, representing more than 110 countries. SPC has received a top award from the Community Colleges for International Development in recognition of its international education activities.

SPC is proud to act on the local and world stages. Offering specialized training, SPC currently houses one of the largest homeland security training centers in the United States. In April 2004, SPC administrators were invited to Russia by the state department to share the college's antiterrorism program with Russian government and education leaders.

IMPLICATIONS AND OPPORTUNITIES FOR THE ENTREPRENEURIAL COMMUNITY COLLEGE

The Web page of the National Dialogue on Entrepreneurship suggests that entrepreneurship applies to a business or idea:

> What is an entrepreneur? An individual engaged in the process of starting and growing one's own business or idea. Dozens of definitions exist; but in the end, this one seems to best fit the research and findings on the issue. Success in entrepreneurship requires not only knowledge, but practice and skill in the process of doing. (Public Forum Institute, 2003, paras. 1 & 2)

Entrepreneurial ideas are about doing. Entrepreneurship applies to education institutions, as well as to businesses. Community colleges, in particular, are skilled in the process of doing and are known for creatively and efficiently applying resources and getting a quality job done quickly. Many times the process of doing, or carrying out entrepreneurial ideas, brings incredible challenges. E-spirited institutions, however, tend to view challenges as opportunities. Drucker (1985) wrote, "Entrepreneurs see change as the norm and as healthy. He or she always searches for change, responds to it, and exploits it as an opportunity." SPC further identifies with a statement made by *Washington Post* columnist William Raspberry (2004), who described an entrepreneurial college as "one who looks for new markets as old ones dry up."

A collective e-spirit among leadership, faculty, staff, and students, like the e-spirit at SPC, creates the desire and right combination of resources to move an entrepreneurial idea forward. Then, success inspires greater success and entrepreneurship is contagious. As SPC pursues entrepreneurial opportunities, including those cited in this chapter, new ideas and opportunities are spawned throughout the college and noted by the community. Businesses, hospitals, and government agencies frequently approach SPC with ideas and requests for entrepreneurial partnerships. The e-spirit is a shared spirit, benefiting all college constituents.

SPC's leaders encourage and support entrepreneurial initiatives, and its board members are active at state and national levels and respond positively to entrepreneurial ideas presented by the college leadership. The board inspires the college to be alert to any next steps as plans and ideas unfold. Additionally, the board encourages hiring people who are entering the next generation of leadership. More than 20 SPC administrators have become college presidents, chancellors, and national association leaders.

Cultivating an entrepreneurial spirit can breathe new life into a community college. At SPC, entrepreneurial activity generates high energy and renewed appreciation for the mission and contributes to the economic and social health of the entire community. As Kuratko stated in *Entrepreneurship Education: Emerging Trends and Challenges for the 21st Century,*

> Perhaps the entrepreneur is leading all of corporate America to a rediscovery of business as enterprise, a rediscovery of business as a process limited only by the boundaries of each individual's intelligence, imagination, energy, and daring…Entrepreneurship is more than the mere creation of business. Although that is certainly an important facet, it's not the complete picture. The characteristics of seeking opportunities, taking risks beyond security, and having the tenacity to push an idea through to reality combine into a special perspective that permeates entrepreneurs. An "entrepreneurial perspective" can be developed in individuals. This perspective can be exhibited inside or outside an organization, in profit or not-for-profit enterprises, and in business or non-business activities for the purpose of bringing forth creative ideas. (2003, p. 2)

That perspective, what I call e-spirit, can extend beyond college leaders and staff. Teaching entrepreneurship is warranted and profitable; how much more enriching for students, however, when their education institution also practices entrepreneurship. And going one step further, the entrepreneurial graduate is often a very good resource for college fundraising, thus completing an entrepreneurial cycle of success.

SPC's activities, projects, programs, and initiatives have served as a springboard for success in larger projects, such as the four examples detailed in this chapter. As the college first accomplished smaller objectives, a developing e-spirit among administration, faculty, and staff created a platform for SPC to take greater risks and achieve large-scale success. The foundation was built through the implementation of the ongoing and accomplished objectives described in Tables 4.1 and 4.2.

Table 4.1	Ongoing E-Spirit Objectives
Frequency	**Objective**
Annually	Seek the opinions of the top 25 leaders in the community, state, and nation on critical issues in higher education

Table 4.1	Ongoing E-Spirit Objectives (cont'd)
Frequency	**Objective**
Annually	Bring the entire teaching faculty and counseling and library staffs (500 professionals) to the National Institute of Staff and Organizational Development (NISOD) conference in Austin, Texas
	Achieve near-perfect financial audits for more than 25 years
	Work with John Roueche and USA Today to begin a program of annual recognition of faculty at the NISOD conference, similar to the program *USA Today* sponsors for Phi Theta Kappa students at their national convention
Each semester	Administer international education programs in China, South America, and Russia, and offer travel with credit programs for SPC students
	Recognize students' achievement through scholarships for top performers and recognition for students with high GPAs
Monthly	Host half-hour workshops with the board of trustees to keep them current on college issues and events
As needed	Present gifts—college memorabilia and other items—to people important to the college
Ongoing	Help organize a state plan for energy efficiency—applying for grants and receiving funds—and conserve resources whenever possible
	Actively support Phi Theta Kappa (PTK) honor society, which has resulted in its receipt of PTK's highest award for the most distinguished chapter in the world on five occasions
	Actively assist in addressing some of society's ills, including instituting a court-required course for parents who are divorcing and have children; the course teaches parents how not to make children victims of divorce
	Build creative financial endowments
	Recognize employees with a view toward strengthening the college family through the celebration of birthdays, employment anniversaries, newly earned degrees, and other special events
	Provide, on SPC's campuses, advanced-degree opportunities for faculty
	Provide employee training in e-mail programs, computer advances, and software systems to promote distance education
	Require faculty to have six graduate hours to gain tenure, including courses covering the history of the community college movement (to build appreciation for the institution's mission) and classroom teaching

Table 4.2	Objectives Accomplished at St. Petersburg College
Objective	**Approach**
SPC's National Profile	Hosted two national roundtables for approximately 20 participants each and invited national leaders to critique SPC and give suggestions for improvement
	Co-sponsored with the American Association of Community Colleges (AACC) two presidential library conferences for community college presidents, with former U.S. presidents Gerald Ford and Jimmy Carter
	Rode the wave during the business community's re-engineering era, offering courses, with Florida's governor, to 200 public officials at the state's capitol
	Served with U.S. Secretary of Education Terrell Bell to evaluate outstanding high schools in America and extract best principles
	Co-sponsored, with Harvard University and Microsoft, a 1-day seminar on the future of technology for 75 of Florida's leaders in education, government, business, and technology
	Conducted a seminar for 600 county leaders to address how SPC could work together with the political and business communities in the new millennium
Fundraising	Created an active fundraising office that has received some of America's largest community college gifts (including separate gifts of $22 million and $11.2 million)
	Passed a local one-time tax referendum where no local support is authorized otherwise for community college funding
	Led a health education campaign to double the nursing population and to expand degrees for health-related careers (more than $15 million raised)
	Acquired the largest (at the time of the gift in the 1980s) computer gift in America for faculty from Apple Computer, totaling $2.5 million
	Revitalized donor recognition through lunches at the Florida governor's mansion, naming opportunities on buildings, etc.
	Supported the original idea and applied annually for the Florida legislature's program of matching funds for donor gifts; the program was named for SPC's former board of trustees chairman, Phillip Benjamin
Administration and Board of Trustees	Trimmed the administrative structure through reorganization
	Installed a process for review of AS degrees every 5 years
	Addressed concerns about administrative succession by creating on-campus cohorts of doctoral students from within the college staff for

Table 4.2	Objectives Accomplished at St. Petersburg College (cont'd)
Objective	**Approach**
Administration and Board of Trustees	future leadership roles; participants earned certificates and credit hours toward their doctoral degrees
Students	Developed a 75-point plan for a complete review of academic standards, including a total review of prerequisites and co-requisites; the plan resulted in a requirement of English credits during the first accumulated 24 credit hours, computer literacy (25 years ago), speech, and applied ethics
	Developed an applied ethics course that led to production of a nationally used textbook and adoption of a values-based atmosphere at the college
	Instituted a major dual-credit program for high school students, later adding St. Petersburg Collegiate High School, which took dual credit to a new level
	Supported honors courses, ultimately leading to an SPC honors college
	Instituted a system of awarding honorary degrees and other major recognition at graduation
Faculty and Staff	In the early 1990s, more than 25 SPC staff members worked with John Roueche, professor and director of the Community College Leadership Program at The University of Texas at Austin on a master plan of change for education in the 21st century; former Secretary of Education Terrell Bell served as chairman of this research effort
	Produced and co-edited with John Roueche and Dale Parnell *1001 Exemplary Practices in America's Two-Year Colleges* (McGraw-Hill, 1994) as a learning exercise and to share with others
	Co-sponsored with Unisys a national conference for community colleges—a first-time conference of its kind in technology
	Produced a set of videos as a training tool for our adjunct faculty; later sold the videos to other colleges across America

THE ALLSTATE CENTER

The heart of SPC's Allstate Center beats with synergy and entrepreneurship; in this story a few resources were parlayed into many. The center, an attractive complex on Florida's west coast, once served as Allstate Insurance Company's regional headquarters. It is now a state, regional, and national training facility for criminal justice, fire safety, emergency management, and homeland security programs. Allstate has attracted millions of dollars in state support and federal grants and contracts.

In the 1980s, the Pinellas County sheriff suggested that the community's public safety education needs were not being met. During the 1950s and 1960s, a high school diploma and technical school certificate were adequate for entry into public safety employment. However, by the 1980s, the Pinellas County police and sheriff departments decided that they preferred a 2-year degree for their law enforcement officers. The Pinellas County school board, which provided the training, had difficulty understanding the new trend. However, once the criminal justice community clarified its need for better-educated personnel, the college and school board completed an articulation agreement. Plans began for finding a new home and staffing to support the entrepreneurial endeavor.

School board personnel and college faculty and staff brought creative energy and dynamic spirit to the new program. Criminal justice, fire, and other public safety officials at local, state, and federal levels joined in a partnership to develop a career ladder giving students an opportunity to earn higher degrees and to address a void. The college, seeking a physical plant to house newly collected resources, identified a promising property. The site of Allstate Insurance Company's former regional offices was for sale. The property seemed well suited, because it included 20 acres and more than 130,000 square feet, including meeting and dining facilities. In 1988, it was valued at $11.15 million. SPC set to acquire this mega-center as a gift to the college.

Others shared SPC's vision, among them were the chief of the St. Petersburg police department, the city of St. Petersburg's redevelopment specialist, and CEO of Florida Progress Corporation (one of the state's most successful companies). At the time, the site was in a redevelopment area, and the Florida Department of Community Affairs had a little-known program of tax credits to encourage private donations to upgrade economically depressed areas. With this information, the group approached Allstate and offered to transform the former insurance processing facility and its regional offices for public use.

Allstate leaders recognized the opportunity and elected to invest in the college and community, provided the details could be worked out. These included Allstate's need for an adjustment in the timing of the tax credit program, an alteration that would make a large contribution more beneficial to the donor. This required passage of special legislation. Guided by college trustees and Governor Bob Martinez, SPC's plan was bolstered by members of the Pinellas legislative delegation, whose bipartisan spirit infused the effort to compress the tax credit time frame from 6 to 2 years—a proposal ultimately approved by the legislature.

At a 1988 press conference, at which Governor Martinez was the keynote speaker, Allstate's regional vice president presented college officials with the keys to the new building. The Florida cabinet cited Allstate Insurance Company as a model of corporate citizenship. Allstate's senior vice president for corporate relations announced an additional gift (the first in a series) of $30,000 for a planned drug resource center and 25 videotapes of Allstate's *Drug-Free Kids* television production. Copyrights of these videos were transferred to the college for future royalties. Later, Allstate, through the Sears Foundation, gave $400,000 for needed asbestos removal in the build-out of the structure.

Extensive renovations were necessary to comply with state building standards and to make the site usable as a law enforcement training center. To maintain the momentum, the SPC administration made the work part of a project already in the legislative approval process. It then sought and was awarded $4.5 million for the renovation. The center, almost completely refurbished, opened in June 1991, to students and professionals. Since the acquisition of the site, more than $20 million has been raised to improve and expand Allstate Center initiatives.

The college pursued one of its dreams—establishing a criminal justice training center that provides federal, state, and local training in one location. Today, the program participates in the nation's war on drugs for the reduction of demand and supply. Additional programs were quick to follow. Through the leadership of U.S. congressman C. W. Bill Young, SPC's National Terrorism Preparedness Institute was initiated prior to September 11, 2001, and the national cry for home-land security. Ongoing initiatives for training emergency responders to prepare for, respond to, and mitigate incidents involving weapons of mass destruction (WMD) include port security, medical strategies for WMD incidents, and development of experimental software and training projects that allow for the interface of military and civilian information from local, state, and federal first-responders during a WMD incident in a major city such as Washington, DC, or New York.

Additionally, SPC has partnerships with the Federal Emergency Management Administration; Secret Service; Department of Justice; Internal Revenue Service; Coast Guard; Social Security Administration; Federal Law Enforcement Training Center (Glencoe, GA); Department of Alcohol, Tobacco, and Firearms; and others. Programs are offered over the Internet and through satellite distribution. Enrollments and viewers in these specialized presentations grew from a few students to more than 5 million participants.

The SPC Allstate story provided the impetus to reverse a stagnant education program, eliminate serious potential competition, and create soaring revenues. A public safety curriculum was enlarged to handle additional programs in law enforcement, corrections and fire science, computer fraud, crime scene technology, security management, crime analysis, forensics, and emergency administration. These programs offered 2-year degrees that can lead to a bachelor's degree in public safety administration.

It is anticipated that when SPC's bachelor of applied science in public safety administration degree is offered over the Internet, beginning January 2005, it will be one of the most sought-after degrees in Florida. The entrepreneurial spirit of public safety communities, and SPC's board of trustees, administration, and faculty converged with the local business community and its leaders to achieve an incredible set of goals. Such partnerships help stabilize the overall college budget.

DISTANCE LEARNING

For 60 years, SPC, like many other colleges, was steeped in the tradition of offering courses mostly on campus, between 8:00 a.m. and 1:00 p.m. As a demand for evening classes increased, the shift in scheduling was difficult to staff. Eventually, it was difficult to provide classrooms and other plant facilities for students who required flexible scheduling.

SPC reports indicate that although students have shown limited interest in or need for classes on campus between 1:00 p.m. and 6:00 p.m., evening classes are increasingly popular. SPC students are older—the average age of students is 28—and have families and job responsibilities. Likewise, many of SPC's instructors are balancing more than one job; approximately 35% of the classes are taught by adjunct or part-time faculty. Having adjunct faculty, who make up 50% or more of the American community college teaching staff, available to teach in the evening helps alleviate a dilemma for many full-time faculty members who still prefer to have the majority of their work scheduled during the day.

Attempting to serve students with family and job responsibilities, along with the challenge of providing adequate and efficient use of plant facilities, led to creative solutions for meeting special needs and to alternative course delivery modes. With energy, creativity, and entrepreneurship, faculty use myriad instructional platforms, including face-to-face instruction and distance learning, to ensure students' success. SPC's commitment to providing service any time, any place has created a nationally recognized model known as Project Eagle.

Project Eagle is a multiyear strategic initiative, funded with federal, state, and private money totaling approximately $10 million. The college has built a national model for increasing access to 2-year degrees and workforce training, and now offers 4-year degrees or higher. Access is enhanced with flexible courses, programs, and support services delivered at a time, place, and pace suited to the needs of the individual learner.

SPC realizes that colleges relying on proprietary approaches operate at their own peril. Since 1999, the college has developed, implemented, and evaluated 262 technology-mediated (primarily Web-based) associate degree and certificate courses, as well as baccalaureate courses. Also, in conjunction with college and university partners, the college developed and delivered innovative, integrated student and academic support services for upper-division, distance, and other flexible-access students (e.g., open-entry/open-exit). Another Project Eagle component was the task of determining distance learning best practices, incorporating those practices into program development, and then disseminating the results and outcomes with evaluated findings nationally.

Project Eagle established a model organization to train, develop, and support online and flexible delivery of courses and programs and to provide the infrastructure, equipment, and support for ready access to upper-division and workforce courses and programs throughout Pinellas County. The number of courses developed to date far exceeds the number first promised. SPC's eCampus is the largest distance learning program among all community colleges in the state, with 12,781 students served in spring 2004.

Important to SPC's distance learning successes are the electronic academic and administrative support services developed with Project Eagle funding. A robust portal to e-learning appears on the eCampus Web site (http://www.spcollege.edu). The site provides a gateway to course logins, plus access to a wide range of cyberservices, including cyberadvisors. Distance learning students (along with those in face-to-face classes) can access SPC's full range of support services—admissions, orientation, testing, advising, financial aid, and registration—without ever coming to a physical campus.

A previously mentioned Project Eagle component, research and dissemination, is another area of exemplary accomplishment. A series of research questions about e-learning was crafted, and internal and external evaluators were used to identify best practices for the college to emulate. The concept of researching best practices led to the publication of *Best Educational E-Practices (BEEP),* a monthly online newsletter that focuses on one subject related to e-learning each month. *BEEP* has become a nationally recognized authority on the topic and has subscribers on every continent except Antarctica (to subscribe, contact Project Eagle coordinator Jennifer Lechner at lechnerj@spcollege.edu).

SPC's Project Eagle and other endeavors have spun off into other successful entrepreneurial benefits for the college:

- College faculty and staff are sometimes frustrated but mostly invigorated by constant technological advances in education and the marketplace and continually upgrade hardware and software accordingly.

- It soon became apparent that many students do not perform well in e-learning environments; likewise, many are less suited to traditional lecture modes. Along with many other colleges, SPC continues to identify and develop appropriate placement criteria and assistance to ensure that students are in the learning environment that best suits them.
- On-campus classes benefit from college distance learning initiatives. Help desk and video services and educational technology departments assist all faculty—not just those who teach online.
- Another by-product of this entrepreneurial activity is facilities' cost savings and budgetary redistribution. The college has saved some dollars by not having to build as many classrooms; however, the classrooms newly built or renovated are more costly. Classrooms are equipped with computers, projectors, high-speed Internet connections, two-way interactive technology, smart boards, and more.
- Project Eagle and eCampus experiences raised college consciousness about the need for more flexible access to college courses and programs. For example,
  – The college has revisited its rather limited roster of honors courses and now has a coordinated honors college (including online honors classes).
  – SPC has responded to a statewide appeal to create a collegiate high school. Taking the dual-credit program to a new level, St. Petersburg Collegiate High School is bringing 150 students to the college for 3 years of study. These students, who enrolled in the fall of 2004, will receive an AA degree as they graduate from high school.

SPC's eCampus activity is exciting and dynamic. The rapid pace of change in the education and technology marketplaces, and college clientele's demand for quick response, challenges and invigorates SPC.

THE UNIVERSITY PARTNERSHIP CENTER

Whether community colleges offer degrees beyond the associate's continues to be the subject for debate. In 2002, while maintaining a commitment to its 2-year mission, SPC began offering 4-year degrees in education, nursing, and technology management. The college has since added or is planning for more than 10 additional bachelor's programs, mostly converting AS to BS degrees. There are nearly 200 AS degrees offered at community colleges in Florida. Only five of them are articulated for successful transfer to Florida's university system. SPC offers or will offer bachelor's degrees in areas including public safety administration, dental hygiene, orthotics and prosthetics, and veterinary technology. SPC offers the occasional AA to BA degree, but those degrees are left primarily to the universities.

SPC opted to venture into this entrepreneurial area from yet another direction. SPC's University Partnership Center (UPC) was inspired by a state senator who documented a need for baccalaureate access in Pinellas County. This partnership model was not new. For years, colleges have brought higher degree offerings to their campuses, though only one or two have larger, more complex partnership centers than SPC.

Coordination is key for a university partnership center. SPC sent staff to Texas, Michigan, and Ohio to study what were at the time thought to be the most comprehensive partnerships in America. The college team interviewed faculty, students, university staff, and residents of the communities to determine the strengths and weaknesses of this approach. Learning from others' experiences, the college, in fall 1999, opened the UPC with seven university partners, offering 33 courses in 16 bachelor's programs and boasting an enrollment of 251. By spring 2004, the UPC had 14 partners offering 315 courses in 40 bachelor's and 24 graduate programs with an enrollment of nearly 3,000 students.

In a short time, SPC created a model in which, in addition to hosting university partners' existing programs, new programs could be produced within months. This was a contrast to the usual several years of waiting that is common for new university-level programs. Examples of new programs include dentistry and pharmacy, offered in tandem with the University of Florida, and hospitality, offered with Florida International University. Pinellas County government officials asked the college to offer a hospitality program to assist the county's tourism-dependent local economy. SPC responded by creating a 2-year program and partnering with Florida International University (FIU) to offer higher degrees. FIU is regarded as the number-one hospitality program in the United States. A medical building for the two University of Florida doctoral programs is under construction now on one SPC campus.

In 1 year, the college has received approval for and raised more than $3 million to offer a bachelor's degree in orthotics and prosthetics (O&P). SPC and the University of South Florida (USF) have an understanding that USF will partner with the UPC to house a master's and a PhD program, operated by USF. Florida will become a major education center for O&P education, offering the first O&P doctoral program in the United States. Major U.S. and international manufacturers of O&P technology and equipment have made generous contributions, and partnering opportunities exist with Walter Reed Hospital in Washington, DC, the only provider of O&P treatment for returning military service men and women, and Tampa Bay area hospitals and clinics. Finally, two cities have partnered with the college to build state-of-the-art, joint-use libraries. In both cases, the cities will pay a portion of the library's operating costs, resulting in savings for the cities and revenue for the college. In one case, the city is paying for the majority of personnel costs as well.

The EpiCenter

In the mid-1970s, with a few AS degrees and a small continuing education program, SPC was primarily a transfer 2+2 college. In 1978, the college sought to enlarge its continuing education program and expand services to business communities with continuing educations units. At the time, SPC's continuing education activities were not organized centrally. Rather, traditional academic departments were in charge of continuing education initiatives for their areas. Faculty members were not able to support continuing education course development and delivery, in addition to primary program responsibilities, adequately.

The college reorganized, and a new provost was assigned the task of developing SPC's Open Campus. In a few years, Open Campus enrollment exceeded 20,000 students. A workforce, hungry for educational opportunity, received up-to-date knowledge, opportunities to earn certificates, and an expanded number of degrees. SPC's reorganization of continuing education initiatives was an improvement and, for a number of years, met community need.

Emboldened by a number of successful ventures, including a local tax referendum that revitalized the college's facilities and equipment acquisitions, SPC crafted a new plan. A

Corporate Training Center was established in the mid-1980s (about the time the personal computer entered the workforce), and a wide variety of computer and management training programs were offered to the workforce. As the 1990s approached, computer certifications became a primary ticket for employment promotions, and computer training became a significant pillar of SPC revenue.

By the early 2000s, the college had become a primary purveyor of educational opportunities for technology-based industries that flooded the county. But the SPC Corporate Training Center was just the warm-up. The college realized it was actually on a treadmill of change and that America's workforce and technology training needs would continue to evolve and create even greater entrepreneurial opportunities.

In June 2000, the Pinellas County economic development department surveyed approximately 35,000 businesses. The survey revealed that the number-one challenge in business was finding qualified workers. Other survey information indicated high satisfaction among those employing SPC students and graduates and a specific need for qualified electrical engineers.

Meanwhile, Florida had established a unique matching-funds program for scholarships, facilities, and certain specific academic endeavors, with funds matched dollar-for-dollar by the Florida legislature. American community colleges were experiencing a shake-up in workforce education dollars—redefining what constituted one-stop education centers and other workforce-related matters. Changes in funding patterns and opportunities for matched dollars prompted SPC leaders to think of new ways to serve customers, such as electrical engineering degrees, an area into which the college had not yet expanded.

One idea came from a presentation at a Florida Community Colleges Council of Presidents retreat in Orlando. At the invitation of Seminole Community College president E. Ann McGee (one of the retreat's organizers and the author of chapter 8), a private company selling its education services to major employers showcased its collaborative learning center. The collaborative learning center presentation sparked SPC's desire to own a facility in Pinellas County that would include such a center.

Relying on a successful history of activities sponsored by SPC and the Pinellas County government, including the county's request for the tourism and hospitality program at SPC, the college approached the county as a potential partner for this new plan. County and college leaders began discussing the EpiCenter, envisioned to be unique in county government and college circles. The EpiCenter would be a full-service center for business and workforce development. It would house the county's economic development headquarters in a custom-renovated building along with the SPC administration and its burgeoning corporate training center. As the plans solidified, the local WorkNet (Workforce) Board agreed to join the collaboration.

The learning center concept brought a new enterprise to higher education: a 10,000 to 12,000 square-foot think tank, designed with a common meeting area where 100 people could gather and break-out rooms for smaller group meetings. With the unusual combination of county and college talent, technology, and consulting expertise available in a single setting, the EpiCenter will serve its mutual constituents well. Corporate training and full presentation topics, ranging from how to begin a new business to making good business better and curing the ailing business, will be provided.

The EpiCenter, scheduled to open December 2004, benefited from the county's contribution of $8 million, matched by another $8 million from the state legislature. The sale of

SPC's old administration building completed the project budget with $32 million earmarked for the EpiCenter. Revenues from the EpiCenter are expected to cover operating expenses and enhance the college's budget. As the opening of the EpiCenter drew near in fall 2004, the list of departments and agencies serving clientele side-by-side at the center continued to grow. The college looks forward to creating and re-creating services and combinations of services and cultivating monetary savings for taxpayers at the same time. The EpiCenter is poised to become a premier education center for businesses in the southeast. SPC expects that dollars will be conserved, as business owners and investors discover this efficient and economical vehicle, not only for building and training their workforce, but also for assisting their workers with retention, counseling, and technical support.

CONCLUSION

The entrepreneurial community college inherently accepts challenges. As president of an e-spirited college, I am well aware that one of those challenges is to meld principles and practices from the marketplace carefully with the ethical and social values that for centuries have been central to the mission of the academic enterprise. In other words, although I concede my entrepreneurial bias, I also accept the college's obligation to choose carefully from the array of entrepreneurial opportunities that are available.

Bok has said that educators need to "be very clear about what the fundamental academic values are . . . because there are a lot of profit-making or commercial activities that are innocuous and even beneficial. It's when they begin to result in compromises of basic academic values that you get into trouble" (cited in Olson, 2004, p. 20). Whether academic institutions should engage in entrepreneurial activity continues to be a debated subject. Not everyone in the academic community is a believer, even though it is clear that many e-spirited colleges are thriving, serving their constituents well at a time when traditional resources continue to shrink. Competition is forcing traditional colleges and universities to review the concept of entrepreneurship.

The academic institution best positioned to capture entrepreneurial opportunity is the community college. Community colleges are known to be lean-staffed, get-it-done institutions with a short turn-around time for accomplishing new and high-quality initiatives. The e-spirit is not just a spirit—it equates to lower operating costs and increased revenues. The challenge is to keep the e-spirit alive—identifying and implementing ways to continually encourage everyone involved, moving the college along—and ready for the next entrepreneurial idea.

In *Why Entrepreneurship Has Won!* Stevenson, of Harvard University, stated: "We can no longer simply say 'entrepreneurship is different.' *Entrepreneurship is now a part of the mainstream*" [emphasis added] (2000, p. 7). SPC's entrepreneurial spirit creates a continued sense of renewal for all involved in its entrepreneurial projects and initiatives. The e-spirit is felt in the college, community, state, and nation. In a study on entrepreneurial leadership, Burrows (2002) found SPC leadership to be entrepreneurial and SPC a "make it happen" college. Florida's Governor Jeb Bush, in an impromptu speech to more than 80 SPC students visiting the capitol in spring 2004, said: "You can be proud. SPC is one of the most entrepreneurial colleges in America."

REFERENCES

Burrows, B. A. (2002). *The vertical extension of Florida's community college system: A case study of politics and entrepreneurial leadership.* Unpublished doctoral dissertation, The University of Texas at Austin.

Drucker, P. F. (1985). *Innovation and entrepreneurship.* New York: HarperBusiness.

Farrel, L. C. (2001). *The entrepreneurial age: Awakening the spirit of enterprise in people, companies, and countries.* New York: Allworth Press.

Kuratko, D. F. (2003). *Entrepreneurship education: Emerging trends and challenges for the 21st century.* (2003 Coleman Foundation White Paper Series for the U.S. Association of Small Business and Entrepreneurship). Retrieved June 3, 2004, from http://www.usasbe.org/pdf/CWP-2003-kuratko.pdf

Leatherman, S. P. (2003). *America's best beaches.* Gainesville, FL: University Press of Florida.

Olson, M. (2004, June). *What price profit? Former Harvard University president Derek Bok talks about evaluating entrepreneurial ideas in light of their impact on academic values.* Washington, DC: National Association of College and University Business Officers. Available from http://www.nacubo.org

Public Forum Institute. (2003). Understanding entrepreneurship. In *National dialogue on entrepreneurship.* Retrieved June 3, 2004, from http://www.publicforuminstitute.org/nde/ under/index.htm.

Raspberry, W. (2004, April). *Great American potential that remains to be realized.* Keynote address presented at the annual meeting of the American Association of Community Colleges, Minneapolis, MN.

Roueche, J. E., & Parnell, D. (1994). *1001 exemplary practices in America's two-year colleges.* New York: McGraw Hill.

Stevenson, H. H. (2000, February). *Why entrepreneurship has won!* (Coleman Foundation White Paper plenary address). Retrieved June 3, 2004, from http://www.usasbe.org/pdf/CWP-2000-stevenson.pdf

With special thanks to Dr. Ian C. Barker, education consultant, Florida Department of Education, and the following St. Petersburg staff: Dr. Kay Adkins, associate vice president, Educational and Student Services; Ms. Marsha Barlow, senior executive staff assistant, President's Office; Ms. Amelia W. Carey, director, Institutional Advancement; Dr. Carol C. Copenhaver, senior vice president, Educational and Student Services; Dr. Thomas E. Furlong, senior vice president, Baccalaureate Programs and University Partnerships; Mr. Lars A. Hafner, vice president, University Partnership Center Athletic Director; Mr. Jim Moorhead, information coordinator, Institutional Advancement; Dr. Esther Oliver, provost, Allstate Center; Dr. James Olliver, provost, Seminole Campus and eCampus; Ms. Junetta Smith, executive staff assistant, President's Office; and Dr. Karen K. White, acting special assistant to the president.

CHAPTER 5

ENTREPRENEURIAL PARTNERSHIPS

Donald W. Cameron

—Guilford Technical and Community College, Jamestown, North Carolina

---

Coming together is a beginning, staying together is progress, and working together is success.

—*Henry Ford*

Guilford Technical Community College (GTCC), located in Guilford County, North Carolina, serves a large urban county that includes two of the state's largest cities, Greensboro and High Point. GTCC opened in 1958, as one of North Carolina's first industrial education centers that collectively evolved into the present North Carolina Community College System. The industrial education centers were established to prepare people for jobs created by the rapid transition of North Carolina's post–World War II, agrarian economy to a new economy dominated by manufacturing. Guilford County was home to many of the nation's best-known textile and furniture industries. High Point, which hosts the International Home Furnishings Market, is still known as the Furniture Capital of the World.

In 1965, the Guilford County Industrial Education Center was granted the authority to award associate degrees and, subsequently, became Guilford Technical Institute. In 1983, despite considerable opposition at the local and system levels, GTI added a college transfer program, becoming Guilford Technical Community College. Because of its long history of providing vocational and technical education, and to demonstrate the continuing commitment to that aspect of its expanding mission, GTCC trustees insisted that technical remain a part of the institution's name.

Today, GTCC has four campuses and enrolls more than 12,000 (unduplicated) students in curriculum programs and 30,000 (unduplicated) students in continuing education programs annually. More than 50% of the curriculum students are over 24 years of age, and 75% of those students work full or part time. GTCC is the fourth largest community college in the North Carolina Community College System. Guilford County is also the home of two branches of the University of North Carolina, four private colleges, and numerous proprietary educational enterprises. More than 90% of GTCC graduates remain in the area following graduation.

PRESIDENTIAL LEADERSHIP: PROMOTING AN ENTREPRENEURIAL COMMUNITY COLLEGE

GTCC's board of trustees has long been known for encouraging entrepreneurial activity. Rather than staying the established course, GTCC's board encourages innovative programs, community partnerships, and a broad range of student activities. Early in my presidency, I became involved heavily in a variety of community activities: civic clubs, economic development organizations, and chambers of commerce. These associations not only allowed me a pulpit from which to educate the community about GTCC and its mission, but also they gave me the opportunity to develop a broad and influential circle of contacts who could benefit the college.

Within the college community, I encouraged all campus employees to assume a role in collegewide planning processes. Through their participation, individual employees were able to demonstrate a high regard for initiative, creativity, and risk taking. The employee-of-the-month award was established to recognize creativity in performing jobs more effectively, conserving college resources, and providing improved customer service. As a result of a spirit of creativity and thinking beyond the limitations of its resources, GTCC can boast of accomplishments otherwise impossible. The three case studies included here grew from the college's planning process, and none of them would have been possible without additional funding beyond county and state allocations.

A New Culinary Technology Facility

In 1983, the college implemented a commercial food service program. Although a feasibility study had clearly documented the need, there was no funding available for a facility in which to house the program. The college decided to renovate an existing kitchen facility that served as the food preparation area for the college's on-campus day-care center. In 1989, the college received approval to offer a 2-year culinary technology curriculum. A classroom next to the kitchen became a dining facility in which meals could be served to college employees, students, and, at times, the general public. These limited facilities created other limitations, including the types of equipment to which students could be exposed and the number of students the program could serve.

The culinary technology advisory committee became especially active as the culinary industry in Guilford County, and the surrounding area boomed. Demand for trained chefs, food service managers, and other personnel increased rapidly. The growing hotel and convention center industry in the area also demanded more trained workers. The college administration and board sincerely wanted to respond to the advisory committee's persistent request for more space, but there were no capital funds to purchase, build, or lease it. When the college, with significant input from the advisory committee, successfully passed bond issues in 1990 and 1993, sufficient funds were raised to build a new facility. The board's long-range facilities plan included a building that would house the existing culinary program, a new hospitality management program, and GTCC's theatre arts program.

Invigorated by success, the advisory committee also became involved in the architectural design of the new facility. A 40,000 square-foot facility emerged from the design process and was to be built on the edge of the college's 5-acre lake, a prime location on the Jamestown campus. The new building, which opened in the 1998–1999 academic year, included the following:

- Five teaching kitchens with baking, *garde manger*, front-line, and preparation areas designed to accommodate up to four different classes at one time
- A demonstration kitchen with tiered, auditorium-type seats and equipped with audiovisual equipment for viewing demonstrations
- A dining room with a seating capacity for 100 (along with an outdoor, lakeside area for 30) and a private dining room to seat 25
- A walk-in cooler and freezer, and storage facilities for dry goods, linens, china, silver glassware, kitchen smallwares, cooking utensils, and other items
- General classrooms and office space to accommodate the needs of the curriculum and the new hospitality management program
- Two model hotel rooms
- A small service kitchen adjoining the private dining room
- A 500-seat auditorium and an innovative, black box theatre to accommodate the college's theatre program

Although capital funds were available to replace the makeshift kitchen and dining room, GTCC lacked the funds to equip this new facility with state-of-the-art kitchen appliances and tools that the industry demanded.

The North Carolina Community College System always has struggled with one of the lowest, and now perhaps the lowest, FTE–funding levels in the nation's community college systems. Equipment funding, also provided through an FTE–based formula, is no better. Clearly, a nontraditional funding source was needed if this new facility was to have equipment commensurate with local industry's standards. Again, the advisory committee became pivotal.

I worked closely with the department's faculty and directly with key advisory committee members to find a solution. Staff, working with advisory committee members, developed a list of equipment and implements they needed. The total cost was projected at $600,000—a figure greater than the college's total annual equipment budget. Advisory committee members, working through the college's foundation, set out to raise funds, either through cash donations or donated equipment.

Members of the advisory committee included representatives from the area's two major utility providers—Duke Power and Piedmont Natural Gas. Both companies had an obvious interest in the growth of the area's hospitality industry. Through their contacts and influence, major donations of equipment, tools, and supplies were solicited successfully. In fact, more than 25 companies involved in the hospitality industry contributed equipment and supplies. Several major furniture companies in the High Point area contributed case goods, upholstered furniture, and decorative accessories for the private dining rooms and conference rooms. The donation-raising effort and success were unprecedented in the college's history.

An unusual aspect of these donations was that many of the large kitchen pieces were donated on consignment. The agreement allowed the manufacturers of the equipment to use the facility to demonstrate their equipment to potential customers. As a result, some of the companies, for the first time, had a live kitchen operation in which to demonstrate their products. Moreover, the agreement allowed the manufacturer to replace the consigned equipment with newer models as they developed. So, not only did the college reduce its need for equipment funds, but also it reduced its need for replacing equipment.

In the midst of this solicitation, the college received the largest gift in its history—$500,000 from the area's premier commercial developer, designated for support of the culinary and hospitality management programs. Even before the new facility was occupied, enrollments in the culinary program grew rapidly. In fact, after the facility was occupied, between 1997 and 2003, unduplicated headcount in the program rose from 35 to 145, and the FTE more than doubled.

The advisory committee found other ways to assist the program. The committee instituted an annual open house. Interested high school students and their parents visit the facility for an evening reception at which they enjoy a delicious meal and learn about program and career opportunities in the hospitality industry. The local chapter of the American Culinary Federation hosted a chefs' ball, with some of the proceeds going to scholarships. The advisory committee decided to sponsor golf tournaments jointly with other culinary associations to raise funds for scholarships. One person in the community who regularly dines with friends at the facility recently informed the college's foundation that she had established a $1 million trust in her estate to support the culinary program and facility.

The culinary program, from its more than humble beginnings, has become a flagship program for GTCC and generates inestimable amounts of goodwill for the college. Two days a week the public can make reservations for lunch, and one night a week they can reserve dinner in the main dining room. These events are heavily attended, and reservation slots are filled usually days in advance. For a nominal fee ($6 for lunch, $7.50 for dinner), citizens have a delicious meal prepared and served by GTCC students. Several times a year, a dinner is scheduled before one of GTCC's theatre department productions. In addition to bringing so many people to campus, many of them for the first time, these receipts also help the college recoup almost one third of the total supply budget needed to fund the culinary program annually.

Today, GTCC offers the only culinary program in the North Carolina Community College System that is accredited by the American Culinary Federation. Of all the curriculum programs at GTCC, most of which have been strengthened through partnerships with outside businesses or agencies, the ongoing story of the culinary program is a case study in the success that an active advisory committee can achieve when it engages in entrepreneurial activity.

YMCA Comes to Campus

There was little, if any, interest in a physical education center during GTCC's formative years. In fact, there was no demonstrated interest in such a facility or the programs and activities it might support during the first 25 years of the college's history. Only a few of North Carolina's community colleges ever developed intercollegiate athletics programs, and most community college campuses in this state have no athletic facilities, either gymnasiums or playing fields. Perhaps more important, a large majority of students work at least 20 hours per week in addition to going to school, so they have little time for intercollegiate activities, either as participants or spectators.

At GTCC and throughout the North Carolina Community College System, the funding of athletic or physical education facilities has been a negative issue. Although GTCC has passed all seven bond issues during its history, money was not available for anything resembling a physical education complex. Even if the college's board had proposed such a facility, it is highly unlikely that the county commissioners would have included it on a bond referendum. And, the county's voters would not have approved it had it been on the ballot.

In the early 1980s, as GTCC began to move aggressively toward adding a college transfer program to its technical and vocational offerings, there was some interest, more among college administrators and faculty than among trustees, in adding intramural sports and, perhaps, intercollegiate sports. Using private donations and student government funds, tennis courts, volleyball courts, and basketball courts were added to the campus landscape—and the student government association successfully launched some limited intramural activities.

There was interest in constructing a wellness center on campus—not a gymnasium, but a fitness center. Several board members pushed this idea as a way of providing fitness courses for students, particularly college-transfer students whose 4-year curricula would require physical education credits. In addition, some trustees felt that the wellness center might find a niche in providing wellness programs to area business and industry. This idea fit perfectly with the college's established mission of providing training to local employers, and those same trustees believed that such a facility would allow the college to provide a valuable benefit to college employees interested in a wellness program. Finally, a small but well-organized group of faculty and staff had begun encouraging me (I was then the college's vice president for academic affairs) to support a wellness center for employees. The addition of a college transfer program was the key factor that led to a wellness center on campus.

When the college transfer program was first offered, the only on-campus facilities for physical education courses were tennis courts, a volleyball court, and a basketball court; most of the physical education classes were scheduled at area YMCAs, golf courses, and bowling alleys. Not only did this situation produce transportation and scheduling problems for students, but also it demanded local funds to rent the facilities (state funds cannot be used for such purposes).

In 1984, some unallocated capital funds were used to construct a 6,600 square-foot wellness center. This small building contained a large fitness room with Nautilus equipment, free weights, treadmills, stationary cycles, and open floor space for aerobics, as well as a general classroom, three faculty offices, and shower and locker facilities.

As college-transfer enrollments grew rapidly over the next decade, the college felt the pressure to add more facilities. Although a large number of fitness and wellness classes were offered through the new facility, there was not sufficient space or enough variety to meet the growing demand. A possible solution to the dilemma came 15 years later when YMCA officials approached me, then president, about constructing a facility on the Jamestown Campus.

The YMCA made a presentation to the GTCC board of trustees in spring 1998. Although the Jamestown Campus of GTCC is located 2 miles outside of the city limits of Greensboro, much of Greensboro's growth during the 1990s had been in the southwest area of the city, close to GTCC. The interest of the YMCA was in serving that growing population, most of which lived or worked too great a distance from the existing YMCA facilities to be involved in their programs. The benefits to the YMCA in arranging for a facility on GTCC's campus were clear—it would be located in the heart of suburban growth, associated with a community college with strong community support, and would have access to other college facilities (e.g., auditoriums, classrooms).

The YMCA's proposal was for a 50,000 square-foot facility that would include an indoor aquatic center, an indoor running/walking track, a modern fitness center, an aerobic studio, a community education center (offering nutrition and wellness programs), a nursery, and a multipurpose gymnasium. The proposal asked for 17 acres of college land on a 50-year lease (at $1 per year) and for the college to contribute $1 million toward an estimated construction cost of $6.5 million.

Advantages to the proposal included the following:

- The college could use an on-campus facility for a diversified offering of physical education courses.
- The new YMCA would provide office space, a general classroom, and shower and locker facilities, eliminating the need for the college's existing wellness center.
- The college would be able to reduce significantly the amount of county funds needed annually to rent off-campus physical education facilities.
- GTCC faculty and staff would have access to a modern physical fitness facility.

However, there were reservations. Many trustees questioned whether the college could afford, in the long-term, to give up so much land on its main campus. Moreover, the board calculated that the college would not be able to provide the $1 million requested for construction of the complex.

In the months following the presentation of the proposal to the board, several major roadblocks developed. The High Point YMCA, separate from the Greensboro YMCA, raised questions about whether the proposed site violated national YMCA policy on service areas. Additionally, owners of local private fitness centers (developed in the fitness boom of the 1980s and 1990s) raised questions about being in competition with a community college financed with public funds. North Carolina has a statutory provision that prohibits state-funded entities from competing with private enterprise. This provision has been cited frequently by private businesses that thought state universities were involved in unfair competition. Several years ago, for example, the University of North Carolina at Chapel Hill's bookstore began stocking personal computers for sale, and area computer stores raised this statute to oppose that retail activity.

By December 1998, most of these obstacles had been removed. Local YMCA officials, working with their national office, resolved the issue of territorial boundaries, and the Greensboro YMCA was granted permission to proceed with the plan to serve the southwest area of Guilford County. Within a few months, at least the public opposition from owners of private fitness centers began to vanish. YMCA officials continually stressed that they were serving a different population, and, at least apparently, the private businesses had sufficient memberships that they were not severely threatened by the prospect of a YMCA in the area.

After considerable debate, GTCC's board of trustees agreed that the advantages of entering into such a lease were greater than the loss of land and, in December 1998, the board gave its approval to begin negotiating a lease. In early 1999, the State Board of Community Colleges gave its approval to leasing 7 acres of land. By spring 1999, the YMCA established an organizing committee to raise capital funds. I found myself in a new role—as a member of the executive committee of the YMCA's campaign. Meanwhile, college staff and YMCA staff (and their respective attorneys) began a laborious process of writing an acceptable lease document. This process lasted for more than a year.

The next roadblock was out of the college's control. The Greensboro YMCA was already in the midst of a major capital campaign to establish a facility in downtown Greensboro to replace a dated and undersized facility. Furthermore, the economy, and especially the local economy, turned downward quickly. Initial fundraising efforts were less than successful. In fact, it took almost 3 years before sufficient funding was available with which to enter into a construction contract.

Other problems were encountered along the way—most notably, the YMCA's continuing request to lease additional college land to use as playing fields. The college's trustees, some of whom had been reluctant to lease the original 7 acres, relented and agreed to lease another 7 acres for that purpose. Because of legal complications with leasing so much land purchased with public funds, the college had to work with its local delegation to the North Carolina General Assembly to get a local bill introduced and passed that would allow such a lease.

Perhaps one of the most difficult and unanticipated challenges was the time and energy that I had to commit personally to the YMCA's fundraising activities. Because the college's foundation had simultaneously embarked on its first major endowment campaign, I faced a personal and professional dilemma in approaching potential contributors. As experienced fundraisers know, one organization can approach the same set of contributors only a limited number of times. Although this situation remained a personal dilemma for me throughout the YMCA's campaign, it never became a public issue.

The advantages to the college of having a YMCA facility on campus were clear, and they justified my active participation in the fundraising campaign. The college would have a quality physical education facility available to students and staff, a reality that would never have been possible without such a partnership. The college would save almost $100,000 a year in funds previously used to rent off-campus facilities for physical education classes and approximately $50,000 every 5 or 6 years by not having to replace equipment that had been used in the existing Wellness Center.

An unexpected advantage developed late in the process. As it became clear that the YMCA would succeed in its capital campaign, college staff and board members began to consider what to do with the Wellness Center. Because of size and other facility limitations, there was no opportunity to turn the facility into general classroom space. There was some discussion about turning it into faculty office space for the growing number of adjunct instructors, but most favored demolishing the structure. Ironically, local economic development efforts began to focus on the biotechnology industry since several start-up businesses had emerged in the area. The Wellness Center structure offers a possible temporary home for some biotechnology training; at this time, it appears that the administration and the board will make that decision.

Quick Jobs With a Future
When the Industrial Education Center (IEC) was established in Guilford County in 1958, the first classes were for employees of a hosiery firm. Classes for workers in the scores of furniture manufacturing plants in the county soon followed. For the next 30 years, as the IEC evolved into Guilford Technical Institute and then into Guilford Technical Community College, training for these traditional manufacturers remained a high priority.

In the late 1980s, however, the economy of North Carolina, and of Guilford County in particular, began to change. National and international conglomerates began to acquire locally owned textile and furniture companies. The passage and implementation of the North American Free Trade Agreement in the mid-1990s, although supported by some textile executives, produced major changes in the national economy and a cataclysmic change in North Carolina's economy. Guilford County's manufacturing economy, which for a century had been dominated by textiles, furniture, and tobacco, was especially hard hit.

As these traditional manufacturers began to move more and more operations offshore, local reductions-in-force and entire plant closings became weekly headlines. In the decade from 1994 to 2004, more than 14,000 manufacturing jobs were lost in Guilford County alone. For GTCC, it meant enrolling hundreds of those displaced workers who took advantage of training programs to acquire new skills for new jobs. They used Workforce Investment Act benefits or Pell Grants to pursue traditional degree or diploma programs in a variety of fields, many only remotely connected to their previous employment. For a large number of those unemployed citizens, though, traditional offerings were not attractive. The programs were too long, or at least seemed too long, for many unemployed adults who were struggling to keep up with bills and family responsibilities.

After numerous informal discussions with college staff, community leaders, and members of the board, in late 2003, I decided to launch a formal initiative that would focus on short-term training, designed for jobs already available in the local economy. At my urging, a local coalition, which currently has at least a dozen organizations as active members, began to meet and discuss possible strategies. The coalition included representatives from the county's Department of Social Services, local Employment Security Commission, local chambers of commerce, United Way, and the local Workforce Development Board.

From these meetings, the coalition adopted a purpose statement "to develop a cooperative effort between interested parties that links the displaced worker with assessment, counseling, and placement in specialized training, empowering the candidate to return to the workplace within 90 days." Because of its recognized history of being the major source of job training in the county, GTCC quickly became the focus of the coalition's efforts; the other coalition members became an advisory group.

An immediate problem I faced, along with my leadership team, was how to fund such a program. Although North Carolina, as many community college historians have noted, has led the nation in providing customized training for new and expanding industries, there is no similar funding source for displaced workers. Moreover, the FTE–based funding structure for North Carolina's community colleges for short-term, occupational training is even less than that provided for curriculum programs (which itself is among the lowest in the nation). Furthermore, funding for North Carolina community colleges is provided in the budgetary year after the FTE is earned. Put another way, there is no start-up funding for new programs, curricula, or continuing education.

I engaged in informal conversations with leaders of local foundations to see if I could identify foundation support for the effort. I was not surprised, given the severity of the problem, that I found support, but I was surprised at the speed with which it developed. Four local foundations, with long histories of providing support for economic and community development, committed $350,000 to the effort. These gifts were remarkable; however, it was clear that this was a one-time grant. For the program to be ongoing, a means had to be identified and designed to make the program self-sustaining.

Because of a long-time friendship with Thomas Barton, president at Greenville Technical College in South Carolina, I was familiar with a similar (and successful) initiative undertaken there. In its first 2 years of operation, Greenville Tech's Quick Jobs program had trained more than 3,000 students and successfully placed 70% of those graduates into jobs. Several GTCC leaders and I traveled to Greenville and intensively studied the operations and history of the program. We found that the local economies of Greenville, South Carolina, and Guilford County, North Carolina, are remarkably similar. Whereas the South Carolina system provides a better funding formula for short-term (nondegree) occupational training, Greenville Tech's other program matched up perfectly with Guilford County's needs. Barton and his staff generously shared their program and results and gave permission for GTCC to export any of their ideas.

Back home in North Carolina, I presented the Greenville Tech program as a model for the coalition. Within a month of that visit and within 3 months of the original discussions, the coalition adopted the following three goals:

1. Establish the infrastructure (administration, governance, and instruction) to launch Quick Jobs (the same name used by Greenville Tech) by February 1, 2004.
2. Identify and package training for 10 in-demand jobs that fit the 90-day requirement for the launch on February 1, 2004.
3. Measure the job placement rate for the participants who complete the training with targeted achievement of greater than 70% placed.

The coalition continued its work and focused on identifying jobs in the local economy that had high vacancy rates. In addition, the coalition partners ensured that all sources would have the same information about training opportunities. Finally, the coalition agreed that all agencies would be involved in the development of an accountability process to track results of this new program.

The work of the coalition and the funding provided by the local foundations generated considerable attention in the local media. Local newspapers carried articles about the coalition's plans and about the foundations' monetary support. Editorial endorsements of the plans also appeared. Displaced workers interested in the program began to call the college before a formal operation had been established.

I admit that some of my senior staff and I were apprehensive about being able to respond within such a tight timeline to the high expectations that were developing rapidly. Previously when the college had undertaken a new program, months and often years went into planning, feasibility studies, and curriculum design before the program was publicized, much less initiated. Fortunately, GTCC was in the process of hiring a new dean of business and industry; quickly, that selection process began to include, as a major criterion, the ability to direct and coordinate this new program. In addition, I identified an experienced faculty member who had a long and successful record of classroom teaching and special project coordination to begin working with curriculum design and other details. With this support in place, I was at least partially freed up from the organizational details and could continue building public support for the program.

By late December 2003, GTCC had modified Greenville Tech's Quick Jobs into GTCC's Quick Jobs With a Future. A major press briefing was held on campus to inform local media about the new project. In press releases and advertisements, the college promised a variety of courses at affordable prices and at convenient times and locations. To appeal to displaced workers facing financial responsibilities, the college focused on the theme that the training would be skills-specific and would take 3 months or less. In addition, publicity emphasized that many of the classes would not require a high school diploma or GED. Financial assistance, through scholarships, grants, or loans, was promised.

In the month following the media's announcement of Quick Jobs With a Future, GTCC received more than 300 calls requesting information. Because of this overwhelming response, the college decided to hold a public information session on January 16, 2004. The college advertised the session in local newspapers, including block ads in the classified sections. Local television stations carried the stories. At least 1,000 people turned out for the session.

Next, the college developed a comprehensive link on its Web page to the Quick Jobs With a Future Web site. There interested citizens were able to explore a description of the initiative, the curriculum for each of the programs, a schedule of the course offerings, and information about financial aid and job placement.

The course offerings began in early February 2004. As planned, the first offerings were in identified fields where relatively fast training would result in jobs currently available in substantial numbers in the local economy. Those first 10 fields included truck driver, welder, administrative medical specialist, call center representative, warehouse technician, office specialist, medical receptionist, certified nursing assistant, automotive maintenance technician, and retail sales associate.

Offered on a self-supporting basis, some of the courses were brief (2–4 weeks in the case of retail sales associate and call center associate). Each student's cost ranged from $78 to $1,400, but many qualified for financial aid. Most of the courses were offered on an intensive schedule of 5 days a week and 4–8 hours a day. Although registration was on a first-come, first-served basis, preference was given to people who were unemployed at the time of registration. Today, more than 300 students are enrolled in one of the programs. Some of the shorter courses have ended, and most of the graduates have found employment.

Curriculum plans for additional offerings are in the design phase. During the next 4 years, the college's goals are for the program to become self-supporting and to enroll 3,500 participants, with a 70% job placement rate for graduates. College officials have completed a 3-year financial plan that includes a phase-out of foundation support in the third year, with the program becoming self-supporting in the fourth year. Whatever the long-term results, one immediate success is clear. The college is being applauded by local business and government officials for its quick response to a crisis in the local economy. The program will be evaluated closely through the college's regular program evaluation process; early indications point to its success.

CONCLUSION

If entrepreneurial activity is generating income that will supplement the overall operation of the college, none of the three case studies described in this chapter qualifies as entrepreneurial. However, these projects are entrepreneurial in several other ways. First, none of the three projects would have been possible if those involved had limited their thinking to the boundaries of existing financial resources available to the college. Entering into the partnerships just described involved moving beyond boundaries and taking on a certain amount of risk. There was also the risk that successfully initiated projects would not live up to their long-term promise.

These projects are also entrepreneurial in that their successful implementation saved the college substantial amounts of county operating funds and state equipment funds. It is difficult to estimate accurately the annual savings to the college in facility rental funds, utility and maintenance funds, and equipment funds—conservatively, $200,000 annually in operating funds and $250,000 annually in equipment funds. More important than these savings, however, are the improvements in facilities, instructional equipment, and services to students and the general public that resulted from each project.

Unfortunately, improved funding for North Carolina's community colleges is not likely. If GTCC is to continue its legacy of providing instructional programs that rise to the level of excellence expected by business and industry and the general public, it will be possible only with additional entrepreneurial partnerships in the college's future.

CHAPTER 6

EMBEDDING ENTREPRENEURIALISM:
A CANADIAN CASE STUDY

Robert A. Gordon

—Humber College Institute of Technology and Advanced Learning, Toronto, Canada

They see the pattern, understand the order, experience the vision.

—*Peter Drucker, business strategist and author*

The globalizing higher education market means that entrepreneurial activity has become a mainstay of how colleges compete. To be competitive in their markets, colleges need to adopt and adapt business tools that build on their unique advantages and positions within their markets. Humber College Institute of Technology and Advanced Learning addressed these market changes. Our experiences are presented as a case study by which to outline a framework for adopting entrepreneurial principles and for implementing successful practices in any college setting.

Founded in 1967, Humber College Institute of Technology and Advanced Learning (until 2003, College of Applied Arts and Technology) is located in the northwestern quadrant of Toronto, Canada's largest city, with a population of almost 6 million. The city is considered one of the world's most ethnically diverse and cosmopolitan, with a constant influx of immigrants adding to and enriching that mix. Humber's population is broadly reflective of the city's ethnic mosaic and includes people from numerous countries around the world.

Humber is 1 of 24 public colleges in Ontario, a province with more than 12 million inhabitants; 8 of these colleges are located in the Greater Toronto Area (GTA). Unlike in the United States, Canadian colleges, particularly in the Toronto region, do not have to operate in precisely defined geographical districts. Students have always been free to attend any college in the system, subject only to meeting admissions criteria and availability of adequate space in specific programs. Tuition fees generally are standardized across the province by the government. Humber has two major campuses—one, the North, located some 10 minutes from Pearson International Airport; the other, Lakeshore, situated on the shores of Lake Ontario, within 20 minutes of downtown Toronto.

Humber offers the most comprehensive menu of programs in Ontario, with some 160 full-time diplomas, 200 certificates, 9 degrees (with more under development), and more than 1,000 courses in continuing education. In September 2003, almost 16,000 students were enrolled full-time, with another 60,000 part-time registrants and corporate clients in eight schools, including applied technology, business, hospitality, recreation and tourism, social and community services, creative and performing arts, health sciences, media studies and information technology, and liberal arts and science. To meet the constantly growing enrollment demand, the institution currently is completing a $130 million capital improvement program, including two additional student residences, bringing the total number of rooms to 1,400.

Humber is one of the two largest colleges in Canada; Seneca, in the north quadrant of the GTA, is the other. Although transfer programs to universities have not been a major focus generally, to serve an ever-growing number of diploma-seeking graduates, Humber has transfer agreements with 41 universities in Canada, the United States, and internationally. Humber is the only Canadian member of the League for Innovation in the Community College and was selected as one of 12 Vanguard Learning Colleges in North America (see http://www.league.org/league/projects/lcp/vanguard.htm).

THE IMPETUS FOR ENTREPRENEURSHIP AT HUMBER COLLEGE

Humber has long operated in an entrepreneurial way, partly because of the impact of local and environmental conditions and partly because of the commitment of its leadership and management. Indeed, by playing on the opportunities presented by these two factors, Humber has been able to identify and engage in many creative agreements and relationships that have provided the impetus for successful entrepreneurship at Humber. Five examples are described in the following sections.

Labor and Economic Forces

Colleges in Ontario were structured initially to educate students in the skills needed for direct entry to the labor markets. Because job placement has held such a high premium, the institution always has nurtured strong relations with potential employers. Also, paying considerable attention to developing a workforce for private sector firms and to customized training has enabled the college to cement strong working relationships based on competence and trust over many years. These relationships have been critical to Humber's success, because public colleges are not allowed to gain revenues from local taxation, unlike in most U.S. jurisdictions, nor are there any provisions to allow them to generate capital through methods such as floating bond issues.

Because programs are unique, as well as capital-intensive, and because government grants are insufficient to cover constantly escalating requirements, the squeeze on finances always has been an issue. Lately, with government grants in decline and tuition frozen, this serious situation has reached crisis proportions. Thus, Humber has sought tangible support from its satisfied customers in the private sector and has tried to develop mutually beneficial relationships by providing outstanding services to countless companies, which, in turn, helped the college meet its needs for equipment, software, internships, and cooperative opportunities. These economic pushes have compelled Humber to hone its abilities as an entrepreneurial college.

Population Shifts

The official, geographical catch basin (i.e., northwest Toronto) allocated to Humber by the Ontario Colleges Act, 1965, stipulated that members of the Board of Governors must live or work in the area and that the college could not have physical facilities outside the catch basin. In the beginning, the geographic limitations did not appear problematic. Since 1967, populations have grown, and because of this, there have been problems. Whereas the two boroughs of Toronto assigned to Humber—Etobicoke and York—had a population of about 400,000 in 1967 and remain essentially at that level today, the catch basins of contiguous colleges have grown exponentially. Seneca's region, for example, has grown to about 1.8 million, whereas Sheridan College, immediately to the west of Humber, has grown to about 1.7 million. That growth combined with a precipitous decline in high school enrollment, caused by an aging population and low birth rates in the 1980s, led Humber had to seek students from other geographical areas aggressively. It was that or risk a serious decline in enrollment, staffing, and operating revenues and a weakened position in terms of programming choices and critical mass.

As a result, Humber made the conscious decision to maintain steady enrollment growth by becoming the college for the entire province of Ontario, extending its reach even beyond the immediate regions of nearby colleges. Humber, therefore, embarked on a two-pronged strategy to develop and specialize in new programs not offered anywhere else (e.g., funeral services) and to make the college a destination of choice for its high-quality education programs and student life. In short, Humber developed reasons for prospective students to realize that it was worth their effort to enroll at the college. Although this strategy caused some resentment in some colleges, it has been successful and has contributed to the development of Humber's entrepreneurial transformation.

Government Policy Changes

In the early 1990s, both the federal and provincial governments changed the manner in which training contracts were to be made available. For many years, colleges had been preferred providers of curriculum relating to skills upgrading, English as a second language training, immigrant integration, and apprenticeship. These contracts had provided a steady stream of revenue that could be used to supplement or complement regular resources to purchase equipment and refit labs. In a move to create a more competitive environment, contracts were now to be tendered more broadly.

As a result, more contracts were awarded to private sector trainers and to the unions, largely because of their lower overheads, with most colleges, as a corollary, receiving fewer contacts. This development—when coupled with the Ontario government's drive to increase accountability for public institutions and its introduction of key performance indicators, which tied performance to operating grants—increased the pressure on colleges that depended on more stable and guaranteed revenues. The most crippling blow occurred in 1995, when the newly elected provincial government carried through on its pledge to cut operating budgets across the public sector by 15%. For Humber, this meant an annual loss of about $13 million (exclusive of one-time money spent on early retirement and lay-off packages) and a challenge to adjust to this loss in subsequent years, even as enrollments continued to rise.

These developments, which essentially dropped dependence on government funding from more than 70% to less than 50%, forced Humber to rely less on public funding and to become even more entrepreneurial so that the college's financial and physical resource position could be enhanced. Fortunately, this called only for an augmentation of how Humber acted in the marketplace, rather than for a complete paradigm shift. Humber continued to adapt creatively to preserve its institutional vibrancy and health and to embrace an exciting, if sometimes not clearly known, future. Reiterating that it would not deviate from the institutional values adopted in 1982 (when the current president assumed his position), Humber focused on those relating to entrepreneurship, including customer service, student and staff growth and development, and, most important, innovation and risk taking—the latter being a value not shared widely with many public sector organizations.

A Supportive Board of Governors

The fact that members of the board of governors are appointed, rather than elected, is a positive benefit for Humber. Although elected board members reflect a sense of transparent democracy, some members may arrive with vested interests or single-issue biases that might act as an impediment to the college's flexibility. However, Humber's ability to recruit, recommend, and have appointed candidates from the many sophisticated citizens found in Toronto—in other words, those generally familiar with the global economy and the challenges of doing business today—has mitigated this problem. It has enabled the administration to adopt a larger worldview than might be otherwise possible. Equally as important, carefully appointed board members tend to understand the distinction between policy setting and strategy approval and the involvement in the day-to-day management of the college. Moreover, freed from the constraints that a defined district and local taxation sometimes present, the college administration, with the solid support of its board, has been able to entertain a broad vision of what Humber could accomplish.

This broad vision has been very important as the college developed activities in the international arena. Rather than being critical that entrepreneurial values drew Humber away from local priorities, the board has understood the value, both financially and culturally, of bringing the world to Humber and vice versa. Indeed, board members have taken great pride in the college's active participation in many parts of the world. In short, it is evident that whereas a parochial board can act to restrain entrepreneurial initiatives, particularly internationally, an open-minded and worldly one can be a stimulus to seize opportunities and embrace new ventures. Moreover, if the president is forced to spend a great deal of time trying to defend his or her recommendations, gaining support, or convincing a sceptical board of proposed actions, too much energy can be wasted and, as a result, many interesting possibilities remain undeveloped and nonoperational.

Continuity of Leadership

Humber has benefited from the continuity and stability of long-serving and committed leaders. The president is beginning his 23rd year in office, one vice president has just retired after 36 years at Humber (18 as academic vice president), and a vice president of business development has been in place for more than 15 years. Four vice presidents, recently retired, still serve the college on part-time assignments in areas where their expertise and understanding of how the college functions can be put to good use. They also help new people become acclimated to Humber and adjust to the accepted managerial style and value proposition. Additionally, many other senior academic administrators, such as deans, who could easily obtain promotions (e.g., to academic vice president) at other colleges, have chosen to stay at

Humber, contributing to the accumulated experience and leadership of the institution. This continuity of leadership has provided real stability, and the collective focus on entrepreneurial values has prevented stagnation.

In the context of nurturing internal leadership within a framework of respecting people and instilling a self-sustaining entrepreneurial tone throughout the organization, some key management principles are fundamental to the Humber way. The first is that long-standing college values have been fully embedded in the culture of the institution. Everyone working at Humber is expected to adopt the principles on which the college operates. It has been the responsibility of the president to be fully committed to establishing the culture and atmosphere of the college; to implanting the roots of key values and strategic direction; and to monitoring progress, maintaining morale, and making mid-course corrections. It is clear this matter could not be delegated away; indeed, other key administrative leaders have had to accept joint ownership and to spread the concept broadly throughout the institution so that the buy-in occurs collegewide. Developing an entrepreneurial culture does not have to be mutually exclusive of developing a learning culture, but it does mean that some different principles must be stressed, including the following:

- Establishing a culture (and comfort) with change that respects the successful past but constantly sets new directions to meet emerging issues
- Focusing on ensuring that followers are engaged in carrying out the strategic vision and adopting ownership (i.e., getting the agenda accomplished through others, while minimizing the influence of leaders' egos)
- Maximizing individual potential through personalized, professional development throughout the organization and providing exposure to external stimuli frequently
- Hiring the best people available; delegating widely; allowing staff the freedom to do optimum work while encouraging the use of creative, if unorthodox, approaches; and demanding accountability in a climate of support, trust, and mutual respect
- Promoting conditions for self-actualization for all staff—high morale, self-esteem, a sense of worth, and pride in work are strong motivators
- Respecting all staff for their competencies and role differences; always ensuring that staff are treated with compassion and can maintain personal dignity, regardless of the situation
- Actively developing disciples from all areas of the institution (e.g., opinion leaders in faculty who fully embrace values and style—i.e., entrepreneurial attitude) and building support by increasing leadership circle
- Acting as a visible role model and mentor, and walking the talk of the stated goals and philosophy
- Constantly restating and reinforcing the college's vision and values (e.g., innovation and risk taking)
- Rewarding behavior that reflects trying something different or learning from mistakes, minimizing punitive actions with those who try their best, establishing reward and recognition programs for those who take initiative and live college values (e.g., extra mile award, innovator of the year)

- Communicating and consulting regularly—people can never have too much information and want to be part of the decision-making process—and encouraging everyone to be in the loop and to accept ownership (e.g., the importance of revenue diversification is everyone's issue)
- Calculating risks and downsides for all entrepreneurial activities by remembering that the college is dealing with the public trust and accountability
- Moving quickly to assess new trends and courses of action and avoiding quick hits in favor of longer-term viability
- Ensuring that staff members are assertive, competitive, ethical, and acting with integrity

HUMBER'S DEFINITION AND MODEL OF ENTREPRENEURIALISM

Through trial and error, and the evolution of behaviors and actions, Humber has settled on an all-encompassing definition of what entrepreneurship means in the Humber context. For Humber, entrepreneurship is the constant pursuit to initiate, establish, and sustain ventures, relationships, and partnerships that expand, or add value to, the institution's overall well-being; to increase relevance or support for target markets; to broaden the public profile and enhance its reputation as a provider of high-quality programming; to contribute to cutting costs, increasing revenues, or improving physical and academic capital resources; and to reinforce the institution's reputation for focused, imaginative programming and avant garde activities.

Based on Humber's values and principles, a basic model has been developed to shape its entrepreneurial activities. The model includes six features:

1. Focus is not just on increasing revenues and making money; it includes augmenting the academic profile of the college in times of restraint. Ensure that staff takes pride in serving the common good at optimum levels.
2. Entrepreneurial initiatives are directly linked to, and at the core of, Humber's mission, values, and strategic goals. Specifically, initiatives can, and should, support three of Humber's goals—namely, lifelong learning, market responsiveness, and financial sustainability.
3. External focus and unswerving commitment to satisfying clients are as important as sound management internally.
4. Value-added potential of entrepreneurial initiatives is key in terms of leveraging active support of academic schools, new curricula, and other internal resources.
5. Combinations of existing college assets should be packaged with new external initiatives to provide greater leverage and a competitive advantage for the Humber brand.
6. A long-term focus needs to be maintained. Sustaining entrepreneurial initiatives builds value-added relationships and helps staff manage relationships over the long term.

Years of trial and error have suggested ways to expedite and facilitate new initiatives. Structurally, the college employs a vice president of business development, who acts as leader and enabler for corporate and continuing education and guides many business units and a corporate sales team. All deans are expected to pursue promising opportunities to enhance the ongoing activities of their schools.

Cooperation between and among the deans and vice presidents is expected, particularly at a time when new academic activities must cross existing institutional academic sectors. The college has created cross-functional teams to ensure one-stop shopping for Humber's clients, as well as to develop new, multidisciplinary activities that can provide skills development opportunities to serve the requirements of the new economy. In addition, the college has instituted the following actions to improve its service and ability to maintain influence in important sectors.

- Established stand-alone units in various areas, such as sailing, truck driving, and motorcycling. Without financial support from the college, these units often operate nationwide and are expected to be self-sufficient, preferably creating operating surpluses.
- Established sector-specific programming (e.g., plastics, automotive, pharmaceutical), in addition to company-specific programming, where possible. Firms in the same field have similar staffing issues and find stealing each other's employees a wasteful exercise. They are prepared to cooperate with Humber to achieve mutual benefit.
- Established CEOs' councils in important sectors, such as pharmaceuticals, manufacturing, and hospitality, to give strategic advice for human capital needs, build credibility and emotional attachment to Humber, and create legitimacy for future political and capital requirements for Humber.

Examples of Successful Risk Taking at Humber

Humber's calculated entrepreneurship is linked directly to its planning processes, and its initiatives often are emulated by other institutions once the value of the initiatives has been established. Humber's ground-breaking initiatives in Ontario include the following:

- An 1895 heritage site was converted, at little cost to Humber, to a state-of-the-art modern facility that now accommodates 3,000 additional full-time students at the Lakeshore campus. This was accomplished through land swaps, heritage funds, and other sources of money other than the college's own resources.
- Humber is the first college to build its own residences, increasing the ability to attract students from greater distances.
- Humber is the only college to conclude a joint venture with a major university (Guelph) to offer full honors and baccalaureate programs and to integrate college curricula so that two credentials could be granted in 4 years in two separate, but compatible, fields. The entire activity for the 3,000 full-time students is offered exclusively at Humber, and all programs are funded at university level.
- Humber is the first college to receive the government's authorization to establish a holding company that operates at arm's length from the college because it needs to have different rules than those of the public-regulated college in order to enter into investments, etc.

- Humber is a forward-thinking college that promoted legislative change to allow colleges to offer baccalaureates with an applied focus.
- Humber is the first college to receive the government's authorization to change its designation from a college of applied arts and technology to an institute of technology and advanced learning, with a revised mandate to offer 15% of programming at the baccalaureate level; Humber can now offer 25 degrees.
- Humber is the first college to offer accelerated 1-year programs for university graduates only.
- Humber is the only college to receive ministerial consent to offer a 4-year nursing degree, using Humber faculty, and to have the degree granted by a university outside Ontario (University of New Brunswick).
- In 1986, Humber purchased a 100-acre farm, some 30 miles north of the North Campus. The property was purchased in 1986; Humber is waiting for a development opportunity that fits its strategic plan.

INTERNATIONAL ENTREPRENEURIAL VENTURES

To appreciate the development of international entrepreneurial activities at Humber, it is important to view where the college has come from and some of the driving forces that have precipitated growth and change. Humber's international activities date from the early 1970s, shortly after it opened its doors, at which time the focus was on small projects aimed at strengthening both educational and management practices in selected overseas institutions. Most of these activities were staffed by faculty volunteers because there was limited or no funding available. Generally, the expectation was that Humber would provide, pro bono, the human and physical resources to support such activities.

In the late 1970s, modest levels of funding became available through Canadian government agencies. This enabled projects to be undertaken on a cost-shared basis, primarily to establish twin relationships between Canadian and overseas institutions in designated areas of the world. Although this funding grew slowly over the next decade, the 1990s brought a reverse trend, and there was a decline in government funding of this nature. Interestingly and significantly, this forced colleges and, to a smaller extent, universities to become entrepreneurial. Cost-recovery projects, sometimes referred to as fee-for-service, became increasingly common in order for colleges to continue with international development activities. Also critical to an understanding of this context is the fact that colleges wanted to be on the international stage, not simply to provide assistance, but to enhance the profile of the institution very specifically, provide professional development opportunities for faculty, and broaden the educational experience for Canadian students.

Fee-for-service activities provided international clients with custom-designed programming and drew on deep resources of Humber staff for implementation. Most recently, and in the last 10 years in particular, Humber has been engaged in joint education partnerships where training and education are developed and delivered in a variety of models that speak directly to the needs of students and funding agencies. For example, short programs, intensive training, late and early starts, advanced credit evaluation, partnership delivery, and articulation across borders have become the norm. On this basis, Humber has marketed and promoted its programs globally and now recruits international students from all corners of the globe.

The modus operandi has shifted from the voluntarism of the 1970s, through the partial funding models of the 1980s, to today's more pragmatic approach, which requires projects to cover all costs plus contribute to the institution's bottom line. In essence, Humber has become entrepreneurial in its approach and expectations. Furthermore, that approach, although resting on a financial platform, continues to serve faculty development needs and local students' interests in terms of providing a broader, globally enhanced educational experience. Currently, Humber has completed or is continuing international delivery of a variety of training and education models in 25 countries with a total value in the mid-six figures. The major areas of focus have included clients and partners in Bangladesh, Botswana, Brunei, China, Egypt, Guyana, India, Indonesia, Kenya, Lesotho, Malaysia, Philippines, Singapore, South Africa, Swaziland, Taiwan, Tanzania, Thailand, Ukraine, and Zimbabwe. In addition, Humber is home to 700 international students from 70 countries studying in 2- and 3-year diploma programs, 4-year degree programs, and 1-year postgraduate programs.

Ningbo University and Humber Joint Project

In 1995, Humber developed a partnership with Ningbo University to implement a joint program in which Chinese students have the combined benefits of a local and Canadian education. A model was developed for selected Chinese students to take part in a 2-year business management diploma program hosted by Ningbo University. The program is taught by a combination of Ningbo and Humber professors. The model allowed for the recognition of business courses taught in Chinese and English and a parallel English language development program; successful students then transfer to Humber for the third year of the business administration diploma. This 2+1 model allows each institution to maintain the integrity of its own program and offer an opportunity not normally available to Chinese students.

The overall goal is to provide a blend of education and cultural experiences to students that prepare them for the world of work. The graduates of this joint program are people who have had the benefits of a local university education, been exposed to Canadian teaching methods and courses, enhanced their language capabilities, and been exposed in-depth to Western culture. As compared to students who gain their education through a traditional program and remain local, the students of the joint program have distinct advantages when they return home and seek jobs. They have an international education and strong language skills. They are culturally adept and more confident, generally, than are their counterparts who took the traditional path.

From a financial perspective, the joint program provides benefits to both partners. Ningbo University, by means of offering a premium program, can attract students at tuition rates far greater than those paid by students in its regular programs. Ningbo University is providing a service beyond the usual scope of their programming that is very much in demand by an ever-increasingly consumer-centered society. Humber derives financial benefits in the form of a negotiated fee paid by Ningbo University for each student enrolled in the joint program and also enjoys the benefits of enrolling more than 50 students each year who pay international student fees. The revenues Humber generates through the partnership are used to cover all operating expenses, including teachers' salaries in Canada and in China, airline transportation, project administration, and student services. The expenses of the International Office that coordinates the joint program and the school that provides the training are covered adequately by the revenues generated. The reputations of Ningbo University and Humber have been enhanced greatly through this partnership, particularly in China, where the joint program is held out as a model of true partnership, friendship, and sound education. Humber has been asked to replicate the model on numerous occasions by a broad variety of public and private institutions.

Recruiting International Students to Humber

Humber recruits international students for three important reasons. First, the integration of foreign students within Humber's classrooms provides an educational and learning context that otherwise would not be achieved. Humber students learn about the world through their interaction with students from around the world. Second, faculty are energized by the opportunities and ideas that spring from multicultural teaching environments. Third, the revenue generated by additional students supports the institutional bottom line and helps counteract ever-decreasing government grants.

The benefits of having international students in Humber's programs are significant. The interaction between domestic and international students in an educational setting is a very enriching experience in which perspectives are shared to the benefit of all. Although Humber is situated in one of the most culturally diverse cities in the world, there is still a great deal to be learned from visitors from abroad. Hosting these students at Humber constitutes cultural entrepreneurship.

The revenue generated through the recruitment of international students is significant. Tuition revenue from local students studying at the diploma level is approximately $4,500 Canadian per year, whereas each international student is charged approximately $11,000 Canadian per year. International student tuition revenue has grown from $1.9 million in 1998 to $8.1 million in the 2003 fiscal year and is projected to be $9 million for the 2004–2005 fiscal year. A significant portion of the revenue generated through international recruitment is retained for central operations at Humber; however, modest remaining funds are distributed directly to the academic schools. To provide an incentive for the schools to support international students directly, this secondary distribution is accomplished pro rata. Currently, the budget allocated for the recruitment of international students is approximately 10% of the total revenue generated in the fiscal year.

THE CENTER FOR EMPLOYEE BENEFITS

Business Model

The 1970s was a decade of tremendous growth in the benefits and pension industry in Canada. Economic, employment, and union growth spurred most employers to expand their benefit and pension programs. Insurance, trust, consulting, and union organizations were enjoying a booming base of clientele. The federal government continued to support the private pension system by linking old-age security payments to inflation, introducing the spouse allowance, increasing registered retirement pension plan limits, and introducing the registered retirement income fund as an alternative to the traditional annuity. In the United States, ERISA was introduced to regulate qualified pension plans.

This growth in business and legislation, however, outstripped the growth in benefits and pension knowledge in the industry. Product providers and organizational buyers experienced a severe shortage of employees with a solid working knowledge of pensions and benefits. As the demand outstripped the supply, both private and public sector employers felt a serious need to address their competency gap. Also, consulting firms were facing challenges in recruiting qualified support personnel to complement their professional staff services.

This knowledge void presented the opportunity and motivation to create an industry alliance to serve everyone's needs. The concept of creating a center of excellence was conceived by public and private sector partners. The pension and benefits consulting community agreed to provide instructional staff as subject matter experts to provide professional, up-to-date information and business strategies for nominal fees. Humber, in return, agreed to charge reasonable tuition fees for managing, promoting, and sponsoring public seminars and other education services.

With a basic business model now agreed on by all partners, Humber assumed the task of establishing and operating the Center for Employee Benefits (CEB), under the general oversight of the Industry advisory council. Staffing, physical resources, and budget were all Humber's responsibilities; the remaining partners provided general oversight, counsel, and advice through the advisory council. The Certificate of Proficiency in Employee Benefits, more popularly known by the acronym CEB, was launched. The advisory council (representing both instructors' and customers' organizations) expected efficiency, effectiveness, and modest fees. Surpluses and reputation were to be shared by everyone. The CEB was officially launched in 1969; since that time, it has been building its reputation as the premier provider of value-added pension, benefit, and trustee education in Canada.

Revenue Model

The driving force behind CEB's business model has been financial self-sustainability. The center develops and provides fee-for-service solutions to the business community across the country. For the first 20 years of its existence, the center provided its programs in local hotel boardrooms in Toronto. Students were dispatched to Toronto by employers who easily justified the expense with the results their employees were able to demonstrate on the job. It was reinforced by the highly qualified instructors and the demanding standards that had been set by the center. Students soon learned that they could apply the knowledge from the courses directly to the work environment. Improved work performance was noticed quickly by senior management.

Encouraged by this success in the 1970s and 1980s, Humber staff realized that other opportunities were available by building on the success of the CEB program and capitalizing on its rapidly expanding database of students. The best and most cost-effective way to increase business is to serve existing, satisfied customers and then offer additional products that respond to their needs. This, naturally, required a solid understanding of the pension and benefits marketplace and the customer's knowledge gaps and an established ability to deliver the goods. Two new specialty programs were introduced in the late 1980s, targeted specifically at former CEB clients who needed to keep their skills current and were willing to return for more specialized education.

With the arrival of the 1990s came some harsh realities in the pension and benefits marketplace. In spite of soaring stock markets, the numbers of private pension plans continued to decline dramatically, and new plans were virtually nonexistent. Tax legislation in Canada had been introduced to level the playing field, and the fallout from the pension reform decade of the 1980s was becoming more evident. New tax legislation and regulations were being introduced across Canada, creating a challenge for employers but a windfall for CEB. Viewed as an opportunity, CEB immediately responded. Using feedback from both customers and the industry, CEB successfully developed and launched two new programs, the Pension Plan Administration Certificate (PPAC) and the Pension Fund Investment Certificate (PFIC). These were advanced-level training programs designed to respond to the rapidly changing demands of the marketplace and the need for plan sponsors to comply with a plethora of new legislation or face stiff financial penalties. These changes also presented an opportunity to introduce free market pricing.

The market changes brought about in the 1990s resulted in alterations to the center's business strategy. Increasingly, it became evident that new product lines and pricing approaches were needed. With the backing of the advisory council, the center adopted a strategy of taking education to the market and unbundling its programs. It began to promote its public seminars to employers as flexible, modularized units that could be delivered on their premises as an investment by employers and employees in cooperative learning. This new approach provided flexible delivery and timing to suit individual corporate schedules. Employers quickly realized value in the approach resulting from economies of scale. Higher numbers of enrollments were now possible, opening up learning opportunities for other employees who might not have been approved for off-site training involving hotel and travel expenses.

Gains were realized through a reduction in lost productivity, use of flexible schedules, and elimination of direct costs such as hotel and travel expenses. Instructional staff continued to be drawn from the industry. Although direct costs for courses and instructors rose significantly, customers' acceptance of the increased fees, together with more tailored learning solutions, increased gross revenues and net profits for CEB significantly.

Growth of CEB and of revenue have continued into the 2000s with the introduction of the new Trustee Development Program (TDP). TDP was designed to meet an increasing need for educating trustees in Canada, and it sought to capitalize on CEB's reputation for enhancing knowledge of pensions and of programs that had been established over the previous three decades. The program's model reflected the specific requirements of the trustee target market and incorporated feedback from regulators and plan sponsors and content drawn from CEB's successful, advanced-level PPAC. A series of 1-day modules that could also accommodate local on-site delivery was built with a national audience in mind. Each module reflects the specific legislation of the jurisdiction in which it is being provided, enabling the program to provide learning solutions in most jurisdictions across Canada.

Through more than 30 years of operation, CEB has built its success on three major factors.

1. Based on the unique business model that CEB has developed and sustained, new learning products are continuously identified, developed, and provided to the pension and benefits industry by industry experts. This results in a more knowledgeable and professional workforce to serve the industry. Furthermore, CEB has built credibility and confidence in the industry such that CEB now offers several professionally recognized industry certifications based on its course content.

2. CEB is perceived by the industry as a credible knowledge source and expert for pension and benefits learning solutions. Building on 30 years of success, the CEB is recognized as an integral member of the pension and benefits industry in

Canada; thus, there are no degrees of separation to contend with as there might be with a typical service provider.

3. CEB has established significant competitive advantage through developing in-depth knowledge of the market and expertise in the pension and benefits field, as well as through its ability to provide solutions nationally. Humber's reputation as a value-added learning solutions provider also builds and reinforces CEB's credibility. These features serve to make it a more difficult proposition for potential competitors to enter the market or gain a significant market-share foothold.

Testimony to Humber's success is the fact that the core content and standards have received the industry's recognition and support, as evidenced by PPAC's pension program being designated as a condition of employment by major employers across Canada. CEB's strength is in its broad-based expertise in a niche market, buttressed by extensive partnerships with clients and industry stakeholders, focused on providing value-added solutions for the industry. CEB has enjoyed three profitable decades of success built on these sustaining principles and key success factors, and now it is recognized as Canada's leading pension and benefits-learning solutions provider.

THE COMEDY COLLEGE

Humber is the first postsecondary institution to offer a full-fledged program in comedy writing and performance, consisting of courses in sketch, stand-up, improvisation, physical comedy, and script writing. The impetus for such a program was the belief that comedians have a hard time making it out in the harsh world of entertainment and that there is much to learn before one can become a comedy writer or performer. A common saying at the college is "We can't make people funny, but we can make them funnier." It is an important distinction, because the college does not seek to instill talent in any of the creative and performing arts students: It merely shapes and develops it. Another reason for undertaking the teaching of comedy was based on the rich tradition and history of comedy in Canada.

The list of Canadian comedians and comedy creators is impressive: Mike Myers, Dan Aykroyd, Catherine O'Hara, Martin Short, Jim Carrey, Lorne Michaels, and Ivan Reitman, to name a few. And many of these comedians, along with their American counterparts, have become friends of this unique program. The first chair of the program's advisory board, for instance, was Steve Allen. Other advisors include *Second City T.V.* alumni Rick Moranis, Eugene Levy, Joe Flaherty, and Dave Thomas. The college has welcomed Carl Reiner, Chevy Chase, Joan Rivers, Colin Mochrie, and *Seinfeld* producer George Shapiro to its campus, all of whom have thrilled and educated the students.

Humber launched the program in 1996 as a summer workshop to determine whether a market for this kind of programming existed. Recognizing the need for support from the industry, Humber asked a Canadian comedy impresario, Mark Breslin, owner of Yuk Yuk's, the country's largest chain of stand-up clubs, for help. Breslin managed to attract Steve Allen as the first guest presenter. The faculty also included Joe Flaherty and Eugene Levy, as well as Anne Beatts, two-time Emmy award-winning writer of *Saturday Night Live;* Lorne Frohman, Emmy award-winning writer for Richard Pryor; Jay Leno; and Dame Edna. The program administrators found that it had to appeal to people who harbored a secret desire to try comedy but did not have the opportunity to develop this skill. Students came from all walks of life and from all over our country—some from the United States, several from Europe, and one from Japan.

Based on the program's initial success, the college ventured further and created a full, 2-year undergraduate program directed at students coming out of high school and a 1-year postgraduate program for people with prior experience. Today, hundreds of applicants line up at the college's door to audition. And already some of the graduates have gone on to national success. Both Nikki Payne and Jason Rouse have won Gemini Awards for outstanding TV specials. Levi MacDougall and Ryan Belleville have won Canadian Comedy Awards, and the list goes on. Approximately 24 graduates have lucrative careers in commercials, at *Second City*, and in stand-up clubs.

Mark Breslin has opened his famous Yuk Yuk's stand-up club in downtown Toronto to Humber students every Tuesday night, allowing students a chance to ply their comedy wares in a public forum. The Canadian Broadcasting Corporation has bought radio sketches performed by students, and the Comedy Network is about to buy "Humber Comedy Shorts," 2-minute video sketches.

During fall 2003, *The New York Times* sent a reporter to the college to write about the success of this new, unique program. The published article led to a spotlight on *60 Minutes*. Merv Griffin Entertainment, along with Creative Artists Agency, expressed interest in producing a feature film, a situation comedy, inspired by the idea of a comedy college, and a reality series based at the college itself. Creative Artists began pitching the idea to its own stable of directors and producers: Lorne Michaels, Ivan Reitman, Harold Ramis, Ron Howard, and Brian Grazer. Such ventures may not only bring unprecedented attention to an entrepreneurial program but also could vault Humber graduates onto the world stage. It could bring great acclaim to Humber, and royalties could help in times of declining government funding.

One of the senior partners at Creative Artists took *The New York Times* article to one of his meetings, where Jonathan Levin is said to have exclaimed, "Eureka! Of course, comedy college. Why aren't other colleges doing it? It's so simple, so obvious." Such is the way in which this program has been received. It is arguably one of the three or four best-known college programs in Canada. It can be argued that few institutions would have encouraged the development of such a program—even some Humber people chuckled (for the wrong reason) at the mere mention of it; however, it was conceptualized and grounded in the same way as any traditional academic program. Moreover, some of the early critics are now wondering what sort of lustre they might add to their own schools to make them shine as brightly and gain the kind of attention comedy attracts. The Comedy College has been a valuable addition to the School of Creative and Performing Arts at Humber, and it is a valuable destination for class clowns who, until now, had nowhere else to go.

HUMBER AND DAIMLERCHRYSLER SOLVE A CORPORATE LEARNING CHALLENGE

DaimlerChrysler's key position in the global automotive industry has been attributed to the knowledge and expertise of its workforce. It is no surprise then that continuing education and corporate training are well-supported initiatives in the company. In 1997, DaimlerChrysler established a new policy that required all management employees to possess degrees. As a long-standing Humber corporate client, DaimlerChrysler asked Humber to assist it in meeting this target and devised a tuition reimbursement program for its staff. Humber had been its corporate training provider for some years, so it was natural for DaimlerChrysler to approach the college to help it address this challenge.

At that time Humber did not have the authority to grant degrees, but it had developed a favorable reputation within the university sector for upholding high academic standards, a proven ability to develop and deliver curriculum at the baccalaureate level, and an entrepreneurial spirit and track record that challenged the traditional boundaries for Ontario colleges. Because of its highly developed mechanism for transferring external credits to its degrees, the British Columbia Open University (BCOU) was asked to join the partnership. BCOU was considered an appropriate partner because of its full membership with the Association of Universities and Colleges of Canada and as a division of the former Open Learning Agency.

Key Aspects of the Solution

The program architecture was built around four critical components:

- An innovative approach to prior learning assessment (PLA)
- Flexible on-site course delivery that accommodated shift changes
- A tight articulation agreement between Humber and BCOU
- A generous employee training tuition reimbursement program for DaimlerChrysler employees

Employees in the management group at DaimlerChrysler's Brampton assembly plant were invited to take part in a unique learning experience and to take college-level courses in general arts and science and business, with full degree transferability, through Humber and BCOU. Prior to in-house training, however, postsecondary academic courses and life experiences needed to be assessed under the PLA process. The process was very labor-intensive and, for students who had not had previous experience with the documentation of PLA credits, time-consuming and frustrating. As a result of lessons learned in this process, both Humber and BCOU implemented changes to their respective PLA processes. By signing an articulation agreement between BCOU and Humber, students were granted degree credits at both lower and upper levels; Humber began to teach articulated courses on site at the plant, and BCOU delivered courses by distance education.

The Dividends of Partnering

Both on-site and distance education courses began April 1999, with 40 employees taking a combination of liberal arts and business courses leading to a Humber certificate (30 credits) or diploma (60 credits) in general arts and science. These credits, when successfully completed, would be transferable to a BCOU degree in general studies (120 credits). Courses were structured to accommodate employees' shifts and thus promote access to learning. Nine class sections were run for three 12-week semesters per year, with six faculty members from Humber providing instruction on site at DaimlerChrysler. This schedule continues today with courses offered at up to three different times each week to accommodate rotating shift schedules.

Because BCOU has a residency requirement of only 6 credits of the 120 required for the bachelor of general studies degree, most employees earn the majority of their credits on site. In response to the increased demand for advanced-level credits, Humber initially developed six new courses for degree credit. The development of Humber courses for advanced-level credit has continued throughout the life of the program to keep up with ongoing demand. Both DaimlerChrysler employees and university-transfer students in regular Humber diploma programs take these courses.

The curriculum was developed initially by faculty and administrators from both partners, based on feedback from DaimlerChrysler's human resources officials at the plant. As the courses progressed, however, the students' feedback became the major determinant of which courses would be provided. With few exceptions, the students' feedback was extremely positive.

With the program's expansion in January 2001 to include hourly production employees, it became necessary to install a portable classroom at DaimlerChrysler's Bramalea site to accommodate the larger numbers of students. As part of its ongoing support for the initiative, DaimlerChrysler provided all heating, electrical service, and maintenance. In January 2002 the program expanded again to the Etobicoke casting plant, where an additional 500 employees became eligible to enroll. In addition, other employees from office locations across the GTA are participating in the program, and a third on-site location at DaimlerChrysler's Mississauga administration office has been added recently. The success of this initiative is clear: The original agreement signed between DaimlerChrysler and Humber, which had a completion date of 2004, has been extended to spring 2005.

Entrepreneurship Contributes to More Than the Bottom Line

What began as a response to a learning challenge faced by a corporate partner yielded far more benefit to Humber than simply the revenue generated through the tuition. Seeing an emerging need for degree-level education with an applied focus, Humber has positioned itself to extend its array of learning solutions by providing polytechnic-type bachelor's degrees. The DaimlerChrysler project became a real-life pilot that enabled Humber to experiment with many of the academic and support systems required to provide this higher level of education.

A Degree Council at Humber was formed for the purpose of establishing standards that would be expected of all degree programs, providing support to faculty teams developing curriculum, and ultimately recommending approval of courses that would be delivered at the degree level. An unexpected benefit accrued as Humber simultaneously sought to secure the opportunity to grant its own degrees: Partnerships with accredited universities and demonstrated acceptance of Humber faculty and curriculum by those universities could help to form an essential component of Humber's strategy.

In the intervening time, Humber has become the polytechnic institute of choice for lifelong students by providing learning solutions appropriate at a wide range of career development stages. Initiatives like the DaimlerChrylser degree program challenged Humber's management to introduce student records systems that provide the foundational support for all types of instruction. Humber is involved in a major review of these systems currently; the lessons learned by supporting DaimlerChryler are proving to be invaluable to that review and will result in systems that are much more accommodating of corporate clients' requirements.

Implications for the Future

With the support of DaimlerChrysler, the initiative has been extended to three plant locations in the GTA, and, to date, more than 180 employees have participated and more than 75 academic credentials have been awarded. The experience gained by Humber has played an important role in helping to change the collective institutional attitude to one that is more open to developing learning opportunities that do not conform to the traditional on-site, classroom-based instruction.

Although Humber has a long and successful history of working with corporate clients and now has a well-developed PLA process, the success of the DaimlerChrysler project has encouraged Humber to seek more aggressively corporate partners who could benefit from customized degree completion programs for their workforce. The college is working actively with several other organizations, such as the Ontario Provincial Police, to develop a diploma/degree completion program that builds on the lessons of the DaimlerChrysler project. The additional learning models, coupled with increasing requirements of clients for higher-level credentials, will enable Humber to channel its entrepreneurial know how into a variety of new initiatives.

CONCLUSION

Entrepreneurial activity at Humber is rooted in economic, political, and environmental influences that have changed permanently how colleges do business. Furthermore, Humber's entrepreneurial culture demands an evolving and open environment where cookie-cutter solutions are not acceptable to solve either the requirements of the ever-changing economy or the shifting demands of contemporary students. Whereas Humber uses a fluid process based on solid principles to take advantage of emerging opportunities, it also recognizes that it must develop unique solutions for specific situations. In that context, and by employing broad, lateral thinking, the only limitations to Humber's entrepreneurial activities are imagination and a willingness to try something different.

As Humber engages in entrepreneurial activities, it has learned from its successes and failures, and it has used its experiences to develop and apply new techniques to future cases. Entrepreneurial activity benefits not just Humber. At the college we have learned to ask, "What is in it for our potential partner?" without regard for whether that partner is one person or an entire sector of the economy. Focusing on the expectations of both sides of the partnership ensures mutual benefit rather than a zero-sum win. This approach also builds trust-based relationships and the sustainability of new partnerships over the long term. Certainly, Humber's experience has demonstrated that quick hits tend to be short term and, generally, only once, whereas carefully nurtured long-term solutions can ensure future and expanding gains. It is clear that funding from public sources will not increase significantly in the foreseeable future. Healthy, thriving colleges must sustain and, preferably, increase their resourcefulness and net worth in order to ensure adequate revenues, viability of programming, and the ability to move into new ventures with the confidence that institutional stability will not be threatened.

The author acknowledges the contributions of Kris Gataveckas, Frank Franklin, Ian Smith, Ted Patterson, and Joe Kertes for their assistance in the preparation of this chapter.

CHAPTER 7

A HISTORY OF ENTREPRENEURSHIP AT KIRKWOOD COMMUNITY COLLEGE

Norm Nielsen

—Kirkwood Community College, Cedar Rapids, Iowa

Never before have we had so little time in which to do so much.

—*Franklin D. Roosevelt*

In 1967, Kirkwood Community College purchased 315 acres for its campus in Cedar Rapids. Soon after, founding President Selby A. Ballantyne engaged in one of Kirkwood's first entrepreneurial acts—forming a 501(c)(3)-status facilities foundation and directing the foundation to lease space from Kirkwood to house food- and beverage-vending services. Net profits were used by the foundation to buy agricultural land adjacent to the campus. After paying the mortgages with farmland rental income and revenue from the vending services, the facilities foundation donated an additional 320 acres to the college. In doing so, a vision was cast for a college, which is now the largest of 15 Iowa community colleges and the third largest college in Iowa.

For nearly 40 years, Kirkwood has continued to cultivate the entrepreneurial ethos initially modeled by its founding president. College leaders think creatively about ways to enhance Kirkwood's financial position through sharing or reducing expenses and increasing and generating revenue. As in Ballantyne's day, the vision and mission of the college drive entrepreneurial efforts. The current vision is to invent, develop, and deliver learning solutions for the 21st century. The mission is to identify community needs, provide accessible quality education and training, and promote opportunities for lifelong learning.

In keeping with the college's mission and entrepreneurial spirit, Bill F. Stewart, Kirkwood's second president, led the development of a distance learning system. With a federal grant, in 1981, the college built the first microwave audio–video system in the country. This system allowed Kirkwood to deliver credit classes to its rural counties and is still in operation today, serving more than 3,000 students at 10 sites each semester.

Located in Cedar Rapids, Iowa—the second-largest city in Iowa and number one in manufacturing—Kirkwood serves a seven-county area in eastern Iowa with a population of

400,000 and an immediate urban area of 140,000. Since 1966, the college has grown from an enrollment of 199 students to 15,000 enrolled in college-credit classes and another 50,000 annually in noncredit, continuing education classes. Kirkwood employs more than 700 highly qualified, full-time employees and 1,150 part-time employees who teach and support the college. The college possesses more than 1 million square feet of facilities, with 640 acres of land, a central campus, and 11 learning centers connected via an advanced technology distance learning system.

Kirkwood is a member of the League for Innovation in the Community College, a consortium of 20 of the nation's finest 2-year colleges. In addition to being a leader in the liberal arts and sciences, Kirkwood is the largest 2-year agricultural campus in the midwest and the second largest in the nation. The college is the headquarters for AgrowKnowledge, a national consortium of major universities, colleges, and agribusiness partners focused on geospatial technology and food-chain protection. Kirkwood is also a national leader in emergency preparation and response training.

Kirkwood has faced major challenges including decreased state funding and the need to be responsive to local businesses and industries. However, the college has created an entrepreneurial environment and celebrates its entrepreneurial programs, some of which are described in this chapter.

An Entrepreneurial Environment

Whereas the Kirkwood ethos has always been entrepreneurial, the college's approach, out of necessity, evolved to embrace increased innovation and entrepreneurship. Under Ballantyne's presidency (1966–1977), Kirkwood could count on state revenue and property taxes to cover 60% of the college's budget. Today, these two traditional funding streams cover less than 40% of the total college budget. With the need for vibrant education programs greater than ever, innovative ways of reducing expenses and increasing revenue are crucial to achieving success.

One of Kirkwood's enduring strengths is a supportive board that has made ambitious decisions in the college's 38-year history. The board has allowed and encouraged entrepreneurial risk taking to serve the college's vision and accomplish its mission. Each of the nine elected board members serves a 3-year term. Because Kirkwood does not limit membership terms, the longevity of institutional board members and chairs contributes to trust and stability within the community.

Board members understand that one of their primary roles is maintaining an environment in which the image of the college is enhanced in the community. Frequent split votes by the board or reports of divisiveness can affect efforts to pass or renew levies or other fundraising campaigns, negatively. A board presenting a united front to the community not only activates potential donors but also stimulates a climate of innovative, creative thinking on the part of community leaders about ways to partner with Kirkwood.

The entrepreneurial style of the board of trustees has helped keep Kirkwood financially solvent. The college's new Equestrian Center, initially planned as a $2 million education facility, is an example of innovative thinking. Encouragement from horse enthusiasts in the region prompted the board to recommend upgrading the plan to a $5 million education and events center for weekend horse shows. The facility was built with significant funds donated or otherwise contributed by businesses and industries because of the board's involvement in the community. The project illustrates a principle that has held true over time that when the college has the right cause, a creative plan, and a solid reputation for delivering quality, investors will materialize.

Another board-supported example is the AGEON Corporate Data Center, located on campus. The college's partnership with AEGON USA, a Cedar Rapids–based insurance company, dates back 20 years to 1985, when Kirkwood began to provide customized training for the company's employees with a credit program at the AEGON USA site. When Kirkwood launched its first major college fund drive in 1990, the AEGON USA CEO agreed to co-chair the $5 million campaign. This company pledged $100,000 to initiate the effort, which eventually generated more than $6 million.

Since 1992, AEGON USA and Kirkwood have partnered to create customized training, benefiting both partners. On campus, there is a 50,000 square-foot facility that initially served as a corporate data center for AEGON USA and that Kirkwood used for computer classrooms and labs. When AEGON USA needed more space, the company invested $1.6 million toward the construction of another facility on campus: a 75,000 square-foot major business education and information technology facility. The college now occupies the new center, completed in 2002, allowing AEGON USA access to the former Kirkwood-occupied area to meet its growing technology and space needs.

During the initial discussions, college leaders had qualms about putting the corporate data center on campus. It was a difficult time, financially, to be making such a big budgetary commitment. However, the determination of the trustees kept the project afloat. From Kirkwood's inception, the board of trustees has maintained a forward-moving philosophy that has set the tone for innovation at the college.

The Role of the President

My history with this vibrant college began in 1979. After serving a number of years as assistant to the president, vice president of administration, and vice president of instruction, I was named president in 1985 and experienced the adjustment of extricating myself from details with which I was involved as vice president. I quickly realized that a president of a college the size of Kirkwood could not afford to manage the numerous programs, departments, and concerns in detail. Good people must be hired, given appropriate positions, and then trusted to do their work. I see my responsibility as one of facilitation and motivation. I facilitate the process and try to motivate people to do their best. If leaders acknowledge accomplishments, employees stay motivated. I strongly believe in the notion that there is no limit to what can be accomplished if it does not matter who gets the credit.

Described in the next section are programs such as the Resource Center and the Kirkwood Training and Outreach Center. I was involved with both projects at their inception, but I no longer oversee them in detail. Many capable people run these centers. I am kept abreast of all activities at Kirkwood, and I help where possible in a supportive role but not in a directive, detailed sense. Of course, crucial to this style of leadership is effective communication. I meet weekly with the operations team: five vice presidents and an executive director who report to me directly and four directors who report to the vice presidents. I depend heavily on input from this team.

Although Kirkwood has very capable leaders who are knowledgeable about facilities, I stay involved because I am passionate about maintaining a clean and attractive campus. I am also active in external relationships with the community, working with the Chamber of Commerce and economic development groups of our two major population centers, along with various hospital, bank, and social service boards. My community involvement, and that of other key Kirkwood leaders, encourages many community members to explore innovative partnership ideas with the college. A high percentage of donations and ideas for new or improved education programs is a result of connections made by these activities. Being involved in the community, college leaders help convey an image of Kirkwood as an institution that has integrity and the ability to deliver. This external activity contributes to Kirkwood's entrepreneurial environment.

Decreased Funding

Like other education institutions across the country, decreased state funding is an issue for Kirkwood. State general aid and property taxes are low. The state has not funded the FTE for the last 8 years, during which time Kirkwood's enrollment has increased by 6,000. Because state revenues have not kept up with enrollment growth, Kirkwood has raised tuition and employed more part-time faculty and staff than is considered desirable. Currently, nearly 60% of the revenue stream is from tuition income, which concerns college leaders. Profit centers, such as contracted training and continuing education, have had to raise fees for services. The Kirkwood foundation and grant acquisitions office are under pressure to find additional sources of revenue.

Meeting Changing Needs of the Workplace

In 1998, during a time of economic expansion and low unemployment, Kirkwood initiated a study of 33 major area businesses and their projected needs for employment and skills. The study, funded by administrative fees from an economic development program, resulted in the Skills 2000 Report, which stimulated new workforce training programs offered by Kirkwood, secondary schools, and businesses. The Iowa Legislature responded to the Skills 2000 Report and other community college lobbying efforts by establishing the Accelerated Career Education (ACE) program in 1999.

Under current guidelines, the state contributes to this program by allowing sponsoring employers to divert a percentage of Iowa withholding from their aggregate withholding payments. Sponsoring employers make quarterly employee state income tax withholding diversion payments to Kirkwood, as required by state law. Thus, ACE programs, established by Kirkwood, are funded by the state, employer sponsorships, and tuition.

Kirkwood's ACE programs lead to 1-year diplomas or 2-year associate of applied sciences degrees. These college-credit programs incorporate the successful characteristics of customized job training programs. Sponsoring employers help design the curricula and ensure that the programs are responsive to employers' and students' needs. Kirkwood faculty and other industry experts provide instruction. Kirkwood's ACE programs include degrees in nursing, automotive technology, computer programming, diesel truck technology, heating and cooling technology, local area networking, manufacturing technology, microcomputer technology, plumbing technology, surgical technology, and telecommunications technology.

The employers provide cash or in-kind contributions to Kirkwood equaling 20% of the cost for each sponsored student's position. Employers help develop and modify the ACE curriculum, as well as provide assistance in marketing the program. Employers agree to interview and provide hiring preferences for sponsored program graduates; if sponsoring five or more student's positions, employers agree to offer full-time employment to no less than 25% of the sponsored program graduates. Employers provide a wage level for program jobs of no less than $22,500 per year. State funds are available to qualifying ACE program students to apply toward tuition, travel, room, board, and child care.

Benefits to sponsoring partners include tax deductibility of cash and in-kind contributions to the program, enhanced access to program graduates through employer partner job connections, technical education programs aligned with the employers' needs, an increased labor pool resulting from new or expanded programs, and community visibility through inclusion in program marketing efforts. Benefits to Kirkwood include technical support from employer partners, financial support from employer partners and the state, increased enrollment in high-demand technical and career education programs, and enhanced job placement for students.

Kirkwood's ACE programs are coordinated with new Career Edge Academies, which help local high school students gain relevant job skills and experience for employment in Iowa. Organized as schools-within-schools, the academies help students develop and integrate career skills with their traditional academic studies. In most cases, high school instructors who meet community college certification teach the courses, thus providing dual (high school and college) credit.

Using Perkins Tech Prep federal funds, the Career Edge Academy programs were created initially through a consortium of six high schools—Kirkwood, the area education agency, and The Workplace Learning Connection (a Kirkwood-based office that organizes job shadowing and internships for academy students). Corporate funding from local businesses such as Rockwell Collins and McLeod USA supported start-up costs. Other critical funding sources included the Grow Iowa Values Fund and a U.S. Department of Labor H1B grant. Local district funds cover ongoing instructional and program costs. Academy programs offer dual-credit courses in the form of high school and college credit, with college tuition paid by local school districts.

The Career Edge Academies currently offer programs in agriscience, automotive technology, computer programming, education and human services, engineering, graphics and media, health sciences, information management systems, and local area networking. Approximately 1,113 local high school students enrolled in one or more of these academies during the 2003–2004 school year, earning up to 18 semester hours of college credit before graduating from high school. Incumbent worker and pre-employment training programs have been implemented as a result of the Skills 2000 Report. Ultimately, the report serves as an entrepreneurial tool in stimulating the Iowa Legislature to think creatively about keeping up with the state's needs for a high-skilled workforce, not only for Kirkwood, but for other community colleges across Iowa.

Since 1999, the ACE program has provided $13 million in operational funding, via the income tax withholding diversion, and $23 million in infrastructure appropriations to community colleges for the creation or expansion of high-wage, high-skill technical degree education programs. For both the ACE programs and the Career Edge Academies, the Iowa legislature created a weighted-factor funding system that provides additional funding for jointly administered programs in vocational education. These programs are now part of an effective portfolio of workforce development programs in Iowa. Clearly, the Iowa legislature's willingness to think creatively has enhanced the ability of its community colleges to respond effectively to the state's needs for a highly trained workforce.

In 2003, in less vigorous economic conditions, it was time for a reassessment of employers' future employment and workforce skill needs. Kirkwood initiated another study, funded by administration fees from an economic development program. Once again, the information would help provide a curricular blueprint for the community college and local schools to help students become valuable employees. The information would be used for economic development planning by businesses, chambers of commerce, and the Iowa legislature.

The Cedar Rapids/Iowa City Technology Corridor committee, of which Kirkwood is a member, sponsored the 2003 study. The committee is made up of representatives from chambers of commerce, economic development groups, higher education, and government. More than 150 companies from 10 industry sectors, located throughout Kirkwood Community College's seven-county service area, participated in the study. Industry sectors included advanced manufacturing/electronics, agriculture/biotechnology, educational services, financial services/software, food/health and beauty products, government, health care, plastics/packaging, printing, and others. The goals of the survey included

- Determining replacement and new job growth projections by occupational categories
- Identifying education levels desired and skills gaps
- Identifying training methods to be used and identifying what gaps exist in regional higher education and internship programs

The Skills 2006 Technology Corridor Report asserts that near-term increases in employment are evident in survey responses. Companies participating in the survey projected a 7% increase in new jobs and a 13% increase in replacement positions, through the year 2006. Based on this and other information gathered in the Skills 2006 report, the Technology Corridor committee recommended that businesses, in partnership with local education institutions, should do the following:

- Require assessments or certifications for hiring in the area of essential and technical skills
- Continue to invest in essential and technical skill training for existing workers
- Place more priority on work-based learning experiences for area high school and college students to improve retention
- Make more efforts to improve the number of women and minorities in technical program areas
- Continue to address quality-of-life issues in order to attract and retain qualified workers

Kirkwood is using the updated Skills 2006 report to reinforce the role of community colleges in the Grow Iowa Values Fund, a $503 million economic stimulus package, and to lobby for increased funding for other programs. The college anticipates that the Skills 2006 report, like the 2000 report, will serve as an important tool for designing and offering innovative education programs in the Cedar Rapids/Iowa City corridor, as well as for continued economic development across Iowa. Across the country, there are few state-aided workforce and economic development portfolios like those found currently in Iowa.

THE CREATION OF POSSIBILITY

The programs described in this section are entrepreneurial—they share or otherwise reduce expenses or increase and generate revenue. Kirkwood's compass for these innovative programs is its mission of identifying community needs; providing accessible, quality education and training; and promoting opportunities for lifelong learning. When the college mission is combined with innovation, positive results can occur, even in challenging economic times.

Kirkwood Resource Center

In 1997, a 60,000 square-foot commercial building on Fifth Avenue near the downtown area of Cedar Rapids had been repossessed by a bank and was for sale. Tenants included medical professionals and United Way. There was wide community support for finding a way to continue providing United Way with a reduced rental configuration. Kirkwood leaders envisioned buying and using the building's third floor for an education resource center and revenue from the commercial tenants to cover the costs of operating the building. A resource center near the downtown area held the possibility of better accessibility for the underserved, lower socioeconomic population living near the downtown area.

Kirkwood purchased the building for $2.2 million. The Hall-Perrine Foundation, a Cedar Rapids organization dedicated to improving the quality of life for people in Linn County, contributed $750,000, based on Kirkwood's reduced rental agreement with United Way. After renovating the third floor of the building, as well as other publicly used areas, and adding landscaping to enhance the appearance, Kirkwood opened the Resource Center in 1998. The other three floors of the building house United Way, medical and pharmaceutical offices and businesses, human service agencies, and the Workplace Learning Connection (WLC). WLC—a synergetic partnership of area businesses, other education institutions, and Kirkwood—organizes work-based learning experiences such as internships, job-shadowing, tours, career fairs, and summer career camps for area K–12 students.

At the Resource Center, students take arts and sciences classes for college credit. The center is the location for all of the ADVANCE courses offered at the college. ADVANCE, a business degree program with courses offered in accelerated format, is designed for working adults who want to continue their education while maintaining a balance with work and family. An associate or bachelor's degree can be obtained with several options for business majors. Through an articulation agreement between Kirkwood and a local 4-year college, ADVANCE students experience a smooth transition to Mt. Mercy's ADVANCE program. In addition to the ADVANCE and traditional college-credit classes, high school completion, adult basic education, and English as a second language instruction are offered at the Resource Center.

The Kirkwood Resource Center houses the college's Skills-to-Employment division, which serves unemployed and underemployed clients and welfare recipients. The location of the center in an urban low-income neighborhood provides access and resources for the downtown area and beyond. The Skills-to-Employment division uses programs such as the Workforce Investment Act and Promise Jobs to reach out to more than 2,000 clients. Services include assessment, guidance, and training to assist clients in achieving self-sufficiency, job placement, and job retention.

The Resource Center represents Kirkwood's first foray as a landlord, and it has been successful. The private renters in the building understand and accept the differential in rent among the tenants. Because the Resource Center is open some evenings, there is more traffic around the buildings, thus contributing to enhanced security and a safer neighborhood. It is a development that all tenants appreciate.

The college bought the Resource Center, but the facilities foundation manages it by running the lease agreements with the tenants and contracting with Kirkwood for custodial services, maintenance, utilities, and property taxes. The lease agreements generate $450,000 per year; since the operating expenses total approximately $225,000, the facilities foundation has another $225,000 profit center besides the vending services in place since Ballantyne's presidency. The facilities foundation makes a total annual profit of approximately $400,000, which is fed back into the college. The foundation recently bought another 60 acres near the campus that it leases back to the college for $110 per acre—yet another income producer that benefits the college.

National Mass Fatalities Institute

Often it is the unconventional idea that sparks the innovative program in any community college. Prior to September 11, 2001, and increased attention to homeland security, two community members approached Kirkwood leaders with the unthinkable: Cedar Rapids, like most communities, had no cohesive, organized plan for disasters that might result in mass fatalities. A funeral director and a social worker, having responded to mass fatalities through the American Red Cross, had worked in unprepared communities with a lack of space in hospitals for the injured and in morgues for fatalities, as well as those unable to protect crime scenes efficiently. Understanding the need for family assistance centers, these community members warned Kirkwood leaders that all communities need to plan for such events.

Kirkwood has been committed to ensuring the health and safety of community members for many years. In 1975, Kirkwood received a Clean Water Act appropriation to help fund the building of a wastewater training facility to serve the state of Iowa. The Environmental Training Center (ETC) was formed to promote the maintenance of a clean and safe environment through education and training in the areas of municipal water supply, treatment storage and distribution, wastewater collection and treatment, and solid waste management for public sector operators and technicians. ETC was opened in 1976 as the first Environmental Protection Agency–funded wastewater training center in the nation. Besides offering training on site, it provides statewide technical assistance to smaller wastewater plants experiencing operational problems.

In the late 1980s, ETC's efforts expanded from water and wastewater training to hazardous materials training after the Occupational Safety and Health Administration developed worker protection regulations, commonly referred to as the Hazardous Waste Operations and Emergency Response standards. The Hazardous Materials Training and Research Institute (HMTRI) was established in 1987 by Kirkwood and the Eastern Iowa Community College District, headquartered in Davenport, Iowa.

To deliver state-of-the-art curriculum and staff development programs, HMTRI's operation at Kirkwood maintains the nation's most comprehensive environmental, health, and safety program at a 2-year college, offering open-enrollment courses on campus and contracting with business and industry to deliver on-site customized worker training. Kirkwood delivered courses to more than 3,500 students and instructors in the past year. More than 150 colleges and organizations regularly purchase or license the use of texts and learning resources from Kirkwood. The college sponsors a national consortium of colleges funded by the National Institute of Environmental Health Sciences that has trained more than 125,000 students since 1987. Kirkwood's national leadership in the environmental health safety arena has garnered the college $25 million in funding from the National Science Foundation, the U.S. Department of Education, the Environmental Protection Agency, the Occupational Safety and Health Administration, and other federal agencies.

From wastewater to hazardous materials training, the logical next step was mass fatality and terrorism response training, with the two community members serving as catalysts. Kirkwood's National Mass Fatalities Institute (NMFI) began operation October 1, 2000, with funding from the Iowa Division of Emergency Management and, more recently, from the federal Centers for Disease Control and Prevention.

NMFI provides advanced-level mass fatalities incident-response training to prepare emergency planners and responders from all disaster management professions to plan to manage incidents effectively while providing proper care for victims, surviving family members, and responders. Personnel to be trained include emergency management professionals, mental health professionals, funeral directors, firefighters, law enforcement personnel, military staff, medical practitioners, clergy, and representatives of industry and disaster response organizations across the country.

After the events of September 11, 2001, college leaders noted the sad irony when one month before, in the August 10, 2001, edition of *The Chronicle of Higher Education,* Curry accused Kirkwood of "feasting at the pork barrel" because federal support for NMFI came from a congressional appropriation. The September 11, 2001, tragedy made the importance of community preparation for mass fatalities obvious. Kirkwood responded by implementing terrorism-response training for communities all over the country, using online training, including a database with case studies, to help plan and build awareness programs.

All of these programs are now housed in a new 16,224 square-foot facility on the north campus of Kirkwood, the Community Training and Response Center. It houses the Linn County Emergency Management Agency, which coordinates emergency responses in Linn County and surrounding counties, and the East Central Iowa Regional Fire Service Training Center, which provides training for volunteer firefighters and first responders. To create an efficient and effective resource, all of the programs share common resources, including facilities and equipment. The operations provide a comprehensive approach for preparing, training, assessing, and tracking a local community's ability to plan, prevent, mitigate, respond to, and recover from emergency situations. In time of emergency, the center will draw on other college capacities including its satellite uplink, fiber optic and microwave communications networks, computer labs, food service facility, gym and child-care center, and many technology programs and laboratories.

Funding this $2 million facility was a congregate effort, with $850,000 coming from Kirkwood Community College and HMTRI, $800,000 from Linn County, $100,000 from the City of Cedar Rapids, and $250,000 from PMX, a local industry. Community partners are responsible for a portion of the operating costs for the facility, approximately $30,000 per year. All training costs are paid by revenue from businesses and industries whose workers are receiving the training, as well as from state and federal grants. Presently, 80% of the federal and state homeland security funds must go to the local government, rather than to education institutions. Kirkwood, by partnering with the city and county agencies, stays in the information loop and gains access to shared funds.

Kirkwood Training and Outreach Services Center

Another realm of entrepreneurial activity is partnerships with businesses and industries. As already illustrated, Kirkwood is fortunate to have numerous associates in the college's seven-county area. There are many partnerships that could be highlighted here, but the spotlight will shine on one of the college's longest-term allies: AEGON USA, the Cedar Rapids-based insurance company described earlier in this chapter.

In addition to the facility on campus built by AEGON USA, a more recent development in this partnership is the Kirkwood Training and Outreach Service (KTOS) Center. In 1991, AEGON USA acquired a 35,000 square-foot former grocery store in Marion, Iowa, to house a call center and office complex. By 1996, operations had outgrown the facility and moved elsewhere. The remaining building, not large enough to complement the company's other existing operations, was leased to another company. AEGON USA needed a business resumption plan, given the crucial role of technology in the case of a disaster, such as flood or tornado. In the unlikely event of damage to the company's area facilities caused by weather or other factors, the company needed to create a site for recovering its customer service operations.

During this time, Kirkwood Community College administrators identified the need for a showcase site to combine Kirkwood's training and business consultation services into one easily accessible location. To provide high-quality services to local businesses and other institutions, this location needed to be an attractive facility with updated technology for up-to-date training in a comfortable, corporate learning environment. The new facility, the KTOS Center, is an off-campus, 35,000 square-foot building in Marion, owned by AEGON USA but used by Kirkwood as a center for training for business and industry. Kirkwood uses approximately 21,000 square feet as the corporate training and education center, whereas AEGON USA uses approximately 14,000 square feet as a business resumption center. The college renovated and now maintains the building. In exchange, AEGON USA retains the right to claim part of the building as a resumption center, in case of natural or other disasters.

The facility houses the KTOS Center staff and is uniquely designed to facilitate business with a variety of modern facilities for hosting training seminars and programs and with approximately 7,000 square feet of meeting room space with the option to use AEGON USA's 14,000 square feet as well. High-speed telecommunications allow companies to connect with remote sites for extended training programs. Multiple digital phone lines and computer connections, computer labs, lecture and presentation classrooms, an executive boardroom, and a cafeteria lend a corporate environment to this facility.

The KTOS Center provides critical technical assistance to local businesses and industry via several programs housed at the center, including the Small Business Development Center, providing confidential, free management counseling to help businesses grow; the Iowa Quality Center, a nonprofit organization providing leadership for performance excellence by connecting individuals, organizations, and communities; the Iowa Waste Exchange, providing Iowa industries with smart waste management alternatives and business assistance services; and the ACT Center, providing comprehensive, computer-delivered training and testing at affordable costs in areas such as adult literacy, information technology, English as a second language, industrial technology and safety skills, and professional and personal development.

The KTOS Center is in an accessible location with ample parking. It allows for small to mid-size conferences and education programs that can be developed rapidly as needed. For example, in 2002, the Cedar Rapids community was one of the hardest hit lay-off areas in the state. KTOS Center personnel quickly developed a job-hunting seminar and job fairs for the more than 400 people expected to lose their jobs.

AEGON USA owns the building, and Kirkwood holds the master lease for $10 per year. The U.S. Department of Labor facilitated a congressional appropriation of $500,000 for high-speed telecommunications connections between the KTOS Center and Kirkwood's learning centers in the seven-county service area. In keeping with the need for funds to benefit Kirkwood's corporate clients, the college invested $750,000 from job-training administrative funds toward the building's renovation. Rent from clients, including AGEON USA, which pays for their training and meeting needs, covers Kirkwood's operating costs. Moreover, AEGON USA is willing to cooperate and help financially as the college evaluates ongoing facility needs.

The KTOS Center has proven to be a successful partnership for Kirkwood and AEGON USA. The facility serves a dual purpose, enabling both organizations to achieve desired objectives in a cost-efficient and functionally effective manner. As the KTOS Center educates and trains Kirkwood clients daily, it stands prepared for resumption activities for AEGON USA business units should needs arise.

CONCLUSION

Kirkwood's mission and vision serve the community. The culture created by college leaders supports autonomy and risk taking. Kirkwood's leaders are interested in external relations; therefore, opportunities for partnerships at all levels continue to surface. Kirkwood has become an indispensable part of the seven-county area it serves in eastern Iowa.

The Cedar Rapids community is fortunate that Kirkwood's first president, Selby A. Ballantyne, and its board of trustees, set the tone for an entrepreneurial, innovative spirit that supported the college's comprehensive mission to meet the needs of the community. College leaders have worked to preserve Kirkwood's entrepreneurial ethos, and trustees and CEOs have remained committed to that philosophy. Two years ago the board of trustees commissioned the creation of an hour-long video, *From a Cornfield to a College*, in which many original employees and trustees were interviewed about the college's beginnings and Ballantyne's leadership. A snapshot historical booklet was commissioned as well. To preserve the founding spirit of Kirkwood, new full-time employees are given these materials during their orientation to the college.

Faced with declining government aid, community colleges must be creative and proactive to meeting their communities' needs in the 21st century and beyond. In the past, colleges were able to remain dependent on the primary sources of income: state general aid, local property taxes, and tuition income. But the days of relying on traditional sources of funding are over. Colleges today will not experience the level of state revenue they enjoyed in the 1970s and 1980s again. Now more than ever, Kirkwood, and other community colleges across the country, must be willing to take risks—they must become entrepreneurial.

REFERENCES

Curry, D. (2001, August 10). Earmarks that make you scratch your head. *The Chronicle of Higher Education.*

CHAPTER 8

LEVERAGING RESOURCES: ENTREPRENEURSHIP AT SEMINOLE COMMUNITY COLLEGE

E. Ann McGee

—Seminole Community College, Sanford, Florida

> Keep on sowing your seed, for you never know which will grow—
> perhaps it all will.
>
> —*Albert Einstein*

Over the years, community colleges nationwide have been referred to as the best-kept secret in the community, establishing a reputation for being all things to all people. However, during the past few years, this status has been reversed, and community colleges are receiving national attention. This exposure not only has been fueled partially by politics, but also it has been enhanced by business and government partnerships that have made expansion of resources possible to better serve our communities.

Florida's 28 community colleges have enjoyed local and state support for many years through matching funds provided by the state. These matching funds attract donors who leverage their contributions—in some cases, doubling their charitable intent. Seminole Community College (SCC) has been the recipient of such generosity, enabling the college to raise funds to equip smart classrooms, award scholarships, establish an endowed teaching chair program, and ultimately build education facilities.

SCC was established in 1965, in Sanford, Florida. Located north of Orlando, the college has two primary campuses and an off-campus center. With enrollment approaching 35,000 credit and noncredit students, the college offers a variety of programs from adult education to transfer. Over the years, SCC has established a reputation as the training engine for the community and is viewed as one of the most comprehensive community colleges in the state, setting the stage for SCC to attract support from business and industry.

SCC's offerings vary from traditional transfer courses to career-oriented training in construction trades, automotive technology, respiratory therapy, nursing, information technology, and child care. The college encourages students' success, as is evident in its slogan—Be Yourself. Only Better. The college is involved with the community and seeks business supporters to generate additional funds for program support.

SETTING THE STAGE: THE ROLE OF A NEW PRESIDENT

With 10 years of experience as the vice president responsible for marketing and fundraising at a community college located in the southern part of the state, I had been involved in a community effort that had increased that foundation's assets from $800,000 to more than $21 million. Such success required a powerful and connected foundation board and an institutional philosophy that fundraising was everyone's responsibility. The expectation of the trustees for SCC was that I would replicate that model.

Prior to my being named president, SCC was an institution living in the shadow of a neighboring community college. SCC's emphasis on its adult high school career programs made it seem less an institution of higher education and more a trade school to the local residents. In reality, the programs were state-of-the-art and achieving national recognition. However, this fact had not been marketed to the local community.

After 30 years of service to the college, SCC's founding president retired. The board's goals in hiring the college's second president were to improve SCC's image and to increase the college's resources. With a background in marketing and fundraising, I set my first goal to connect the college to the community so that the community would take pride in SCC and seek ways to enhance the college's financial position.

SCC had few established links to the community. The college was not a member of chamber boards, and the five foundation officers were college employees. The foundation had less than $1 million; it was difficult for college employees to ask for donations from individuals who did not consider them peers. Marketing efforts were nearly nonexistent, and the neighboring community college was overwhelming the market with slogans that created enormous interest in that institution, making compelling arguments and increasing enrollment.

Knowing that establishing a public presence was essential to any marketing or fundraising success, my goal during the first year was to reintroduce the college to the community, with what eventually became known as 120 days and 120 speeches. Every chamber, Rotary Club, Kiwanis, and city council meeting was an opportunity to advance the cause of the college. By taking SCC's story on the road, I was hoping to increase the community's awareness of the college.

During my first 2 years as president, I worked with college staff and consultants, and we accomplished the following:

- Redesigned the college logo
- Established collegewide celebrations
- Recognized individual achievement
- Changed the organizational structure
- Expanded local publicity

The college also established a foundation board of community leaders who knew that they were agreeing to support and be a part of a "give, get, or get off" philosophy. Individuals were hired for key leadership positions, with the expectation that they would represent the college in the community. Chamber membership and regular public presentations were part of their job descriptions. Fundraising was understood to be everyone's responsibility.

COMMUNITY CONNECTIVITY

Because continuity was critical, the foundation's new chair, a well-connected business leader, agreed to serve a 4-year term. The college's goal was to create a working board that was connected to the college and its mission. SCC hoped to find 18 to 20 people who would be passionate, be willing to contribute financially, and take the college's message to the community.

The college's first entrepreneurial opportunity resulted from 1 of those 120 speeches in 120 days. As the training engine for Seminole County, SCC has strong occupational programs that support the construction industry. Given the substantial growth of Seminole County, the city of Orlando, and Disney World, specifically, the construction industry has become the key to the economic health of the region.

Recognizing the role that SCC played in the region's growth, the college had established programs in carpentry, fire sprinkler installation, electrical engineering, sheet metal fabrication, building construction technology, welding, and plumbing. Approximately 15% of students were enrolled in apprenticeship programs that directly supported the industry. Therefore, I welcomed the invitation to speak at a conference for the construction industry. Following my remarks, a member of the audience pointed out one of the weaknesses in SCC's current construction technology program: The construction programs were housed in 30-year-old portables that were literally falling down. The next comment from the audience included the observation that the heads of the state's two legislative branches were both from the Orlando area and in the construction field. It was suggested that because this group helped the two politicians get elected, they should play a key role in securing a new SCC training facility.

Shortly after this meeting, I walked into the office of the senate president and asked for a new construction trades building. It was a gutsy move for someone who had been a president for such 2 months. Although the president was committed to helping, she wanted to see what the industry would do for us. She turned me around, ushered me out of her office, and sent me back to the community to see how committed they were to a new facility.

Raising approximately $6 million for a new construction trades facility would take nearly 3 years and involve countless trips to Tallahassee for discussions with industry and legislative representatives. This project would become a reality because the industry wanted it. After 2 years of discussion, a key leader in the construction industry asked the college to invite 200 building contractors to a turkey dinner in the college cafeteria. He worked with the college team to make sure that the guest list was complete and then offered to chair the meeting. With almost religious zeal, we held a revival in the college cafeteria that resulted in signatures pledging in-kind services totaling $2.8 million in labor and materials, if the state would match the donation with $2.8 million in cash. Armed with the pledge cards, another trip to Tallahassee secured the necessary support from the president of the senate and the speaker of the house. At the end of the legislative session, SCC was awarded $5.6 million for the construction of a state-of-the art Center for Building Construction.

Other than the dilapidated condition of the training facilities, the industry's discussion with the college was rife with the concern that high school students were not entering these programs. Parents were not anxious to have their children go into construction as a profession. And they certainly were not excited about seeing them attend classes in 30-year-old portables. Industry representatives felt that a state-of-the-art facility would help increase enrollment in a field that was critical to the industry's survival.

More than 90 professionals, contractors, and vendors donated their professional services, materials, and time to construct the Center for Building Construction, which opened in summer 2001. Eight state-of-the-art building construction labs, 19 general classrooms, a computer lab, and 22 office spaces occupy the 46,418 square-foot building. It is a visible tribute to the partnership that exists among education, industry, and government.

The Center for Building Construction is an example of what can happen when business partners join with educators to provide training. What began as a speech to a group of construction representatives resulted in a lifelong partnership that is providing state-of-the-art instruction to more than 700 construction trades apprentices each year. Additionally, the college has partnered with the local high schools. Dual-enrollment students are transported to the site each day for instruction in the construction fields. High school program enrollment in construction trades has doubled in 1 year as students have shared their experiences, recruiting friends to the college.

A convergence of factors made this an incredible opportunity available to SCC: The college faculty and staff had built a reputation for excellence in instruction in the construction field; the industry recognized its need for workers and its reliance on the college; the industry had a strong partnership with the college that included honest communication about the need for workers and its image as a profession; the legislature had the foresight to establish a matching program that would encourage private gifts to colleges; and individuals from legislators to construction industry personnel were willing to pledge their money and influence to ensure that this project would be successful. As a postscript, the Center for Building Construction competed for the 2004 Bellwether Award sponsored by the Community College Futures Assembly at the University of Florida. The construction program won in the planning, governance, and finance category for the role it has played in contributing to the efficiency and effectiveness of the college.

REPLICATING THE EFFORT

As the college worked to secure funding for the Center for Building Construction, the automotive industry approached SCC about its desire to fund a new training facility that would not only expand the automotive training programs but also provide the Central Florida Auto Dealers Association (CFADA) with a permanent home. Faced with the need for 9,000 new technicians over the next 10 years, in Florida alone, CFADA insisted that it wanted to lead the design and development of a new training facility.

Each year, CFADA hosts the Central Florida Auto Show at the Orlando Convention Center, one of the largest convention centers in the world. The proceeds from the show are used to fund CFADA's projects, which include scholarships and competitions at the high school and college levels. Previously, SCC had received $15,000 in scholarship funds at this event. This all changed in 1997 when a check for $250,000 was presented at the auto show, representing the first installment on the $5 million needed to build a state-of-the-art training facility.

With the leadership of CFADA's executive director, the association formed a fundraising committee, hired a professional fundraiser, worked with the executive director of the SCC Foundation to develop a membership campaign, and began soliciting donations. What all thought would take 2 years, became a 7-year project that only recently has realized success.

In retrospect, the two projects had similar goals and support. However, one of the key differences was that the construction trades facility was a hands-on project that required the donors to be physically present as they built the facility. The automotive project required only money from the industry. The auto dealers were not as committed to the project as were their construction counterparts. Also, the auto dealers wanted assurance that the project actually would happen and that their contributions would be in proportion to those of their peers.

The passion and commitment of only a few can inspire others to support a worthwhile project. As case in point, a core group of auto dealers, ably and passionately assisted by the CFADA executive director, staunchly supported the project and refused to be discouraged from achieving the goal. Over a period of 6 years, this group raised more than $2.5 million in cash from their membership, donated it to the SCC foundation, and waited for the state of Florida to match its contribution.

Difficult economic times in Florida threatened the matching funds. The legislature deviated from previous formulas and allocated funds based not on what had been raised, but on the institution's percentage of the state budget. Therefore, instead of the much-anticipated $2.5 million, SCC received only $832,000 to be shared among programs ranging from facilities to scholarships to endowed teaching chairs.

Fearing that the auto dealers would withdraw their contribution, as some other donors in Florida were doing, the college pledged $500,000 of the $832,000 to the project. Letting the donors know that their match would be delayed, college leaders set up a series of meetings with the auto dealers to communicate their commitment to the project. In response, the auto dealers assisted the college in lobbying for the funds, sending a delegation of 12 dealers to the session in Tallahassee to deliver model cars and cookies to the legislators, along with the message, "Match our funds." It was the first time in Florida's history that auto dealers, from any part of the state, had exercised such clout with the legislature. One of the legislators, who had previously championed the construction trades project when he was speaker of the house, asked the college if he could put an additional $1.5 million into the automotive project to assist with the increased cost of this 7-year project. The legislative session resulted in SCC securing $6.5 million to build a world-class automotive training facility that will provide a permanent home for CFADA.

Lessons learned from this endeavor mirror those from the construction trades project. It took committed and talented faculty and staff to establish a training program that would attract the support of industry. It took someone inside both the construction trades and automotive industries to be the driving force. In the case of the automotive project, the executive director of CFADA never gave up on something that she knew would help to ensure the future health and well-being of her industry.

LEVERAGING RESOURCES

Successful entrepreneurship is intertwined with how well a college leverages its human and financial resources. At SCC, we have cultivated an environment of pride. This environment celebrates successes and enables staff to wear their SCC pins proudly. Internal and external marketing are critical to success.

The SCC Foundation and college leaders should receive credit for the financial success. The college has established the expectation that fundraising is everyone's responsibility.

From giving cash awards to career employees for their exemplary efforts to awarding endowed teaching chairs for faculty excellence, foundation-sponsored programs have been excellent ways to improve morale and encourage and support entrepreneurial thinking by faculty and staff about all of our fundraising efforts. For example, a retiring faculty member, who served as the faculty's representative to the foundation board, recently funded an endowed teaching chair. Scholarships are being endowed by faculty and staff in honor of loved ones; a staff member recently donated a piece of heirloom jewelry to the annual Dream Auction with the stipulation that the proceeds be used to establish a scholarship in her family's name.

Members of the foundation board have been tireless in their efforts to support a $10 million capital campaign and establish a presidents' club annual giving program. Envisioned as a way to generate a minimum of $100,000 annually through $1,000 individual contributions, the presidents' club, named for SCC's two presidents, has exceeded expectations and enrolled 132 members in only 2 years. Funds are used to purchase classroom equipment, provide scholarships and emergency assistance to students, and award small grants to every graduate from SCC's Adult High School to entice them to continue their education.

The college needs to secure its future; entrepreneurship is essential to continued success. Attracting a strong foundation board that understands and supports the institution, shares the college's vision with the community, provides ways for people to participate, and leverages all of the college's resources are critical characteristics. SCC is fortunate to be in a state that values private contributions to education, matches contributions, and celebrates the entrepreneurial spirit.

CHAPTER 9

FRIEND RAISING AND THE ENTREPRENEURIAL PRESIDENT

David E. Daniel
—Midland College, Texas

One aspect of serendipity to bear in mind is that you have to be looking for something in order to find something else.

—*Lawrence Block, noted author*

My first job as a fundraiser, a profession I knew little about, was at a small junior college in eastern North Carolina. One day, as it was nearing 5:00 p.m., I decided, after a somewhat unsuccessful day, to make one more call. I drove my car onto a building supply company parking lot. As the 26-year-old director of college relations, I introduced myself to the office manager, Cliff Bensen, and began to present the case for investments in the college. Waiting patiently until I finished, Bensen shared the fact that his mother and aunt both attended Louisburg College. "I have always thought that I should do something for that junior college," he said as he pulled out a checkbook, making the first of several significant investments in the college. Later, his financial contributions led to a new college auditorium that currently bears his name. He became a college trustee and eventually chairman of the board. This is a lesson for a college seeking entrepreneurial status—when there is time for one more call, just do it. Another lesson is that people pursuing a career in resource development will benefit from training.

I learned from Harvey Sharron (Sante Fe Community College in Gainesville, FL)—one of the first gurus of community college fundraising—who conducted a week of training for beginners. What I learned 35 years ago and while subsequently serving as the president and chief fundraiser at two colleges is relevant today. Community colleges have a long way to go in resource development, but for those who will commit themselves to the challenge of change, there are many rewards. The entrepreneurial president will make that commitment.

Entrepreneur is defined as "one who organizes, manages and assumes the risk of a business or enterprise" (*Merriam-Webster's*, 1990, p. 146), although this definition applies more to a commercial business than to a community college. A good businessperson, particularly one who has begun an enterprise from scratch, had a dream or a vision that spawned the venture. Anyone who would become president of a community college today has a choice: Either maintain a steady-as-you-go—or status quo—administration or give due diligence to a comprehensive study of the community and the college as the first step in formulating a vision for the future of the college. Any community should be proud to have a community college. Not only does it provide extraordinary opportunities for its citizens, but also it has significant economic impact. A new president should assess opportunities and devise ways for the college to capitalize on its community's strengths, weaknesses, or shortcomings.

THE ROLE OF THE ENTREPRENEURIAL PRESIDENT

The entrepreneurial president will make certain that key administrative positions are filled with the right people. Fundamentally, the president must compare job descriptions with what is actually being done—a revealing exercise—and identify employees who are over- or under-employed, which involves some weeding out or reorganization of the administrative structure. The results provide opportunity for the president to concentrate on the overall mission of the college. If the president has not completed this process in the first year, the opportunity to do so has been diminished greatly. This is not abdication on the part of the president. It is setting the stage for responsible leadership.

With this accomplished, the president is prepared to continue formulation and articulation of a vision for the college. This vision is colored by the perceived personality of the college. Each member of the governing board must be an integral part of this process, and many presidents have found retreats to be a critical part of the process for bonding and establishing a comprehensive game plan.

A perennial question about the presidency is, How much time should be spent on external matters, such as the procurement of external funds? Although it is the president's job to feel the pulse of operations, too much micromanaging is a waste of time. However, keeping fingers on the pulse can be accomplished by weekly briefing meetings with vice presidents or deans. Assuming that the president has chosen administrators well and that they understand their roles and functions, the question still remains: How much time should today's community college president devote to such matters as the cultivation of friends who have the capacity to contribute some of their resources to the college?

The answer is that the commitment of time in fundraising is situational. If there is a campaign in the planning stages, or in some state of implementation, the president is expected to lead the effort. Prospects who have the capacity to make significant contributions want to be solicited by the president, or at least they want the president on site and involved in the request. A recent conversation with a prospect ended with "If you want money from me, *you* come after it." Be assured that I did that and came away with $100,000. It is possible, maybe even mandatory, that presidents spend most of their time on a campaign. When not involved in a campaign, presidents must spend time in friend raising. The wise president will visit prospects even when not asking for a contribution. Such friend raising paves the way for successful visits when the campaign is on.

Resource development is a must for today's community college president. The early days of ample state and local funding may be gone forever or at least for the foreseeable future. But the future can be bright for colleges where the presidents realize the great potential of a comprehensive development program and then sell it to the governing board and to the community.

WILKES COMMUNITY COLLEGE

Wilkes Community College (WCC) is located in the foothills of western North Carolina, some 150 miles from Raleigh to the east and 30 miles from the picturesque Blue Ridge Parkway to the west. The college service area consists of three sparsely populated contiguous counties. Enrollment is approximately 4,000 credit students. On becoming president in 1977, I was surprised that the college had a foundation with 20 directors, no assets, no minutes, and no record of ever having met. So I suggested to the vice president of administrative services that we open an account in the name of the foundation and make the first contributions, becoming the first investors in the life of the college. Then I set out to visit each of the foundation directors to determine their levels of interest in remaining on the board. With a charge to develop a plan of work, beginning with a retreat in which the annual plan would be developed, I gave them notice that the group would meet several times during the year. At the retreat, during the first portion of the day, the plan would be developed, after which they would play golf and tennis. To my surprise, every member agreed to maintain membership on the board and seemed excited at the prospect. The planning retreat became an annual event.

Their first project was not particularly glamorous, but it was one that was needed immediately. A new academic building had just been completed, located atop a hillside above the administrative building. A steep incline of land, extending about 100 yards, separated the two buildings, making pedestrian traffic difficult. The new 30,000 square-foot building could be reached only by a roadway that skirted the area. Although the road was convenient for some, it definitely was a problem for those who had no transportation. I learned that a stairway to the new building was an alternate in the bidding process and had to be eliminated because of cost overruns.

Therefore, the foundation's first project focused on generating the funds necessary to build a stairway up the hillside to the new building. Ultimately, $250,000 was raised from donors who gave $1,000 for each step, but not just an ordinary set of steps. The plan called for winding sets of steps separated by landings featuring stone benches. Prospective donors were intrigued with the concept; the money was raised in record time. When the project was completed, the college horticulture department planted hundreds of azaleas and other flowering shrubs on each side of the steps and around the landings. The result was a beautiful walkway—not steps to be scaled, but an experience to enjoy. The landings became meeting places. In good weather, some classes met there, and some wedding proposals were made there, too.

This project spawned another. As the step project was nearing completion, I was conducting a campus tour for a senior official with one of the nation's largest building supply chains. The tour included the new steps. Midway up, I stopped to point out another hilltop that we were considering for a new performing arts center. On this day, the flowers were beautiful; my guest commented that the steps reminding him of a walk he had experienced in Italy. Vibes were good, and I suggested that we finish the visit in his office. The prospect was excited about the idea of a performing arts center and asked, "What would it take to build one—what would you expect me to give?" Because I knew of a gift this individual had made to a nearby university where his name appeared on a building, I suggested the same amount I knew he had given to the university. He agreed to that amount with some conditions. One condition was that the total amount of the project would be paid or pledged within a certain time. The other condition would be met if I remained at the college at least until the project was completed. We shook hands, and the deal was done.

The John A. Walker Center is now a wonderful asset for the college and the community. In this case, a potential hard sale (the steps) became a launching pad for a much larger project. The new facility now brings the very best entertainment and enrichment to a rural community in North Carolina. Students in every grade of the public school system enjoy performances and lectures in the facility. Although there were several major gifts funding these projects, hundreds of citizens participated and have a sense of ownership. For example, every seat in the 1,100-seat auditorium was purchased by citizens; their names are etched on the arms of the seats. Lesson learned: It is important to do one's homework and to take advantage of the moment when it comes.

Reciprocal Friendships

Arthel "Doc" Watson is known the world over as a writer, singer, and instrumentalist. He lives just 30 miles from WCC on a farm where his only son, Merle, was killed when his tractor rolled over him while he was preparing land for the coming crop season. A member of the faculty knew something of Doc Watson's bluegrass virtuosity. He suggested that we visit Watson to discuss memorializing his son Merle through a garden for the blind at WCC, where the visually impaired could experience the touch and smell of native flowers and shrubs and could read their Braille descriptions. Watson, himself blind, loved the idea.

When the garden was completed, it was accepted widely as a first step in developing other gardens on the campus. The same faculty member, a professor of horticulture, developed a comprehensive plan for gardens throughout the campus, with the stipulation that all gardens would be endowed for perpetual care. I had doubts that in this area of relatively low per capita income such a large project could be funded. Rather than quash the entire project, I suggested that the instructor construct one garden and secure an appropriate endowment for its care. He did so. It was completed and funded in short order. Today, the entire plan has been implemented and funded. The gardens at WCC are listed among North Carolina's recommended places for tourism, with thousands of garden lovers visiting the campus each year.

This is only a small part of what transpired through the connection with Doc Watson. Watson proposed that the college convene a country and bluegrass festival to which he would invite his friends in the music business. Fortunately, the campus provided a perfect venue, with ample space available, a stream nearby, trees, a winding exercise trail, and plenty of parking. At the first Merle Watson Festival, hundreds of fans paid to see Doc and his friends. That was 20 years ago. Since then, Dolly Parton, Ricky Skaggs, Grandpa Jones, Minnie Pearl, Marty Stuart, and hundreds of other stars have appeared at the Merle Watson Festival. The college was able to fund and build a modern outdoor stage with professional lighting and sound and dressing and rehearsal rooms. The 2004 festival had a record attendance of 81,613 over 4 days. People from every state and from dozens of other countries invested more than $15 million in the local economy. More than $2 million was placed in the college's operating budget. Lesson learned: Trusting a colleague's suggestion will enlarge the college's network.

When an automotive instructor at the college told me about a retired superintendent of schools whom he believed I should visit, I knew it was worth looking into. This superintendent lived in one of the adjoining counties and had been a member of the state legislature decades before. He was the man who changed the one-room school house furniture from benches to desks in the 1920s. Bruce Hash was living alone in a small house in a mountainous part of the county. I drove to the Hash residence on a cold and snowy winter day and knocked on the door. The door opened, and there stood Hash, in his late 80s, with unkempt hair, and a loosened tie spotted with dried eggs and other stains of unknown origin. He ushered me into a back room where a potbellied stove roared, providing plenty of heat.

We sat on either side of the stove. Hash had an empty dog food can stuffed with tissue into which he expectorated from his chew of Red Man tobacco. "Don't mind if I chew?" he asked. I also chewed back then, and I happened to have a pouch of Red Man in my coat pocket. I responded, "No, and I hope that you don't mind if I join you." "Let me get you a can," said Hash. And there we sat, bonded by a bad habit. From this serendipitous beginning, our conversation covered the years of Hash's career. He was well read and had a personal interest in college scholarships—he had two grandnieces he wanted to help—but he also had much broader interests that led to the establishment of a generously funded scholarship program at the college. Two weeks later, I received Hash's check for $50,000, with the admonition that I deposit it in a particular bank or send it back to him. It was deposited as he specified. Until his death, Hash sent regular checks to the college. When he died, his estate was divided between his nieces and the college. I was asked to preside at his funeral. Lesson learned: Take the time to get acquainted personally with the people who can help the college.

MIDLAND COLLEGE

Midland College is located in West Texas, in the heart of the Permian Basin where oil and gas production is the major industry. The college services Midland County, which is the taxing district and provides approximately one third of operational funding. The service area includes three other remote or distant counties, and a portion of another, covering 10,803 square miles, home to almost 150,000. Hispanics represent 48% of the population and are the fastest-growing segment of the area's population.

Established in 1972, Midland College is governed by a nine-member board of trustees, who are elected by the taxing district. The main campus covers 220 acres and has 16 major buildings. Another smaller campus is located in Ft. Stockton, some 110 miles from Midland. The college also maintains the Advanced Technology Center, the Cogdell Learning Center, the West Facility, and hangars at the Midland International Airport and at the municipal airport located adjacent to the college.

Midland is an oil and gas town. Once oil was discovered in the Permian Basin, Midland became the centerpiece for major oil companies. Their presence was a moving force in the city's progressive attitude; these companies invested in all segments of the area's quality of life. The symphony, the community theatre, museums of the western culture including the Petroleum Museum, and all area schools were the beneficiaries of their financial support. The "doo-dah days," as they were called, were replete with extravagance. As thousands of people moved into the area, they brought degrees from prestigious colleges and a drive to create more wealth. But the doo-dah days were not to last. Although the production of energy resources had its highs, the depressed market was inevitable. Whereas the early 1980s were awash in affluence, the late 1980s brought economic depression. By 1991, a semblance of optimism appeared when recovery seemed to be on the way. It was then that I arrived at Midland College as its new president.

Midland College was created as a free-standing community college in 1972. Its programs focused on the liberal arts and several vocational areas, as well as on a noncredit continuing education program, primarily in vocational areas. For almost 20 years the college experienced moderate growth in these program areas. But times were changing. By 1991, a major technological revolution was under way, a revolution that would dwarf any previous period of pervasive change in the world. It was my responsibility to build on the excellent leadership of two former presidents and redirect the college's mission in new technology, while continuing the excellence of programs in the liberal arts.

At the outset of my tenure, the board of trustees unanimously agreed with my assessment of the changing times and what should be accomplished. Fortunately, I knew about the situation, because I had received reams of materials before arriving on campus. During the interview process my assessments had been confirmed, as faculty and staff members related the institution's strengths and shortcomings.

Midland College had a foundation with about $3 million in assets and an active board. At this time, state funding, which accounted for about 35% to 40% of the institutional budgets in Texas's 50 districts, was facing tough times in the legislature. It was apparent that a new revenue stream needed to be identified. I presented a plan to the college foundation to provide funds that would replace lost state funds. Knowing that the 20 members of the foundation were all successful businesspeople who understood the ebb and flow of economic times, I suggested that an endowed fund of $10 million be raised to provide income for the purchase of instructional equipment, a necessity without which the college would fail in its mission. After contemplating the matter for a month, the board met again and adopted a campaign amount of $5,750,000. With this buy in, the directors went to work. The goal was reached soon, and today this fund has a corpus of $6,240,000. The Chaparral Circle Endowment Fund currently provides significant relief from the uncertainties of state funding. Lesson learned: When the climate is just right, it is time for an appropriate challenge.

In order to greet the next millennium at the college, it was apparent that new facilities were needed to address the training required by current and emerging technologies. Advanced technology centers were being established on community college campuses across the country. Members of the board of trustees and I visited several of these campuses and decided that Midland College should make such a project its top priority. A one-story, 85,000 square-foot building was located 3 miles from our main campus. Gutted by the previous owner, it turned out to be the perfect site for the college's expansion. Technical faculty were given the responsibility to design the facility—a task they gladly accepted. The structure was purchased for $850,000 and included 5 acres of land. The plan to create a technology center was widely viewed as a sensible move, because it would provide an incentive for businesses and industries to locate in Midland. Funding partners included the Midland Independent School District, the City of Midland, Midland College, an independent oil and gas producer, and a local foundation.

Now complete, the Advanced Techonology Center serves approximately 1,000 people every day. Students come from the public schools, the community college, and local businesses and industries. The center has trained 1,000 workers for the Cingular Wireless Company, located in Midland primarily because of the training available at the college. This $10 million project has become a major asset to the community and its surrounding area.

The Resource Development Officer

The vice president of resource development, a former division head, was challenged by my proactive visions for the college. Having lived in the community for more than 20 years and having established hundreds of important relationships to open doors and expand the college's influence, she knows the details of the college's service area. She sits on the administrative council with the other vice presidents and has comparable staff and space. Her salary falls in the appropriate range for vice presidents. Presidents understand that success in this area of college operations depends on getting the right start with the appropriate resources. To do less is to diminish results substantially. Lesson learned: It is important to place the resource development function among the highest administrative levels.

On the Heels of Success

A local family foundation, preparing to dissolve, had been in existence for several decades; however, the family members who created the foundation were either deceased or ill, and siblings agreed that it should be dissolved with the remaining assets distributed to community organizations. I learned of this decision and invited the brother and sister to the college to discuss a number of possibilities. The Davidson Distinguished Lecture Series was created, along with an endowment to support the program. The donors requested that the lectures be provided free of charge. Since the series began, the college has hosted luminaries such as Bill Moyers, Ken Burns, David McCullough, and Supreme Court Justice Sandra Day O'Connor.

On the heels of this major triumph, a local attorney and businessman, Robert Cowan, requested that one of the vice presidents and I come to his house to discuss a potential gift to the college. Mrs. Cowan was so impressed with the Davidson lecture series that she and her husband had decided to endow a performing arts series. The couple established the Phyllis and Bob Cowan Performing Arts Series, providing two major performances each year—again, free to the public. The Cowan Series has featured Marvin Hamlisch, the Moscow Boys Choir, the Preservation Hall Jazz Band, and the Ballet Folklorico de Mexico de Amalia Hernandez, among others. Phyllis Cowan died shortly after the series was established, but her husband had peace of mind knowing that her last wishes were fulfilled. It is impossible to overestimate the value of these programs. Students are exposed to the best in entertainment and intellectual commentary. Citizens come by the thousands, and many offer their financial support for these and other endeavors. Lesson learned: Prepare several proposals for whenever and wherever opportunity knocks.

Five miles from the main campus the college was able to open the Cogdell Learning Center as an outreach location in a predominately Hispanic community. Bill Cogdell was a businessman who operated an insurance and loan business in that community and possessed a genuine affinity for all people. He was fluent in Spanish and employed a number of Hispanics. When he approached retirement, he offered to give his business property to the Midland Police Department. I knew that the police department had new, modern quarters and that the city could not use the property being offered to them. The board of trustees agreed that an outreach center should be positioned in that section of the city. I met with a member of the Midland City Council who successfully guided a proposal through the council for the college to own the property.

Today, the learning center is a vital part of the college program. GED and English-as-a-second language classes are taught there regularly. A small business center provides minority entrepreneurs a foundation for establishing their businesses. Credit courses are offered there each semester. On average, 60% to 70% of GED graduates enroll in credit programs on the main campus. Thus, the center is not only an immediate destination but also the gateway to lifelong fulfillment. Cogdell loved the college and what it does for the people in the community. Ultimately, he gave more property to the college and designated that his entire estate go to support scholarships at Midland College and a local university. After a mutually beneficial relationship, I was honored to deliver the eulogy at his funeral.

Forming Relationships With Area Professionals

Another opportunity arose as the office of resource development matured in its operation and expanded its program. At Midland College, lawyers, accountants, and financial planners are invited to campus each spring for a day-long seminar on estate planning. Some of the best minds are invited to make presentations at these functions, each of which draws more than 100 people. The college and the local hospital foundations sponsor the event, and they have the opportunity to present their cases during lunch, each speaking for not more than 10 minutes. It was at one of these events that a CPA saw the advantage for one of his clients of donating $1 million to the college; he knew that his client could do it, and he knew that the client wanted to do something for her parents who had believed strongly in education. Within days after the seminar, he brought her to my office to discuss the possibility of naming a building for her parents. At just that time the college was raising funds for a new science building. The college's policy for the naming of its buildings required the approval of the board of trustees and a gift of $1 million. The woman's wishes and our needs were met.

Midland College always has had an emphasis on the health sciences. Respiratory care, radiography, health information technology, emergency medical service, diagnostic medical sonography, and several levels of nursing education are examples of a vibrant health science emphasis. Additional campus space was needed to house several of these programs. At the same time, Texas Tech University (TTU), located 115 miles to the north, was seeking a location in the Midland area for a physician's assistant program. In a conversation with TTU's chancellor, I proposed that TTU's program be on the community college campus. We agreed that a new building would be constructed at Midland College to house the new TTU program and several of Midland's health science programs. We further agreed that each institution would provide $3 million for the project.

When this agreement appeared in the local newspaper, it received front-page coverage. As the vice president of institutional advancement and I were discussing the project after reading the paper, we thought of a prospect who had an interest in naming a building for himself and his wife. We decided to call the couple's attorney to see if his client had an interest in the project. To everyone's amazement, the prospect had read the paper at breakfast that morning and had called the lawyer to set in motion the events that would lead to The Dorothy and Todd Aaron Medical Science Building. The client's father and grandfather had been medical doctors in the Indian Territory of Oklahoma. A medical sciences building was the perfect project for this couple. This $1 million gift was instrumental in the college's ability to provide its share of the cost. This particular attorney was a well-established estate planner and a regular presenter and attendee at the semiannual seminars held on campus. Lesson learned: It is good to have a working relationship with estate planners.

As the college began the construction and operation of residence halls on campus, it was obvious that a dining hall should be on the list of college priorities. I belonged to an organization known as The Wildcatter's Club, a membership group of people in the oil and gas business. Although I owned no oil wells or oil-related businesses, I did own a few oil stocks and, thus, was qualified for membership. Once a quarter, the Wildcatter members would meet at the Petroleum Club to honor a company that had excelled in the energy business. The meetings always began with a reception, followed by recognition of the honorees. At one of these meetings, I saw a member of the college foundation who operated one of the most successful independent oil and gas operations in the country. Mr. Brown asked, "It takes a million bucks to name a building at the college, right?" I agreed that it did. "Let's talk about it next week," he said.

The next week I met Brown in his office, prepared to present several naming opportunities, among them the much-needed dining hall. After my presentation, Brown said, "I like the idea of that mess hall." He was an Aggie, a Texas A&M graduate. The following week I accepted his personal check for $1 million. The Jack E. Brown Dining Hall stands on the campus today as testimony to an Aggie who had loved the mess hall when he was in college. Lesson learned: Time and money are well spent on the president belonging to organizations where the membership consists of good prospects.

CONCLUSION

Whether a community college is located in an affluent area or an impoverished one, each community has potential assets that may benefit the college and the community. At times a member of the faculty or staff may see a possibility that others may overlook. It is good policy to encourage colleagues to share perceived possibilities with the president or the resource developer. In fact, community college employees should be encouraged to share their thoughts about any potential for strengthening the college and the community through resource development.

The entrepreneurial president is the point person who sets the stage for the procurement of gifts and bequests. It is necessary for the president to delegate responsibility to talented and dedicated people and for the president, with the board of trustees, to have the will and the time to identify the possibilities that could raise the college to new and higher levels of service. Every community college has possibilities yet undiscovered. The community college entrepreneur will know the past and chart the future. This president will move college borders from the expected and the ordinary into the world of the unexpected and the extraordinary.

CHAPTER 10

EDUCATION, ENTERPRISE, AND ENTREPRENEURSHIP

Andrew M. Scibelli

—Springfield Technical Community College, Massachusetts

In times of change, learners inherit the Earth, while the learned find themselves beautifully equipped to deal with a world that no longer exists.

—*Eric Hoffer, American social philosopher (1902–1983)*

Springfield Technical Community College (STCC) in Springfield, Massachusetts, is built on innovation. The campus is located on the 55-acre Springfield Armory National Historic Site—the source not only of famed weapons such as the Springfield Rifle and the M1 rifle but also of important manufacturing processes that led to the innovation of mass production. People with technical skills honed at the armory have spread throughout the Connecticut River Valley, creating what has become known as the Precision Corridor.

In 1967, with the armory closing, STCC established the first state technical community college on the site. Today 6,000 students are enrolled in programs such as engineering technology, lasers and photonics, teleproduction, health sciences, nuclear medicine, and others. Although STCC primarily serves residents of Hampden County, it draws students from a much wider area—including Vermont, Connecticut, and Boston—to its unique technical programs. Through the entrepreneurial efforts of staff and faculty, STCC has become the National Science Foundation–funded National Center for Telecommunications Technologies and the lead college in Verizon's $32 million New England Next Step program, as well as a partner with Microsoft, Intel Corporation, Ford Motor Company, and Cisco Systems. An additional 3,200 adults take noncredit courses through STCC's Center for Business and Technology.

In 1996, STCC opened the first Technology Park associated with a community college on an adjacent 15.3-acre site, once part of the Springfield Armory. Space in the historic brick buildings is leased to private companies, many focused on telecommunications. Also located in the STCC Technology Park is the Andrew M. Scibelli Enterprise Center, home to a business incubator/accelerator, a student business incubator, and the STCC Entrepreneurial Institute. The institute provides entrepreneurship offerings to area K–12 children, including a

1,200-student high school program, as well as an associate degree option in entrepreneurship under the auspices of the college's School of Business and Information Technologies. Well-known nationally for its pioneering efforts in entrepreneurship education, STCC founded the National Association for Community College Entrepreneurship (NACCE) in 2003 to promote entrepreneurship and small business incubation by community colleges throughout America.

A PRESIDENT'S PERSPECTIVE

My affiliation with the college began in 1969 when I became a professor in the biology department. The college was in its fledging years, making it an exciting place to be. I made the transition from faculty to administration, becoming the first registrar, then assistant to the president, director of community relations, and president in 1983. (Editor's note: Scibelli, now president emeritus of STCC, retired in 2004.) Faculty and staff felt that one of their own had taken over at the helm. I was on a first-name basis with most of my colleagues.

In my mind, a successful leader, especially one who will expect others to buy into unusual or risky ventures, must be trusted, and the key to earning trust is integrity. Paying attention to detail, putting people first, trusting in others, and building confidence and pride in performance all go a long way toward ensuring that people will believe in the president and have faith in his or her leadership. Also, building a strong executive team is a requirement for leading an entrepreneurial college. To be successful, the president must encourage freedom of thought, innovation, and risk taking and must discourage a run-of-the-mill caretaker mentality. As much as I have tired of the overused phrase, out-of-the-box thinking, it aptly describes what a leader must encourage for a strong team environment.

Community colleges should have tight and meaningful ties to their communities. The president can establish ties by actively participating on boards and volunteer groups that are related to the college mission. The president must be astute enough to balance the demands by avoiding risk. Otherwise, well-intended efforts will prove counterproductive. The president must establish ties with all constituencies. Getting to know legislative delegations and leaders is vital and requires more than just communicating during crises. Nurturing strong ties means developing relationships, sometimes on a personal and social basis, as well as in formal meetings and at college-sponsored events. It is important to note that a high-risk entrepreneurial venture will be difficult to sell to stakeholders, especially trustees, until or unless one has established a strong faith among leaders with a significant number of victories along the way. Legislative and community leaders must believe in a president's leadership capabilities.

In this chapter I discuss examples of thinking and acting entrepreneurially based on my experiences: STCC created a reorganization scheme with emphasis on revenue sources, developed a technology park, built an entrepreneurial institute, launched a small business incubator and student business incubator, established youth programs and an associate degree in entrepreneurship, founded an Entrepreneurship Hall of Fame, formed NACCE, and spearheaded a brainstorming group, New Ventures Marketing.

LEADERSHIP AND THE ENTREPRENEURIAL ENVIRONMENT

I have never heard a community college president say, "I have too much money!" In fact, from the start of my presidency, it was apparent that the college could not depend on state support for consistent funding; funding has fallen from 70% of our operating budget to less than 40% in 21 years. I know this is the case in many other states. Clearly, a new way of thinking was essential. Thinking entrepreneurially became part of STCC's culture.

The most important step in addressing the issue of revenue enhancement is to look inside. Is the organization structured to enable access to alternative sources of revenue? In the beginning of my tenure, the answer to the question was unequivocally no. The college developed a plan of action to reorganize itself in a way that would define a new way of thinking. The most significant outcome of this plan was the creation of two vice presidential positions focused on revenue generation—a vice president for grants and development and a vice president for economic and business development. This structural shift enabled the college to demonstrate its commitment to seeking alternative funding sources.

Frequently, I have been asked how STCC managed to do so well with grants and workforce development. The answer, in part, is that STCC invested in the human resources to take the college there. Was this risky? You bet! And it was especially risky when other areas of the college were victims of budget cuts. This was not the most popular move, especially among faculty. But strong leadership requires bold decision making. In this case, it was clear what had to be done in terms of long-term gains, and the risk paid off. A few hundred thousand dollars invested in senior staff and support services returned millions of dollars in grants, general fundraising, and training revenues to the college.

An important aspect of grant writing is to know that the person or entity making the request can deliver. Winning grants is not easy; performing as promised may be just as difficult. Poor performance on a grant can be problematic. Conversely, outstanding performance can leverage more, and often larger, grants. A basic rule of thumb has been to make sure the college is not seeking grants as an end in themselves. There must be a link or synergy with the mission, preferably in areas that are weakened from budget cuts. It is important to note that not all grants are free. Often, there is a matching requirement or a commitment to absorbing all costs over time.

Establishing a vice presidency for economic and business development sent a clear message that STCC was serious about workforce and economic development. Revenues generated through contract training and from workforce development grants can add to the bottom line significantly. State-supported institutions must think and operate more like businesses. The college's noncredit training arm is multifaceted and has been aggressive in pursuing the status of an authorized training center for a multitude of certifications granted by national corporations such as Cisco, Microsoft, Intel, and others. These are high-demand certifications and profitable to run.

The vice president for grants and development created New Ventures Marketing—a diverse group of employees who meet periodically to brainstorm possible new ventures to raise money through the college, or foundation, initiatives. It is a high-energy group of people who identify entrepreneurial ideas. The best ideas are shared with various constituencies and individuals who are knowledgeable of the specific venture. One of these ideas led to a proposal that the college operate a jewelry store that a friend of the college planned to open near campus. Conceptually, the venture would require STCC students who were enrolled in business management to work at the store, getting hands-on experience. The college would have an opportunity to share in the profits. Whether or not this venture becomes a reality, such creative thinking opens new doors and leads to potential funding solutions.

STCC TECHNOLOGY PARK

In 1996, the college purchased the former Digital Equipment Corporation property (460,000 square feet), with the expressed purpose of establishing the STCC Technology Park. During the process of this acquisition, the STCC Assistance Corporation was established by the Massachusetts legislature to allow the college to engage in such an activity. While remaining flexible about tenants, the initial goal for the park was to focus on the telecommunications industry. The less flexible rule was that tenants must have a demonstrable synergy with the college.

This venture was clearly as high risk as it gets for a community college, but it was also evident that the up side was an equally high reward. It was a 4-year (1992–1996) process that required salesmanship, patience, an unbending will, and belief in its viability. The time commitment was enormous; several constituents required a clear and articulate expression of the vision.

The 4-year journey began with Digital's announcement that it was closing its operation and selling the property. I felt that the college had to move quickly to acquire the site. With the sluggish economy, no other buyers emerged. The first step was to convince the board of trustees that this was a prudent move for the college. After seeing the business plan, the board, specifically the chair, was relentless in its support as the college moved to persuade a diverse group of stakeholders. These individuals and groups of the leadership consisted of the Massachusetts house of representatives and senate, the governor, the comptroller, the Division of Capitol Asset Management, the inspector general of the state, the mayor of the city of Springfield, the chamber of commerce, and other local business leaders.

The park was established with a focus on telecommunications, given the nature of the building and the availability of a redundancy of fiber-optic cable running just outside the property along a major thoroughfare in the city. It was the location and availability of that fiber that gave us great confidence that the site would be attractive to those who needed the connectivity. The proximity of the cable, and thus the low cost to connect, was a strong selling point.

As envisioned, the buildings began to fill. The tenants were diverse, but most were involved in some way with the telecommunications industry. Others were more service-oriented, but all had a strong relationship with STCC. In 2003, STCC commissioned an economic impact study of the technology park. The results were revealing, suggesting that the college was one of the major players in economic development in our region. The executive summary of the report (available from http://techpark.stcc.edu/economicimpact.html) is reprinted here.

Executive Summary

The Springfield Technical Community College Assistance Corporation (STCCAC) converted the former Digital Equipment Corporation site into a new Technology Park that encompasses 860 employees, housing 18 tenant companies employing more than 750 workers, and an incubator facility with an additional 21 small businesses with approximately 110 employees. The Park received the Economic Development Administration, US Department of Commerce's 2001 Excellence in Urban or Suburban Economic Development Award, as well as the International Economic Development Council's 2002 Excellence in Economic

Development Award. Even with the relatively slow economy, this Technology Park has been a steady employer and offers the City of Springfield valuable benefits. This report highlights the economic and fiscal impact of the STCC Technology Park on the region, the city, and the college. The assessments in this report are both quantitative and qualitative in nature.

On Employment Impact
- Tenant companies in the STCC Technology Park create a total of approximately 860 direct jobs.
- An additional 1,223 jobs are created in the regional economy due to the multiplier effect.
- A total of 2,083 jobs can be attributed either directly or indirectly to the Park.
- For every one job in the Park, an additional 1.42 jobs in the regional economy will be affected.

On Investment and Purchase Impact
- Tenant companies have invested in excess of $300 million in equipment and technology.
- Since the Park's establishment in 1996, STCCAC has invested approximately $8.5 million in the facility.
- The Park's management company's policy of favoring local contractors and s ervice providers infuses approximately $2.5 million into the local economy each year.
- Park employees have the purchase power to spend $17 million for goods and services. It is estimated that a large share of this amount is spent within the region. The multiplier effect brings this purchase power up by another $24 million that may be spent through indirect job generation within the regional economy.

On Fiscal Impact
- The Technology Park generates $218,000 in property tax revenue annually for the City.
- The City spends approximately $44,500 annually to provide municipal services to the Park.
- The City nets approximately $173,500 in annual tax revenues from the Park.

On the STCC/Technology Park Partnership
- The Partnership has made it possible for hundreds of STCC students to gain practical work experience at technology-based companies in the Park.
- The Park provides an ideal educational setting for three STCC academic programs: the National Center for Telecommunications Technologies, the Department of Mechanical Engineering Technology, and the Verizon New England Next Step Program.
- STCC faculty and staff provide tenant companies with both business expertise and up-to-date technical assistance.

The STCC Technology Park is a place where calculated risk is welcomed, where there is a low cost of entry, where innovation is an asset and where academic assistance is literally next door. It is also a place that welcomes, educates, and trains the City's next workforce in new technologies, and that is very much a part of an exciting, changing neighborhood. In short, there is no place quite like it in the City. It is here that one can see the legacy of Springfield's economic past evolving into Springfield's future.

✦

The first few years of ownership required significant investments in infrastructure needs, most of which are one-time investments. Realtor fees were substantial and will occur again only when tenants renew leases, or when new tenants replace tenants that leave. It is also important to note that, at any given time, more than 100 of STCC students are employed either full or part time, and many have accepted employment upon graduation.

SPRINGFIELD ENTERPRISE CENTER

In 1999, STCC opened the Springfield Enterprise Center. This entrepreneurial venture consisted of a plan to mold, shape, and nurture new entrepreneurs. The center is a small business incubator; a student business incubator; a venture center; a site for introducing entrepreneurship to K–12 students; a home for the Entrepreneurship Hall of Fame; and a venue for a plethora of entrepreneurial programs, including the recently launched NACCE. The Enterprise Center falls under the auspices of the vice president for economic and business development.

As was mentioned previously, the creation of the college's Division of Economic and Business Development is an entrepreneurial activity that has helped the community college overcome fiscal challenges by increasing revenue, decreasing expenses, and streamlining processes to ensure an effective, efficient, and economically managed environment. The division encompasses a myriad of services that generate revenue and leverage fundraising and philanthropic donations to sustain its mission. The following entrepreneurial initiatives are operating currently under the auspices of the division.

Workforce Development

Center for Business and Technology (CBT). CBT provides noncredit instruction and training and generates annual revenues approaching $1 million. Comprehensive workforce programs offered include information technology courses and certifications, Web-based education, high-stakes authorized testing, computer workshops, customized employee training, career training, and College for Kids (which offers fun education courses in the summer for K–12 students).

Deliso Videoconferencing Center. The center provides affordable state-of-the-art videoconferencing services to area businesses, organizations, and education institutions, as well as audio conferencing, video production, Web casting, and high-end presentations. Presently generating $50,000 annually, revenues are increasing steadily as the market becomes more educated to its cost-effectiveness and more comfortable with this application of technology. The center also houses several hundred thousand dollars' worth of cutting-edge technology and equipment, made possible by a generous donation from the Deliso family.

New Venture Creation

Business Incubator. In its fifth year of operation, the Business Incubator provides customized leases and support to grow start-up businesses. Operating as a mixed-use facility, the incubator tenants' combined revenues were $6.5 million in 2003. In addition, 200 jobs have been created, and to date, the Business Incubator has graduated 11 companies. Completed in October 1999, the Business Incubator opened its doors debt-free thanks to a $4 million capital campaign, including a $1 million Economic Development Administration grant.

Student Business Incubator. The Student Business Incubator serves as a hatchery where new entrepreneurial start-ups, created by students, grow up. The original funding of $50,000 helped create the incubator when it was launched in November 2000. Since then, more than $150,000 has been raised through grants and foundations, accelerating the incubator's growth to include 16 graduate student businesses and 9 businesses presently incubating with total revenues of approximately $1.5 million annually.

Entrepreneurship Education

Entrepreneur for a Day. Launched in September 2001, the Entrepreneur for a Day program teaches students from kindergarten through eighth grade the fundamental principles of entrepreneurship and how to start a business. Several foundations donated a total of $100,000, which was used to start and operate the program initially. Future plans include revenue generation of $25,000 annually as the program shifts to a fee-for-service model.

MiddleBiz. Concentrating on students in grades 6 through 8 in an after-school environment, the MiddleBiz program offers students the opportunity to learn the distinct differences between becoming an entrepreneur and being an employee. Funded by several private and public sources, totaling $40,000 over 3 years, the program helps students identify the skills and educational requirements necessary to become a successful entrepreneur and business owner.

Excellence in Youth Entrepreneurship. More than 400 students have graduated from the Excellence in Youth Entrepreneurship (EYE) program over the past 3 years, and a total of $50,000 has been raised to support this effort from various organizations and through a fee-for-service exchange. The EYE program is an online learning system that teaches entrepreneurship, information technology, and workplace literacy through business curriculum enhancements and business plan creation.

Young Entrepreneurial Scholars (Yes!). YES! resembles an MBA course, culminating in a business plan competition for more than 1,000 students in 25 high schools. Seed funding of $10,000 in 1998 created an opportunity to provide entrepreneurship education to high school students. Since 1998, YES! has raised more than $250,000 in funding from successful entrepreneurs, foundations, fundraising events, and grants.

Entrepreneurship Associate Degree. Students enrolled in entrepreneurship studies receive the support of faculty advisors and obtain theoretical knowledge from the classroom experience as they learn about creating and operating a small business. Originally launched in 1999 as a degree offering with only 3 students, the program now enrolls 56 full-time students, which represents a significant revenue generation in tuition and fees for the college.

Entrepreneurship Honors Colloquium. Designed to promote entrepreneurship across the curriculum for all students, regardless of their area of study and concentration, the Honors Colloquium offers a hands-on concept to a commercialization course. This unique interdisciplinary course pulls students together from different disciplines and introduces the concepts of innovation, invention, and entrepreneurship. Originally the program was funded by an initial program grant from a foundation totaling $28,000; today the students can pursue applying for individual funding up to $50,000 to further develop their invention through the creation of a working prototype.

S. Prestley Blake Student Venture Center. The Blake Student Venture Center serves as an intensive business incubation experience for student entrepreneurs who have gross sales of $25,000 or more in their business ventures. The center, created with partial funds from a $100,000 investment in entrepreneurship by S. Prestley Blake, co-founder of Friendly's Ice Cream, is supported by an advisory board of local entrepreneurs and business experts, who provide a wealth of knowledge, mentoring, and individual encouragement to the student entrepreneurs.

National Association for Community College Entrepreneurship. NACCE is a national organization reflecting and disseminating successful entrepreneurship education programs from community colleges across the country. Launched with $100,000 in seed capital in December 2001, NACCE developed a business plan and then went on to hold the NACCE Inaugural Conference in October 2003, with 150 attendees from 38 states, representing 102 community colleges. Additional NACCE funding has been secured, totaling $200,000 from two major foundations. Revenues generated through conferences, membership, and technical assistance will provide needed capital for continued growth and expansion of NACCE's national rollout over the next 5 years.

CONCLUSION

STCC has been describing itself as an entrepreneurial college for almost 15 years. By defining itself as an entrepreneurial college and engaging in entrepreneurial activities, STCC began a culture shift that encouraged the risk taking and unusual thinking needed to reduce dependency on shrinking state resources. For this style of management to work, it is necessary to have a strong team of supporters who can handle this mode of operation, particularly senior staff and trustees who share the vision and are confident in the institution's ability to deliver. STCC has experienced highs and lows over the past 10 years, but the philosophy of achievement guru Napoleon Hill rang true—in effect, opportunity often sneaks in the back door disguised as misfortune. It is how one deals with the perceived misfortune that turns bad luck into opportunity.

Community colleges across this nation are ideally situated to deal with perceived misfortunes and to accept the challenge and the excitement of being, thinking, and acting entrepreneurially. Not every leader is willing to accept the risks involved in large-scale projects such as those that STCC has undertaken, but entrepreneurial thinking can come in many forms. Colleges should start small by creating a marketing group. Then they can think bigger—establishing an entrepreneurial program with the local K–12 system is a logical next step. Or go even bigger and establish a small business incubator. Opportunity awaits.

Special thanks to Thomas Goodrow, vice president of Economic and Business Development, and Setta McCabe, director of Publications/Media Relations, for their assistance.

CHAPTER 11

ENTREPRENEURIAL LEADERS

Michael D. Summers and David H. McGilvray

—Greenville Technical College, South Carolina

The principal goal of education is to create men who are capable of doing new things, not simply of repeating what other generations have done—men who are creative, inventive, and discoverers.

—*Jean Piaget*

What are the leadership characteristics of the president of an entrepreneurial college? What is the president's role in creating an entrepreneurial college? What is the working environment or institutional culture that encourages entrepreneurial activity? What are the results of entrepreneurial activities? And what are the advantages and disadvantages of encouraging and supporting entrepreneurial activities in a public community college? We answer these questions in this chapter from the experiences of a community college in South Carolina—a community college with a solid, highly regarded reputation for innovation and a truly entrepreneurial leader.

A HISTORY AND DESCRIPTION OF THE GREENVILLE TECHNICAL COLLEGE

Entrepreneurial spirit is evident throughout the history and development of Greenville Technical College (GTC). In 1960, a state technical education system was initiated by Governor Ernest F. Hollings, who believed that if South Carolina could offer a well-trained workforce, the state could attract diversified business and industry. Hollings planned for this training to be provided by a statewide system of 13 Technical Education Centers (TECs), which later developed into 16 technical colleges. In 1962, the first of those institutions, the Greenville Technical Center, opened its doors.

The college's beginnings were modest: One building constructed on 8 acres of the city's former landfill, 800 full- and part-time students, 32 full- and part-time faculty, and 3 administrators. One of those administrators was the state's first TEC president, Thomas Barton, Jr. The college began to grow, and by 1965, it had acquired an additional 122 acres of land surrounding the original 8.

Academic offerings were expanding. In 1966, an innovative agreement with Clemson University allowed the university to offer freshman and sophomore courses on the Greenville campus, representing the start of a 2-year transfer program. In 1973, this agreement ended, and GTC formed its own arts and sciences division, offering the same freshman and sophomore courses that had been offered with Clemson, transforming an original technical training institution into a comprehensive community college. The college was accredited in 1968 by the Commission on Colleges of the Southern Association of Colleges and Schools to award associate degrees, diplomas, and certificates; its accreditation has been reaffirmed in each review since.

In 1994, the college received approval from the State Board for Comprehensive and Technical Education to establish satellite campuses in the northeastern region of the county (Greer Campus) and in the southern area of the county (Brashier Campus). One year later, these projects broke ground. The two new campuses, situated on approximately 100 acres each, opened in 1996. Facilities at the former Donaldson Air Force Base were established for aircraft maintenance training and truck driver education.

In 2000, a second building was added to each of the two campuses, and a third satellite campus, housed in a leased facility in the northwest region of the county, opened its doors. A few years later, land was purchased to replace the leased facility and construction began on a permanent Northwest Campus, with an anticipated opening in early 2006. Other expansions since 2000 have included an extensive continuing education facility (100,000 square feet), a regional automotive technology training center (93,000 square feet), and a comprehensive admissions and registration center (62,000 square feet).

GTC has grown to encompass almost 600 acres of land and 40 buildings. The college employs more than 1,200 full- and part-time faculty and staff, operates with an annual budget of more than $62 million, and provides services to 20,000 curriculum and 45,000 continuing education students annually. Presently, the college receives approximately 39% of its revenue from the state of South Carolina. Tuition and fee revenue paid by students is retained locally and contributes nearly 42% of the college's revenue. Other sources of revenue include local government support at 10% and auxiliary services at 9%. The Greenville Tech Foundation (GTF), the college's foundation, provides revenue to the college, including scholarships for many students. GTF is a key element in the college's entrepreneurial activities.

THE PHILOSOPHY AND CHARACTERISTICS OF AN ENTREPRENEURIAL PRESIDENT

Thomas E. Barton, Jr., president of GTC, has the longest tenure as president at the same 2-year college in U.S. history: He has served as GTC's president for 42 years. After serving in the public schools of South Carolina and Georgia as teacher, coach, and school superintendent, he became the founding president of GTC in 1962.

Barton's career at GTC is replete with community service; social and civic board memberships; and committee memberships at the local, state, and national levels. He believes that it is necessary to know what is happening in the community college environment and that one should be active in that environment. He has received recognition on numerous occasions as one of Greenville's 50 most influential people, and *Greenville Magazine* once named him businessperson of the year in recognition of GTC's innovative activities.

Barton attributes much of his leadership philosophy to his legendary Clemson football coach, Frank Howard. Playing competitive Division I college football taught Barton what it was to win and lose. And he hated losing! Howard taught him that hard work, focus, sacrifice, and a passion for what he must do are absolutely essential for winning. He has applied these strategies successfully to community college leadership, and his leadership philosophy has been instrumental in creating an entrepreneurial spirit within the college.

What are the leadership characteristics of the president of an entrepreneurial college? To fully understand the leadership philosophy, it is important to examine Barton's beliefs regarding key operational and managerial aspects of the college. For instance, Barton believes that it is important to establish a workplace philosophy in which all employees believe that every problem has a solution; given the necessary resources, every problem can be solved if the problem is fully examined and understood. He contends that focusing on solutions and solving problems create a mindset in the staff that facilitates innovative solutions and alternatives.

Barton believes that effective colleges hire people who need to work and that in today's constantly changing work environment, people who do not have to work are not as passionate about, committed to, and focused on their jobs as those who must. He believes that it is important to pay attention to people's personal lives; for a community college to be successful, it must find ways to get people focused on their work. Employees have problems that distract them; they may have money, marriage, family, drug and alcohol, and kids' problems. And in the midst all this, they must be focused on their jobs and help the college achieve its goals.

Put simply, Barton believes in inspecting what one expects. Having clear job descriptions and evaluation processes helps ensure that all employees are contributing. "Pulling horses don't kick," he observes. When employees have full, comprehensive jobs that challenge their minds and fill their days, there are less idle moments and fewer frivolous complaints. Employees' criticism, input, and feedback are not discouraged. In fact, meaningful input is always sought, but negative actions and attitudes that result from boredom are minimized if employees are engaged fully. On the surface, these personnel strategies suggest a focus on productivity, accountability, and efficiency, all contributing to institutional success and to successful entrepreneurial ventures.

THE PRESIDENT'S ROLE IN CREATING AN ENTREPRENEURIAL COLLEGE

What role does the president have in creating a working environment where entrepreneurial activity occurs? Simply stated, the president's role is absolutely critical because the president ultimately determines what activities and priorities are focused on daily, weekly, and in the long term. A president who expects accountability and data-driven decision making creates a working environment where assessment is integrated throughout the organization. Similarly, a president who advocates for an entrepreneurial environment will create a workplace where employees engage in regular brainstorming activities, visit other colleges to learn about best practices, generate and attempt new initiatives, and receive various incentives for new ideas. Although many community college presidents' roles have become more externally focused on fundraising and political activities, presidents can and should continue to have a tremendous influence on the college's internal work environment.

Responsible Risk Taking

Entrepreneurial people share the characteristic of being risk takers (Gartner, 1985). Barton is so described. He encourages risk-taking behavior within the college, establishing the expectation that employees are not chastised or disciplined when projects do not succeed. Although people are still held accountable for their actions, projects or ideas that do not prove to be of significant value to the college are considered to be the cost of creativity. An atmosphere where employees are not afraid of failure has encouraged a high level of creative thinking and innovation.

Barton and the leadership team at GTC give recognition and support to those who try new things, borrow and adapt projects from other colleges, and look to business and industry for strategies. And this working environment has encouraged employees to question long-standing assumptions and status quo processes and procedures. Barton's philosophy, "If you aren't making any mistakes, then you're not doing anything," helps to create a supportive environment that allows and encourages GTC employees to try new things and become more creative in their thinking.

Locus of Control

A strong internal locus of control is also a recognizable trait of entrepreneurial leaders (Dollinger, 2003). People who have a strong internal locus of control believe that the future is theirs to control through their own efforts. Barton urges employees to focus on ideas, not the money, saying that the money can always be found. Employees learn to concentrate on the creation of ideas, activities, or projects, not on how they will be funded. His is a working philosophy—if the idea, activity, or project is good enough and has enough benefit to the community, funding will be found to support it. Good ideas attract money. He believes that many colleges miss opportunities to develop worthwhile projects because they focus entirely too much on the money that would be required to implement them. Many great ideas never get developed because people are hung up on the funding sources. So, although it may seem counterintuitive to adopt a don't-worry-about-the-money philosophy in the current fiscal environment, this strategy has encouraged multiple entrepreneurial activities at GTC.

Accountability

The need for achievement is yet another personality characteristic associated with entrepreneurs. Entrepreneurs enjoy setting goals and achieving them through their own efforts. At GTC, Barton focuses on completing all projects. To accomplish that, he believes projects should be assigned to people who are specifically responsible for seeing them through to completion. He contends that many colleges take new innovative projects and add them to existing staff responsibilities—a major mistake. In that situation, employees must allocate their increasingly scarce time to a new project, while also juggling existing projects and responsibilities. This means that no one person is completely accountable for the project or for seeing it through to completion; the project competes for employees' attention, and ultimately no one is held responsible for its success or failure.

Barton believes that one or two employees should be assigned to a new project and follow it through to completion. These flexible project specialists are important resources to an entrepreneurial college. They can focus on and assure that the project gets the attention and resources necessary for success.

Institutional Culture

What working environment or institutional culture encourages entrepreneurial activity? First, the work environment or culture of an organization is reflected in its philosophies, rules, norms, and values. It is played out in the ways an organization provides and cares for employees and customers. The culture of an entrepreneurial organization is

> clearly different from the culture of traditional large organizations. It is future-oriented and emphasizes new ideas, creativity, risk taking, and opportunity identification. People feel empowered to manage their own jobs and time. Everyone can make a contribution to the firm's success, and the common worker is a hero. (Dollinger, 2003, p. 322)

GTC's institutional culture is consistent with this definition.

Barton believes that if the college is not growing, then it is falling behind. He is fond of saying, "We're not satisfied with the status quo." Because the world is constantly developing, changing, and growing, the college must grow to keep up. GTC is a college that resists the status quo and, therefore, is in a constant state of development. Employees know that if they want to work at GTC, they must embrace change. And the college has mastered change.

For example, GTC periodically reorganizes its managerial and operational structure to improve efficiency, capitalize on talents, and achieve goals and objectives. Barton believes that it is healthy for an organization to examine its strengths and weaknesses in terms of job responsibilities and assignments. When managers are moved into new areas of responsibility, such a college readily adjusts. Changes enhance professional development, result in productivity, and stimulate new ideas and thinking—especially important in today's competitive market.

GTC's working environment or institutional culture is difficult to separate from the leadership philosophy of its president. One creates the other, and GTC has found both to be essential to support entrepreneurial activity. Examples of GTC's successful entrepreneurial activities provide compelling pictures of the entrepreneurial spirit and mindset at work.

Buying an Aging Retail Mall: McAlister Square

One of the best examples of a successful entrepreneurial project is GTC's purchase of an aging retail mall. This unique acquisition was complicated to put together, but the purchase has resulted in substantial benefits for the college, the city, and its citizens. McAlister Square mall was the first major retail mall built in South Carolina in 1970. At the time of its opening, it was the largest indoor mall in the state, nearly 500,000 square feet of enclosed shopping space. It also had the dubious distinction of having the largest contiguous parking space in the state, nearly 40 acres of asphalt. However, as has happened to hundreds of other urban malls across America, over a period of less than three decades, the mall lost business to larger and more elaborate suburban malls. By 1998, the anchor stores and most retail shops had closed or moved to suburban malls. The streets near the mall area were deteriorating and property values were declining. Why would GTC be interested in purchasing such a mall? Part of the answer goes back a number of years earlier with GTC's establishment of the University Center.

In 1975, GTC began offering university transfer courses at the freshman and sopho-more levels as a service to its community. In addition, Clemson University—located only 35 miles to the west of Greenville—began offering junior- and senior-level courses in Greenville, using some of GTC's classroom space. Nevertheless, by 1987, Greenville—the largest popula-tion center in South Carolina—still did not have a public senior university. Community lead-ers recognized that continued economic development and attractive quality of life in Greenville would require additional local higher education opportunities—4-year degree pro-grams and postgraduate opportunities. In response to this need, Clemson University, with GTC's cooperation, invited other state-supported institutions to form a consortium for the Greenville area. After considerable planning and negotiation, the proposed new Greenville Higher Education Center was chartered by the South Carolina Commission on Higher Education and moved into an office suite on the GTC campus. This partnership among seven public and private higher education institutions—Clemson University, the University of South Carolina, the Medical University of South Carolina, South Carolina State University, the University of South Carolina-Spartanburg, Furman University, and Lander University—resulted in the noncompetitive offering of a variety of baccalaureate, master's-level, and doctoral-level programs in Greenville proper.

Unlike some consortia ventures in other states, the University Center of Greenville operates as a collaboratively governed minicampus, in which all necessary instructional and student support services are housed in one location. The quasi-private center is empowered to serve as a regional coordinating board, from which a state college intending to deliver courses or programs in the Greenville area must obtain permission before making application to the statewide commission. The University Center's annual operating budget is derived from mem-bership fees and a credit-hour charge paid by each college delivering courses at the center. It does not receive state funds for operations. Since 1987, Clemson University has served as the center's fiduciary agent for budget and human resources matters.

The consortium was originally housed on GTC's campus and later grew to occupy a building across the street from McAlister Square in 1996. The continued enrollment growth of the University Center, however, created the need for a larger facility. McAlister Square was the most logical place.

It should be noted from the outset that GTC and its foundation had multiple inter-ests in acquiring an aging retail mall. The University Center needed more room but, of more importance, the center creates a steady alternative income stream for the college's foundation. Furthermore, the idea of promoting Greenville's economic development, by establishing an education center in what would otherwise remain an neighborhood eyesore, gained support from city, county, and state officials. Barton's tenacity and belief in the project were instru-mental in the completion and ultimate success of the project.

In December 2002, the GTF McAlister Limited Liability Corporation (LLC) was formed to hold and operate property for GTF while effectively reducing the potential tort lia-bility to the foundation. Shortly thereafter, the McAlister LLC purchased the master lease from the third party and began the active management of the interior spaces and common area. This transaction involved a bargain sale and a gift-in-kind contribution to GTF from the third-party leaseholder. The foundation financed its net cost through a private bank loan. The principal reason for this transaction was to reduce expenses for operations to the foundation.

Operationally, McAlister Square has leasing and management consulting through a local realtor. Plant maintenance services are contracted with GTC and GTF. McAlister LLC staff handles tenant relations, accounting, and administrative functions. Long-term projections for the GTF McAlister LLC are to provide income of $20 million over the next 30 years to GTF to support GTC programs, faculty, and students. At present, in its first year of operation, the McAlister Square project has returned a substantial net profit to the foundation.

What made this project successful? Timing, persistence, need, and entrepreneurial vision came together. The re-creation of McAlister Square into an environment containing the University Center, retail, restaurants, a call center, radio stations, a magazine publisher, insurance offices, staffing agencies, school district facility construction offices, government offices, private education centers, the County Literacy Association, and a free dental clinic has been amazing. Furthermore, GTC has renovated the second of the big boxes to become its own comprehensive admissions and registration center.

Barton was the planner, innovator, and ultimate decision maker in a productive enterprise. His vision led a team through the complicated legal, political, and real estate transactions necessary to complete the acquisition of McAlister Square. Barton's entrepreneurial spirit and expertise, artfully combined with the collective wisdom and support of the members of the GTF board, were absolutely critical to the success of this project.

THE GREENVILLE TECH FOUNDATION

Established in 1973, GTF, Inc., is a fully chartered 501(c)(3) nonprofit corporation, separate from GTC, but operating for the benefit of the college. It is governed by a board of directors composed of recognized leaders in business, industry, and the professions. The foundation was established to ensure that the college has the financial support beyond that which can be obtained from state and local funding sources. Funding is acquired through charitable contributions from businesses, industries, foundations, organizations, and individual donors.

Like most foundations, Greenville's accepts tax-deductible contributions in cash, real or personal property, securities, bequests, or by naming the foundation as beneficiary of insurance policies or trusts. Gifts are designated or restricted and are made on a one-time basis or over several years. What is unique about the foundation, however, is its membership. Whereas community leaders in government, social agencies, and area businesses and industries typically comprise community college foundations, Greenville's foundation is composed of entrepreneurs, presidents of companies, and successful business people, all of whom care deeply about the college. Foundation membership is a dynamic combination of innovative and entrepreneurial leaders with polished business savvy.

Barton challenged this group to find ways to make money instead of just raise money. This is a noteworthy difference in how most foundations operate. Essentially, the foundation is able to tap into the collective expertise of its membership to identify and develop business opportunities where revenue can be generated. This entrepreneurial foundation works on projects not normally associated with college foundations. The willingness of these professionals to give time and expertise was essential to the success of this approach.

The foundation provided GTC with the expertise to complete an innovative and risky project that has resulted in sustained value for the college, the city, and the residents of Greenville County. Currently, GTF is exploring other projects that have potential for similar success. Clearly, this is an atypical approach to college foundations.

CONCLUSION

An entrepreneurial spirit creates an environment of innovation that affects all areas of the college. Indeed, innovative academic programs and nontraditional instructional strategies result in benefits to students and the community. Entrepreneurial activities improve linkages between businesses in the service area and the college, creating common interests. To be sure, in addition to supplying a trained and educated workforce, the entrepreneurial college develops a reputation for truly understanding the prevalent business environment—a noteworthy achievement among business and political community leaders. Barton's recognition as businessperson of the year is testimony to the importance that the community places on a college that teaches entrepreneurship and and puts it to work. There is an advantage for the classroom, as well. In colleges offering classes in management or business, especially in entrepreneurship, students appreciate that the college practices what it teaches.

Opportunities and feasibilities for entrepreneurial activities vary across colleges, driven by their missions, priorities, locations, and other even more unique circumstances. However, the spirit of entrepreneurship is critical to success. The constant awareness of opportunities, the willingness to accept reasonable and calculated risks, and the ability and willingness to take an idea from concept to fruition are the keys to successful entrepreneurial ventures. Entrepreneurship is manifested by action and obvious in its spirit.

Greenville Technical College is an entrepreneurial college. Its president's philosophy supports entrepreneurial activities. Its culture and work environment support entrepreneurial projects. The business and industry leaders of the foundation bring first-hand experience in entrepreneurialism. Not all colleges have these elements, but studying such a college might chart the path for others to follow.

REFERENCES

Dollinger, M. J. (2003). *Entrepreneurship: Strategies and resources* (3rd ed.). Upper Saddle River, NJ: Pearson Education.

Gartner, W. B. (1985, October). A conceptual framework for describing the phenomenon of new venture creation. *The Academy of Management Review, 10*(4), 696–706.

CHAPTER 12

ENTREPRENEURIAL RISK TAKING

Millicent Valek
—Brazosport College, Lake Jackson, Texas

No noble thing can be done without risks.
—*Michel de Montaigne, French Renaissance philosopher (1533–1592)*

The critical ingredient in any entrepreneurial enterprise is risk taking. When all the other factors are weighed, measured, and accounted for, the amount of risk one can tolerate must still be considered seriously. In some cases, with careful planning, this risk factor might even be shared, but someone must take that first leap into the unknown. It is important that the leap be made from a solid foundation of trusting relationships, a base of operation that takes time to develop and that must be nurtured constantly. One cannot know or anticipate when an entrepreneurial opportunity will present itself. Readiness is the key.

Consistent, sincere communication with multiple audiences creates relationships that become the bridges between potential partners and entrepreneurial ventures. These relationships must be open and strong to support the shared risk of enterprises—built on knowledge, on clear understanding of one another, and mutual trust. It is this base of respect and connectivity that minimizes the risk of entrepreneurial ventures.

BRAZOSPORT COLLEGE HISTORY

Brazosport College (BC) is a comprehensive community college offering programs that transfer to 4-year universities, as well as 2-year degrees in many career-related fields. Students may begin a college major or complete a degree and seek employment. The college is located in Lake Jackson, a town of moderate growth, approximately 10 miles from the mouth of the Brazos River in South Texas. Lake Jackson marks the nexus of the mid-Gulf Coast's petrochemical industry, just 30 miles south of Houston's famous Texas Medical Center complex.

Formerly a sugar and cotton plantation, Lake Jackson boasted a single schoolhouse and, as late as 1937, only one teacher. In the early 1940s, the plantation was purchased for use as a town site for the employees of what is today the Dow Chemical Company. The new town, named for the original plantation owner Abner Jackson, became a model community, reflecting the skilled architectural plan of Alden B. Dow, son of company founder H. H. Dow and a student of the famed architect Frank Lloyd Wright.

Although primarily designed and planned for employee housing, Dow left room for private development, allowing Lake Jackson to become more than a company town. The first area school districts were consolidated in 1944, and 24 years later, voters approved a taxing district supporting the creation of Brazosport Junior College. In 1968, the college enrolled 879 students in its first fall semester.

BRAZOSPORT COLLEGE TODAY

From its inception in the late 1960s, with just fewer than 900 students enrolled in traditional academic transfer courses, to today's comprehensive and flexible learning environment, BC's leaders, faculty, and staff have worked to keep its programs responsive to the expressed needs of its service communities. College ties to the industrial base of the surrounding environment have always been strong. The first governing board of regents included several business and industrial leaders of the day.

BC serves a student base that numbers in the thousands, including day and evening students. The student body includes credit students planning to transfer to 4-year colleges and seeking technical certification or degrees, noncredit or continuing education students pursuing skills training and lifelong learning opportunities, and business and industry employees receiving customized training through the college's Center for Business/Industry Training.

Annually, the college serves approximately 28,924 students. Seventy-six percent of the credit students are evenly divided between academic and technical majors. Approximately 40% of noncredit/continuing education students are enrolled in specific workforce training programs, with the remainder enrolled in programs of avocational interests. More than 12,000 employees from 25 different companies are enrolled in customized workforce training programs and business-related seminars conducted through the Center for Business/Industry Training.

The BC service area encompasses both densely residential and rural communities and is represented heavily by companies engaged in the petrochemical industry and its auxiliary service industries. BC awards degrees to more than 200 students annually and has become the key provider of a highly trained workforce for these local industrial employers. In a collaborative and responsive partnership with local industry, BC customizes workforce-training services, consistently earning top marks from business community members.

BC's mission and practice have been broadened to embrace aspects of enhanced technology, customized workforce training and business consulting services, and cultural enrichment, in addition to providing the general and traditional academic curriculum offerings. Not unlike the first board of regents in 1968, today's governing board remains representative of service area business and industry leadership. The regents' managerial expertise and multifaceted connections to broad sections of the local culture are vital contributors in maintaining an open dialogue with these communities.

EMBRACING ENVIRONMENTAL FACTORS DRIVING ENTREPRENEURSHIP

As the first decade of this new century unfolds, the world is vastly different than that which challenged the founders of the community college system in America. And although the world has changed considerably as have most of the issues facing colleges, there still may exist one perennial issue for America's community colleges: fluctuating seasons of financial uncertainty. With money matters paramount on any community college list of environmental factors, the other significant influences driving change today can be categorized as a growing global marketplace and increased expectations from businesses and the community.

The recent biennium marked a historic decline in levels of state appropriations for community colleges, and the ripple effects of related decisions are being felt throughout the education environments of Texas. They represent dwindling state appropriations and mid-year revertments for BC. Because state allocations are not adequate to maintain the costs of instruction, new, creative, and flexible approaches have been developed to help continue providing high-quality education services to the people who depend on BC.

It is easy to assume that a relatively remote spot in south Texas might be protected from the effects of massive globalization. But for the local workforce, the ripples of these effects have been and will continue to be quite dramatic. When sweeping changes are made to the international policies of an industrial giant whose Texas operations plant is BC's neighbor, these changes affect the community college directly. They may result in the development of training programs to meet new compliance regulations or hosting meetings with international groups of leaders and engineers. They may signal a more dire situation, such as workforce shifts that affect enrollment patterns with little or no advance notice. BC's response to these global changes must be handled locally and with flexibility. The college must think globally to remain in sync with clients' and students' mindsets.

BC has developed a heightened sensitivity to the local property tax rates: 65% of local taxes are paid by two major industrial taxpayers. The standardized effects of changing business and industrial climates are obvious. Essentially, new guidelines for job requirements are driving the need for a more technologically adept workforce. The process technologies curriculum did not exist when BC began in 1968. Today, however, local industrial hiring standards are requiring that entry-level employees have at minimum a 2-year degree. This industrial–educational interface exists in other arenas, but here at the community college level, its effects are often immediate and powerful. An appropriate response to this discussion is an exploration of managing similar organizations in today's climate. Even in the face of difficulties, a leader can influence and guide processes within an education environment that can enhance the organization as it changes and grows.

LEADING CHANGE USING KEY PHILOSOPHICAL PRINCIPLES

The tools of leadership may be used effectively in the everyday work environment of the community college and in creating an environment encourages entrepreneurship. As BC president, I value interdependence, inclusiveness, flexibility, and communication—key principles that are essential to organizing or managing successfully and that are powerful in encouraging innovation and entrepreneurial activity in broader, collegewide contexts. In a community college environment, finding the right balance of these tools is essential to cultivating an environment in which risk taking is possible. Particular opportunities for applying these leadership tools can be internal or campuswide, external or community related; they must involve the college's governing board on the leadership team. Each interactive communication plan or approach must mirror the particular group or subgroup's relationship with the college as a whole.

When I arrived at BC in 1996, it was clear to me that by tweaking the organizational system and by changing or altering workflow patterns of college leaders, more interaction and productivity might emerge. I was able to include a collegewide element within each dean's functional responsibilities that, when shared, would connect them all as a collaborative group. This connection broadened systematic communications, eventually helping spark the development of a common vision. In practice, this council of deans now meets regularly, and together the group consistently advances a variety of initiatives or strategic intents that benefit from this broadened, shared information base and sets the tone for change.

Beyond the campus, BC leaders are encouraged to be involved in civic activities throughout the local communities. Personal involvement in civic affairs helps leaders develop mutually beneficial lines of communication. Through personal contact and influence, college leaders have the opportunity to affect and, in some cases, set the agenda for change within the community.

Frequent and regular contact, cooperative and sincere sharing of information, and flexibility or readiness to act on an opportunity when it presents itself, are all important subtexts to improving relationships that can help leaders effect and manage change, both campuswide and within communities. A solid relationship with potential partners is the foundation of any successful collaborative initiatives. This relationship must be established slowly and methodically over the long term, through consistent contact and communication, and be firmly in place to make any discussions of shared goal setting possible and productive.

It is possible to create an environment for positive response to entrepreneurial opportunities. The antithesis of a fear of stepping out is having all parties develop trust and interdependence through frequent interaction and sincere communication. Inclusiveness is strengthened through interaction, encourages the development of a shared vision, and increases the tolerance for assuming risk. In this climate, opportunities can be pursued. The ability to respond by capitalizing on and pursuing an opportunity does not guard against losing ground; it only creates a momentum for new ventures and more risk taking. In a changing world, depending on the status quo and traditional responses ultimately may prove more risky than venturing forth.

RESPONDING TO FUNDING CHALLENGES

The first step in responding to the converging forces of need and opportunity is participation in one-on-one communication. The ability to share risks is paramount, and eventually, funding challenges influence changes in the way community colleges conduct business. Responding to need and opportunity is prompting an organizational change within BC, and I believe the final outcome of this process will be positive.

BC has received numerous requests from service-area residents for more 4-year degree program opportunities. Although the University of Houston has branch campuses near BC, when the traffic, parking, and travel times are factored into the equation, most students are facing a 2-hour commute each way for one evening class. This is a major impediment for students who are balancing the responsibilities of raising families with the demands of full-time jobs.

When we explored the possible alternatives our college might pursue, we discovered roadblocks to traditional partnerships. One of these roadblocks was a low level of interest among potential 4-year college partners—which probably reflected their concerns about competing demands on faculty resources and about the comparatively small numbers of BC students who might be expected to matriculate. Concurrently, as we talked with local business and industry partners, we discovered that these companies were seeking to identify and promote supervisory-caliber employees who had strong technical skills. They did not want to import these potential managers, but desired a career path for their own high performers who were well settled in the community. These employees typically exhibited maturity, had stable and strong attachments to the area, and, in many cases, were juggling the demands of full-time employment and family responsibilities.

An expressed need (of the local employer) and a defined strategic intent (of the college) effectively emerged. Simply, we were able to share subsequent decisions because we were working from an established base of understanding, mutual respect, and goodwill built over the years. The interdependence and inclusiveness of all concerned parties, strengthened through frequent communication, had established a mutual credibility base. From there we agreed to collaborate and chose to face the risk of addressing this challenge together.

JOINING FORCES

Our initial research indicated that community colleges in other parts of the country had lobbied successfully for legislative approval to offer limited numbers of bachelor's degrees. If this could be done in other states, why not here in Texas? Our focus was on effectively leveraging the combined reputations of the college and local industry with the political support necessary to effect change at the state legislative level.

With support from other higher education leaders in Texas, local business leaders and legislators, and BC's governing board, we were able to secure legislative approval for a pilot program that allowed BC and two other Texas community colleges to develop the first baccalaureate programs in applied technology. Memorable highlights of this experience were witnessing representatives of our own local industry partner testify at the state legislature on behalf of Texas's community colleges and celebrating the accomplishment of the legislation's author, the state representative from our district.

We fought the battle to advance this particular initiative on many fronts. We fought resistance all the way, through the legislature, through the state coordinating board, and through the accreditation process. There were challenges and risks, and we faced tremendous territorialism that threatened to preserve the status quo. But when a venture like this succeeds, everyone benefits. The college receives support and heightened interest from its service-area communities because of its proven ability to respond with a plan that meets expressed needs. All parties have collaborated to contribute to the enterprise, and each group enjoys the satisfaction of involvement in the success.

The new degree program affected BC organizationally. And although not part of the original intent, it is interesting to note that these actions have had a historic impact on how the community college system in Texas does business. We acknowledge, of course, that further organizational and systematic changes are likely to be in store for us as we develop this program, seek accreditation approval, and struggle with implementing the start-up of the program entirely with local funds.

This challenge has encouraged us to assess our existing resource bases and work to redirect these resources. For example, our library has holdings that will support the 4-year degree requirements but will need some enhancements. Many of our faculty members' credentials meet the accreditation standards for the baccalaureate, and the discipline we have chosen for the degree is process technology. By capitalizing on these existing resources, and adding new ones, we are finding ways to offer new programs to our students and our community employers to meet their expressed needs. We are examining faculty credentials in most program areas, measured against 4-year degree standards, and determining the effects on our long-term hiring practices.

ENTREPRENEURIAL ACTIVITIES AT BRAZOSPORT

Two critical activities that BC is developing currently contribute to the college's entrepreneurial status. The first illustrates how we were able to face the risk of changing how we do business organizationally, by modifying our education delivery system. The second describes how we used an entrepreneurial approach to fund the expansion and renovation of our aging physical plant.

The Center for Business/Industry Training

Can radically different types of education delivery systems coexist cordially on a community college campus? From its creation in 1992, the Center for Business/Industry Training has been defined informally as our entrepreneurial arm. We believe that the center is a unique service center within the community college environment. Essentially, it is a business run within the college; its purpose is to develop and provide customized training classes, workshops, and seminars for business clients. It competes with external commercial training vendors, and because we choose to operate with no state reimbursements, there are no restraints on programming.

The creation of the center was not a simple venture. The inevitably conflicting demands of a business environment (characterized by flexibility and lightning-fast response) and the more traditional academic pace (unfolding in semesters) met head on when it came to serving the training needs of one of BC's important business clients. A major industrial neighbor, this business employs a large segment of the local workforce; it was important for the college to respond to its needs. According to the founding director of the center, the opportunity to respond came when BC's then-president gave the go-ahead to answer a request for proposals for this company's computer training needs. Acknowledging that the college's academic track offerings did not match the company's requirements, the president and a college team, including the current director of the center, the BC vice president, directors of the Community Education and the Occupational Technology departments, and a faculty member went to work. This group fashioned a plan to provide customized computer training.

Flexibility and timeliness were key ingredients of the proposal, and the focus was on meeting the client's needs completely, not simply providing a structure or building in which classes would be held. Before the contract was even confirmed, the team was in action. Team members reserved existing classroom space, interviewed potential instructors, and prepared and copied instructional materials, even when it was still not certain that the job would be ours. The center's director aptly calls those the days of whitewater rafting.

In addition to a timely, cost-effective, quality response, this business client was seeking trainers with industry and consulting experience, quality assurance in curriculum, and experts in course delivery, who used the tenets of adult learning theory. The client also wanted a physical environment more like a conference center than a college classroom. The client wanted no excuses for why something could not be accomplished. The proposal was written, and training since has been conducted for 2,880 participants.

The center approached each initiative in terms of providing a turnkey solution that would be financially self-supporting, allowing responders to align the required resources from equipment to supplies to personnel and physical plant requirements to provide a solution for the customer. Although each project had to stand on its own, foundations for future projects were being built as well. This totally self-sufficient unit of the college would operate with none of the restrictions that accompany state aid issues. A new cost structure for all aspects of the operation would need to be designed. It would also mean hiring trainers and consultants outside of academe.

Since its inception, the Center for Business/Industry Training's growth has mimicked a rollercoaster ride, reflecting fluctuating industry needs and requirements. Overall, it has been successful and continues to be so, by several measures. The Center has had an impact on the ability of the college to maintain a balance in its reserves. Financial support from the center's revenue provides an important base to operations at BC; despite decidedly lean economic times, marked by dwindling state appropriations and mid-year revertments, BC has sustained a healthy fund balance ratio in its overall budget, an adequate rainy-day fund for any uncontrollable future events.

Today, the Center for Business/Industry Training is housed in a new, two-story, 45,000 square-foot state-of-the-art Corporate Learning Center on BC's campus. Its staff of part-time trainers works annually with more than 12,000 employees from more than 25 companies, delivering training programs related to computer applications, workforce development, diversity issues, statistical quality control, process technology operations, software conversion projects, individual consulting, job skills assessment, and computer-based instruction, among others. It is continually developing revenue sources to expand programs and working to increase related capacities for new initiatives. The center has applied for Texas Workforce Commission grants and has been awarded four.

Because each year's activity for the center is not plannable, in the business sense, and is driven by immediate client needs, it focuses on the time-honored business directives of building partnerships. Professionals at the center get to know a client company's culture, become allies, and collaborate over the long term. Internal measures for successful outcomes include the following:

- Increasing the number of repeat customers
- Becoming known as an expertise center
- Creating a self-supporting revenue stream from services tailored to each specific company's needs

- Globalizing, multinationally and multiculturally, the college's outreach through its services
- Increasing the number of companies and clients served over the years

Future directions for the Center for Business/Industry Training include continuing consulting services for industry partners and adding a train-the-trainers outreach program. These specialized training services are being developed to include customized consulting for other education institutions that wish to build their own community learning strategies. The center's staff and administrators—their experience levels and their track records—and its unique delivery systems represent valuable mentoring opportunities. Customized consulting services for educational institutions are a natural outgrowth of this progress, particularly as they may apply to universities and other colleges planning to market their unique sets of services. The center's community learning strategy seminar introduces elements of this specialized training.

A Fundraising Initiative to Upgrade Aging Facilities

To address the need to upgrade its facilities, BC moved from an emphasis on process, or how it does business, to the challenge of creating a real bricks and mortar plan. Flexibility is the magic bullet in each successful response to an entrepreneurial opportunity. BC's physical plant presented a major challenge. With only one significant expansion in years—the addition of a new two-story wing of classrooms—the building was stretched to its capacity, and some demands were going unmet. It was time for a serious assessment.

Hesitating to rely on a bond election to pay for any upgrades, renovations, or new construction, we faced the challenge of how to fund expansion and modernization our aging facilities. Analysis of our statistics indicated that 40% of our credit-student base resided outside of our taxing district lines. If we resorted to a typical bond election, this population base would have no obligation to participate, but it would still continue to share equally in all benefits of facility use.

Faced with the reality that no one funding source alone could provide the adequate resources needed to expand, we were required to identify an innovative approach to generating the $22–$24 million needed. Our answer was linked to the pursuit of multiple monetary sources, including the use of reserve funds, private funds, and revenue bonds. Our college never had conducted a capital campaign, nor raised such a large amount of money. It was a risk to count on 25% of the project costs coming from private donations. However, our governing board embraced the idea, developed a plan, and with a bold public declaration, the capital campaign rolled forward.

The campaign unfolded over the next months, planned and implemented with care. With the momentum of our shared vision and a firm proposal of how to pay for the initiatives, our regents and a stellar group of community leaders became the natural guiding forces of this project. Their deep involvement in the campaign to raise community awareness and capital made the effort a success. Unforeseen, however, was the impact of the campaign on the daily business of the office of president, and I found that there was a real shift in my responsibilities. I systemically moved toward expanding the role of president as liaison to the community, particularly in one-on-one fundraising meetings.

Expansion and renovation were planned in phases, and we created a series of opportunities to share facts through local news coverage of each noteworthy milestone. The campaign was structured to reward donations at certain levels, allowing donors to name meeting rooms, fountains, suites of offices, a clock tower, or a formal boardroom. We called our community awareness and capital campaign "Building a Legacy." Between the formal kick-off in September 2000 and the formal closure of the campaign in December 2001, we raised $5.5 million. This amount, and the generosity it represented, pleased us. It was a wonderful feeling: We raised a sum more than double any amount ever raised in a community capital campaign in our area in the space of just 18 months. Monetary support came from a broad composite of large and small industries and businesses, individuals and groups, college departments and student organizations, and wealthy foundations impressed by our success at raising vital matching local funds.

Private talks with individuals in the community allowed me to share, as president, a personal vision of the project and its expected outcomes for our community. It is fair to say that 50% of my time during the 18-month campaign was devoted to meetings of this kind, which meant that other college leaders had to step up to assume some of my responsibilities. This worked particularly well because of the successful channels of communication that were already in place among key leaders. This organizational pattern continues today, even after the campaign, allowing me to stay engaged in a leadership role in the community and with state issues, in addition to leading the college.

The energy and goodwill generated by this accomplishment encourages more success. Many capital campaign contributors have allied themselves closely with the college and are aware of continuing needs. With the generosity of these community members, we are building our general scholarship endowment to augment student financial aid, and we are receiving additional gifts earmarked for specialized types of study or for students who fit certain group profiles. Although I cannot predict where this will lead, by cultivating these positive relationships, we are raising community members' stakes in the college and helping to ensure future shared successes. We are raising the bar on the community's expectations of the college, as well, so the pressure to take on more commitments, begin new programs, and expand services continues to increase with each success—perhaps our biggest challenge yet.

CONCLUSION

So why do we pursue entrepreneurial activities at BC? The simple answer is that we have no other choice. Colleges must continue to reinvent themselves in order to survive. However, if our goal is to do more than survive in today's unforgiving business and social climate, then we must invent the future.

Innovation that is categorized as being entrepreneurial demands some key attributes among college leaders—the ability and drive to build strong relationships, tolerate and encourage risk taking, and remain flexible and open to quick response. Leaders with this mindset are essential at the governing level and must be comfortable within a risk-taking environment. Because they are privy to more information than most and must be able to withstand public scrutiny, their imagination and tolerance for risk and vision will be tested. Leaders who seek to embrace entrepreneurial opportunities must be comfortable in challenging the status quo.

CHAPTER 13

THE ENTREPRENEURIAL COLLEGE: FOCUSING ON THE FUTURE

John E. Roueche and Barbara R. Jones
—The University of Texas at Austin

We have always held to the hope, the belief, the conviction that there is a better life, a better world, beyond the horizon.

—*Franklin D. Roosevelt*

With great anticipation, each generation engages in innovation and invention, determined to enhance technology, advance science, or discover new ways of doing business. In the 21st century the e-generation came of age, so named for its prolific use and control of e-commerce, e-mail, and electronic information in general. Between the ages of 16 and 25, young people in this generation navigate deftly through a digital environment, comfortable with change and optimistic about future possibilities. Current and potential students who will make up a large section of the present and future at America's community colleges are a large part of the e-generation.

E-generation students are much like other generations of community college students: They have little time to contemplate whether colleges receive the same levels of state support; they are disinterested in the number of students who attend colleges; and they care little about the possibility that a significant number of faculty and administrators will retire within the next 10 years. What they do expect and care about is whether or not colleges are responsive to their needs. They want convenient, accessible programs and services, faculty with whom they can relate, and learning that links them to knowledge in familiar ways.

Clearly, entrepreneurial colleges have figured out how to close the generation gap. In fact, they have discovered how to meet the needs of all constituents. With ears open to the voices of change, they hear the frustrations, concerns, and hopes of students and communities. Appreciative of their own past, but focused on their future, entrepreneurial community colleges represent renewed hope and a best-laid plan for the future.

Community colleges have measured, evaluated, and assessed effectiveness and collected volumes of data on the retention, placement, and demographics of students; fiscal health; employee satisfaction; and the like. They have scanned the environment, flattened the organization, and initiated strategies to improve their services. After all, community colleges are champions of managing the education environment. However, what many in community colleges have learned is that sometimes, although data are important in decision making, they do not guarantee future accomplishments or missions fulfilled or achieved.

Entrepreneurial college leaders are not focused only on change; they proactively determine how to meet the challenges of any situation with ease—moving the institution forward through a succession of accomplishments, with small and large strategies. They do this by grasping the wheel of the organization, navigating over current bumps and obstacles, and being discontent to travel the same road. They look beyond the next hill or around the next curve, imagining, often predicting, what waits ahead. The speed at which leaders engage in the journey depends on the extent to which external forces are tailgating the organization and the internal culture of the college, which acts as a gyroscope, keeping the environment stable as the institution moves forward.

Entrepreneurial college leaders have learned to rely on intuition and may, on occasion, foretell their colleges' fortunes. No longer eclipsed by the shadow of declining funds, these colleges have charted their own courses and mapped out directions that move them away from reliance on state funding and toward the pursuit of entrepreneurial endeavors. The 11 colleges profiled in this book have identified strategies to navigate the uncertainty of state support successfully. Findings demonstrate that these entrepreneurial leaders have proven that institutions do not need to be dependent solely on allocations from the traditional state revenue streams. Rather they have proven that entrepreneurial activities can enhance and expand programs and services and can generate sufficient revenues to move the mission of the institution forward.

THE STATUS OF ENTREPRENEURSHIP AT COMMUNITY COLLEGES

There is no magic size or geographic location that guarantees entrepreneurial status. The colleges featured here are located across the United States and Canada. Some colleges are small, serving mostly rural communities; others are located in heavily populated urban cities with populations of 1 million or more. In fact, these colleges are a microcosm of the community college system: Four are located in small residential and rural areas with populations ranging from 26,000 to 56,000; half located in large, metropolitan areas that serve both urban and rural areas with populations ranging from 140,000 to 400,000; and the remaining are located in large urban settings where the population exceeds 1 million. Enrollment mirrors the population and ranges from 6,700 credit enrollment annually at the smallest college to approximately 65,000 at some of the larger, multicampus colleges. We found that most colleges have a significant enrollment in noncredit, continuing education courses, a major factor resulting in the formation of numerous partnerships with business and industry.

Data suggest that entrepreneurial college presidents can be relatively new to this organizational arena or they are veteran, long-term leaders. Among the leaders represented in this book, three presidents have served in this capacity at their present college for 7 to 8 years, three for 13 to 14 years, four for 19 to 26 years, and one for 42 years. We also found that it makes little difference whether the board of trustees is elected or appointed. In our sample, four colleges have elected boards, whereas the remaining have appointed boards. We found modest variance in the role that the board plays in collegewide entrepreneurial activities. All boards were involved actively in building a culture of entrepreneurship. In all cases, the success of a college was dependent, to a large extent, on the vision, support, and participation of the board.

When considering the major challenges or roadblocks to becoming an entrepreneurial college, we found consistent themes throughout the stories told in these chapters. The most obvious challenges were declining state support, increased enrollment, increased need for new training (especially to meet job requirements for the knowledge worker), and inadequate or deteriorating facilities. Other challenges included steady growth in the region, globalization, and accountability issues.

In our analysis of entrepreneurial community colleges, we have determined that the most common roadblocks to becoming entrepreneurial include the following:

- Ineffective organizational structures
- Perceptions that colleges use tax dollars to build facilities to provide services that will compete with those provided by local vendors
- Ideas that partnerships with universities lead students toward community colleges and away from universities
- Imminent mass retirements of faculty and administrators
- Insufficient staff to pursue additional initiatives or a workforce that is too over-burdened with work to take on new projects
- Territorialism
- Parochial boards that restrain entrepreneurial initiatives
- Difficulties securing new funding after poor performance on grant activities, directives, or outcome measures

Most community colleges, whether entrepreneurial or not, have experienced success-ful partnerships with business and industry. In fact, most of the entrepreneurial activities highlighted in this book relate in one way or another to partnerships or strategic alliances. Reviewing the chapters to compile a comprehensive list of business and industry's expressed and anticipated needs, we learned that they want flexible programming and quick turn-around, services and programs that meet their needs, accessible locations, training centers designed as professional conference centers, training provided by qualified faculty and staff, state-of-the-art technology for training, competent graduates, involvement in developing cur-ricula, and ongoing communication and collaboration with the college. The contributors to this book offer numerous strategies for approaching and defining entrepreneurship and describe key ingredients for success.

ENTREPRENEURIAL STRATEGIES, COMPONENTS, AND KEY INGREDIENTS FOR SUCCESS

An entrepreneurial college succeeds when innovative leadership and strategies merge. The entrepreneurial leader is charged with identifying strategies that have the potential to generate additional revenues or reduce current expenditures. However, the leader must ensure that new initiatives align with the mission of the institution and support the learning environment.

The entrepreneurial leader is adept at shaping and molding the environment by iden-tifying opportunities, taking risks, and navigating the institution to new destinations, and by capitalizing on resources, forming successful partnerships, and inspiring others to stretch their imaginations. Presidents in entrepreneurial organizations act more like facilitators than managers. They are comfortable delegating authority and allowing others to receive recognition for successes. They have the instinct to bring constituents together to champion a common cause and demonstrate courage in the face of change.

Throughout the chapters in this book, entrepreneurial presidents and chancellors described their strategies. Drawing on their contributions, we summarize best practices for entrepreneurial leaders in Table 13.1. These strategies offer realistic solutions to addressing declining state support and meeting other serious challenges currently facing community colleges. Implementing these strategies has helped fund new buildings, equipment, and technology. Additionally, entrepreneurial strategies contribute to the expansion of program offerings and services to business, industry, and the community. In Table 13.2, we divide successful entrepreneurial strategies into four categories: strategic alliances, foundations, competitive advantage, and approach.

Table 13.1	Strategies for Entrepreneurial Community College Leaders

- Act as visible role model and mentor.
- Focus on productivity, accountability, and efficiency.
- Formulate a common vision for the future directions of the college.
- Communicate and collaborate effectively and attend to employees' suggestions.
- Maintain long-term focus to sustain entrepreneurial activity.
- Engage in hard work, sacrifice, and risk taking.
- Move quickly to assess new trends and courses of action.
- Be responsible for facilitating and motivating faculty and staff to be entrepreneurial.
- Cultivate a culture that is supportive of autonomy and risk taking.
- Develop trust among constituents.
- View challenges as opportunities.
- Make bold decisions.
- Think outside the traditional box.
- Periodically reorganize managerial and operational structures to capitalize on talents.
- Assign new projects to people who can see them through to completion.
- Develop clear job descriptions and evaluation processes.
- Hire people who are committed to their work.
- Give recognition and funding to those who try new things.
- Discourage a run-of-the-mill caretaker mentality.
- Adopt an institutional philosophy that fundraising is everyone's responsibility.
- Intertwine innovation and invention with how well a college leverages its resources, both human and financial.
- Place decision making at the most appropriate level within the organization—close to point of implementation.
- Place the research and development officer's position among the highest administrative levels.
- Commit a significant amount of time to fundraising.

Table 13.1	Strategies for Entrepreneurial Community College Leaders (cont'd)

- Visit prospects even when not seeking a contribution.
- Know what is happening in the community by being an active part of that environment.
- Lead fundraising activities.
- Establish a public presence to connect or reconnect the college with the community.
- Keep the entrepreneurial momentum going by identifying and implementing ways to encourage everyone to stay involved.

Table 13.2	Crucial Components of Successful Entrepreneurial Strategies

Strategic Alliances

Strategic alliances represent partnerships among colleges and business and industry, communities, state, and other government agencies. Colleges should

- Ascertain what the gain is for the potential partner
- Work with business and industry leaders in lobbying the legislature for funds
- Create industry alliances to meet the needs of employers and students and fill the present knowledge void
- Seek ways to share resources
- Seek advice related to programs and services from business and industry
- Choose to partner with companies that help advance the mission of the college

Foundations

Foundations are the fundraising arms of the institution. They are instrumental in generating revenue through a variety of entrepreneurial strategies. A foundation should

- Have a board consisting of successful businesspeople who understand economic forces
- Ensure the longevity of its chair for continuity
- Participate in annual retreats
- Make money rather than raise money
- Take the lead in raising capital funds
- Prove a valuable link to business and industry, the community, and the state
- Share the president's entrepreneurial vision

Competitive Advantage

Competitive advantages hinge on the philosophy, methodology, and the approach taken to enhancing and expanding a college's entrepreneurial pursuits. A college has a competitive advantage when

- Its programs and services are run like successful businesses
- Business tools that build on its unique advantages and positions within its market are adopted and adapted

Table 13.2	Crucial Components of Successful Entrepreneurial Strategies (cont'd)

- A strategic combination of its existing assets and new external initiatives provide greater leverage
- It is aware of future opportunities before they present themselves
- Assessment of its existing resource base is complete
- Its president belongs to organizations whose members are good funding prospects
- It gets to know other foundations in the community
- Its personnel expand publicity efforts

Approach

To be entrepreneurial the college must

- Focus on the idea, not the money—money can always be found
- Create a formal group that meets to brainstorm about entrepreneurial activities
- Establish an endowed fund to provide a steady flow of revenue
- Ensure long-term relationships with former students

Although an overview of entrepreneurial strategies and components presents an accurate introduction to entrepreneurship and a useful blueprint with which to begin, there are also unique characteristics that are key to ensuring the success of an entrepreneurial college. Drawing on the cumulative wisdom of the contributors, we summarize the key ingredients for identifying, building, and sustaining an entrepreneurial college in Table 13.3.

Table 13.3	Table 13.3 The Entrepreneurial College: Key Ingredients for Success

Human Resources

- Build a strong executive team.
- Select leaders who are most qualified—not just academically prepared.
- Provide stability and a collective focus on entrepreneurship via the continuity of leadership.
- Hire insiders who bring credibility to business relationships.
- Give employees the authority to make key entrepreneurial decisions.
- Understand that the passion and commitment of a few can inspire others to support worthwhile projects.
- Provide an excellent resource development office.
- Focus on generating ideas, not money.

Organization

- Think and operate like a for-profit business.
- Offer programs and services whenever and wherever needed.
- Identify, develop, and specialize in programs not offered anywhere else.

Table 13.3   Table 13.3 The Entrepreneurial College: Key Ingredients for Success (cont'd)

- Use competitive pricing for services.
- Replace fear-based management with risk taking and a supportive environment.
- Build on small successes—a great way to ensure trust and faith in leadership.

Politics

It is helpful if the legislature establishes a matching program for funding new initiatives. Entrepreneurial college presidents lobby legislators and encourage business partners to use their influence to encourage such programs at the state level.

Foundation and Governing Board

The foundation and the board of directors should

- Consist of a dynamic combination of innovative and entrepreneurial leaders
- Not only allow but encourage entrepreneurial activity
- Be active participants in fundraising activities
- Empower the president to make decisions for the college

Relationships

Vital relationships between college leaders and politicians, and business and community leaders

- Offer opportunities to build on college strengths
- Build credibility among partners and serve as the foundation on which additional ventures may be explored
- Focus on the expectations of both sides of the partnership, ensuring mutual benefits rather than a zero sum win
- Play key roles in developing entrepreneurial enterprises with curriculum advisory committees
- Bring the world to the college and the college to the world

Entrepreneurial Vision

Every member of the college community can share in the entrepreneurial vision that ensures success. The entrepreneur

- Invents, develops, and delivers learning solutions for the 21st century
- Knows the past and charts the future
- Links entrepreneurial initiatives to mission—always
- Finds a just cause and creates an environment in which investors will materialize
- Embeds long-standing values into the culture of the institution
- Takes risks
- Is flexible
- Is patient
- Dreams big

CONCLUSION

There are many examples of entrepreneurial leaders and colleges throughout the United States. The 11 featured here represent the images and the voices of a new kind of community college. With agility and precise timing, these entrepreneurial presidents have maneuvered the forces of change successfully, working with their boards, communities, businesses and industries, faculty, staff, and students to transform their institutions.

The rise of the community college entrepreneur represents a new wave in the community college system. And the entrepreneurial college—truly an American invention—represents a new journey, an uncharted path that will lead to new discoveries, helping reshape colleges into self-sustaining, ever-evolving enterprises.

T. S. Eliot (1943) observed, "We shall not cease from exploration and the end of all our exploring will be to arrive where we started and know that place for the first time." The community college began with the vision of entrepreneurial leaders. It was shaped and formed through the creativity and innovation of its leaders to meet the unique challenges of the 1960s generation and beyond. It is an American icon, a constant in ensuring an affordable and accessible education for all citizens. In rediscovering its uniqueness and potential, it is recognizing itself for the first time, after a long and tiring journey. An entrepreneurial spirit lives in the minds and hearts of every community college, and the energy it sustains can play out and live well in missions accomplished and lives enriched.

REFERENCES

Eliot, T. S. (1943). *Four quartets: Quartet no. 4: Little gidding.* Available from
    http://www.americanpoems.com/poets/tseliot/7069

About the Contributors

George R. Boggs is president and CEO of the American Association of Community Colleges (AACC) based in Washington, DC. AACC represents more than 1,100 associate degree–granting institutions and more than 11 million students. Boggs previously served as faculty member, division chair, and associate dean of instruction at Butte College in California, and for 15 years he served as the superintendent/president of Palomar College in California. He served as a member of the Committee on Undergraduate Science Education of the National Research Council and has served on several National Science Foundation panels and committees. He holds a bachelor's degree in chemistry from Ohio State University, a master's degree in chemistry from the University of California at Santa Barbara, and a PhD in educational administration from The University of Texas at Austin.

Donald W. Cameron was appointed interim president of Guilford Technical Community College (GTCC) in Jamestown, North Carolina, in August 1990 and was appointed president in February 1991. Before that, he served as executive vice president of GTCC from 1981 to 1990. Cameron began his career in education as a high school teacher and coach in Robbins, North Carolina. He has served in various faculty and administrative positions in both universities and community colleges during his 30-year career in higher education. Cameron is actively involved in numerous civic activities and has been recognized with awards including the following: Phi Theta Kappa Outstanding College President, Piedmont Triad Regional Leadership Star, the Greensboro Area Chamber of Commerce's Calvin Wiley Award for Excellence in Public School Teaching and Administration, and North Carolina State Board of Community Colleges President of the Year. Cameron holds an AA, bachelor's, and master's degree and a doctorate in education. He completed postgraduate work at Harvard University in educational management for college and university administrators.

David E. Daniel is the third president of Midland College, since 1991. Prior to Midland, he served as executive director of the Pennsylvania Commission on Community Colleges and the Pennsylvania Federation of Community College Trustees. Daniel's first involvement with community colleges was as a sociology instructor. He served as administrative vice president of Louisburg College, as dean of instruction at Isothermal Community College in Spindale, and for 12 years as president of Wilkes Community College in Wilkesboro—all in North Carolina. Daniel was chair of the board of the American Association of Community Colleges 1991–1992 and a board member 1988–1993. He is current president of the Texas Association of Community Colleges. He has served as chair of a Texas statewide committee on workforce training, as a member of the College Commission of the Southern Association of Colleges and Schools, and as a member of the Texas Council of Workforce and Economic Competitiveness 1996–1999. He is a past president of the North Carolina Association of Public Community College Presidents, North Carolina Association of Colleges and

Universities, and the Southern Association of Community and Junior Colleges. He also currently serves on several boards in the Midland community. Daniel is listed in *Who's Who in American Colleges and Universities,* was awarded a Fulbright to China, and was named Fundraiser of the Year (2001) by the Association of Fundraising Professionals. He has authored and coauthored numerous publications about the role of the community college. Daniel received a BA degree from Furman University (Greenville, SC), an MDiv degree from Colgate-Rochester Divinity Schools (NY), and an EdD in community college education from North Carolina State University.

Suzanne L. Flannigan is currently a PhD candidate in the Community College Leadership Program at The University of Texas at Austin. She has 15 years' experience in the community college system, having been a tenured faculty member and a chair of marketing, general management, and public administration. She is an Achieving the Dream research associate and an Edmund Gleazer Scholar. Flannigan has coauthored a chapter in *Leadership Dialogues*, has written numerous articles related to higher education, and has presented at regional national conferences.

Robert A. (Squee) Gordon has been president of Humber College Institute of Technology and Advanced Learning (Toronto) since 1982; prior to that he was president of Dawson College in Montreal. Over his long career, Gordon has held leadership positions in many community groups and national and international organizations, including president of the Association of Canadian Community Colleges; member of the Premier's Council of Ontario, City of Toronto Economic Development Committee; president of the League for Innovation in the Community College; and chair of the Scientific Advisory Panel, the Ontario Technology Fund. He was elected chair of the Committee of Presidents in Ontario for several terms and, since 2001, is the president and chair of the Board of Canada Basketball and a trustee of the Corporation of Bishop's University in Quebec. Gordon holds an honors BA in history, a master's degree in modern British history (Bishop's University), a master's degree in educational administration (University of Massachusetts), a master's degree in public administration (Harvard University), and a doctorate in educational administration (University of Massachusetts).

Thomas G. Greene is a PhD candidate in the Community College Leadership Program at The University of Texas (UT) at Austin. Recognized as a David Bruton, Jr., and University Fellow, he transitioned to UT after 8 years in community college administration, counseling, and instruction. He has coauthored a chapter in *Leadership Dialogues*, written articles on a variety of subjects related to higher education, and presented at national conferences.

Barbara R. Jones is a PhD candidate in the Community College Leadership Program at The University of Texas (UT) at Austin. Recognized as a Senior Roueche Fellow and Edmund Gleazer Scholar, she transitioned to UT after 19 years' administrative experience in the Dallas County Community College District, where she served as assistant to the president at Mountain View College, dean of planning and research for institutional effectiveness, and dean of evening and weekend college. She has coauthored a chapter in *Leadership Dialogues*, written numerous articles related to higher education, and presented at regional and national conferences.

Carl M. Kuttler, Jr., has been president of St. Petersburg College (SPC), formerly St. Petersburg Junior College, since 1978. He is a graduate of St. Petersburg Junior College, Florida State University, and Stetson University College of Law. In 1998, he was named the outstanding community college president in the nation by the National Association of Community College Trustees. In 2003, he was named the outstanding college president in Florida by the Florida Association of Community Colleges. He is a member of the Florida Community Colleges' Hall of Fame. In 1995, he was named the Father of the Community College in Russia after helping establish a postsecondary education system. In May 2004, the Russian Prime Minister named him Honorary Consul to the Russian Federation. In 2001, he led SPC into a new era as a 4-year school offering baccalaureates, the first former community college in Florida to be given such a privilege.

E. Ann McGee has been president of Seminole Community College (SCC), located just north of Orlando, since 1996. SCC enrolls approximately 35,000 students annually in programs that range from adult basic education to workforce education to transfer studies. McGee is a graduate of St. Petersburg Junior College (SPCJ), Florida State University (FSU), and Nova Southeastern University, and she has attended the Air War College. She was named most outstanding graduate at SPJC and was inducted into Phi Beta Kappa at FSU and into the Practitioner's Hall of Fame at Nova. She currently serves as a charter trustee for FSU and is on various local, regional, and national boards. Recently, she was honored by the Seminole Chamber of Commerce with a lifetime achievement award for making a difference in the quality of life in Seminole County. McGee's most coveted award is the 2005 Shirley B. Gordon Award bestowed by Phi Theta Kappa.

David H. McGilvray's first career was as an armor officer in the U.S. Army, serving in numerous command and staff positions in combat arms units, community management, and the inspector general's office. He was deputy commander of the army's technical education institution in Europe and on the faculty at the Command and General Staff College. After the army, McGilvray worked as a program director for 5 years in the San Antonio Metropolitan Health District. After leaving public health, he pursued a community college career full time, beginning as a continuing education instructor. He has taught developmental, technical, and transfer courses as well as serving as a curriculum specialist, education specialist, and director of continuing education. McGilvray has worked at San Antonio College, Northwest Vista, and Palo Alto colleges in San Antonio and at Austin Community College. He received a bachelor's degree in psychology from Texas A&M University in 1970 and master's degree in management from Webster University in 1991. He graduated from the Community College Leadership Program at the University of Texas at Austin in 2004.

Norm Nielsen joined Kirkwood Community College in 1979 as a vice president and served as president from 1985 until retiring on January 1, 2005. Prior to 1979, Nielsen was a teacher, coach, principal, and superintendent of schools in the Iowa public school system. He is a past president of the League for Innovation in the Community College. In 1995 he was awarded Iowa State University's (ISU) Laureate Award for prestigious service, educational leadership, and personal commitment to the teaching profession. ISU also awarded Nielsen the Distinguished Achievement Citation, the highest honor given to alumni through the ISU

Alumni Foundation. The Association of Community College Trustees (ACCT) named Nielsen the Central Region Chief Executive Officer of the Year for 2001 and the Marie Y. Martin Chief Executive Officer for 2001. ACCT also recognized Nielsen for his role as a leader and catalyst in developing public/private partnerships and growing the level and scope of Kirkwood's influence in local, national, and international services. Nielsen serves on several community, state, and national boards. He has worked directly with boards of education at both the K–12 and community college level for the past 30 years. He received advanced degrees from ISU and The University of Iowa.

John Pickelman is chancellor of the North Harris Montgomery Community College District (NHMCCD), a position he has held since March 1, 1991 following a 7-year tenure as president of Galveston College. Pickelman also serves as adjunct professor in the Community College Leadership Program at The University of Texas at Austin. He is a past president of the Association of Texas Colleges and Universities and serves as president of the Texas Association of Community Colleges. He also served as vice chairman of the Commission on Colleges for Southern Association of Colleges and Schools. Pickelman earned a BA in English from Albion College (MI), an MA in education (counseling) from the University of Missouri in Kansas City, and a PhD in educational administration (Community College Leadership Program) from The University of Texas at Austin.

John E. Roueche is the Sid W. Richardson Regents chair and professor and director of the Community College Leadership Program at The University of Texas at Austin. Author of 34 books and more than 150 articles and monographs on educational leadership and teaching effectiveness, Roueche has spoken to more than 1,300 colleges and universities since 1970. He received the 1986 National Leadership Award from the American Association of Community Colleges and the 1999 Career Research Excellence Award from The University of Texas at Austin.

Andrew M. Scibelli, president emeritus of Springfield Technical Community College (STCC), retired in 2004 after 21 years as president. He is a member of the boards of numerous organizations: the Presidents Advisory Council of the National Coalition of Advanced Technology Centers (past chair), the Presidents Council of the Council for Occupational and Research Development, the Community College Research Center, the American Association of Community Colleges, the Massachusetts Telecommunications Council, Mass Ventures, the Economic Development Council, and the Springfield Chamber of Commerce. He also serves as chair of the Statewide Collective Bargaining Negotiating Team for the Massachusetts Community Colleges, vice president of the Regional Employment Board, trustee of the Pioneer Valley Planning Commission, and secretary of the STCC Assistance Corporation. Scibelli is an adjunct professor at the University of Massachusetts and a presenter at many national conferences. Since retiring he has been serving as the interim president at MassBay Community College in Wellesley (MA) and has established a consulting firm specializing in entrepreneurship at community colleges. Most recently he has become president and CEO of Community College Presidential Search Associates, LLC. Scibelli has received numerous professional and community service awards, including the Massachusetts Merit

Award, Entrepreneur of the Year, National Pacesetter of the Year, Workforce Development Leader of the Year, the 1998 Leadership in Workforce Development Award, the Community Builder Award, the Omar T. Pace M.D. Award, the Christopher Cote Award, Distinguished Citizen of the Year Award, and Junior Achievement's Laureate Award in recognition of his outstanding leadership in business and education. Scibelli has a BA from St. Anselm College, an MEd from Boston State College, and an EdD from the University of Massachusetts Amherst.

Michael D. Summers, vice president for Academic and Student Affairs, joined Tidewater Community College in October of 2004 after serving as vice president for Education and Student Affairs at Greenville Technical College in South Carolina from 2000 to 2004. Prior to moving to South Carolina, he worked for several community colleges in Illinois in a variety of faculty and administrative positions from 1981 to 2000. Summers earned a BS in occupational education from the University of Illinois in 1981, an MS in educational administration from Western Illinois University in 1988, and an EdD in community college leadership from the University of Illinois in 2000.

Millicent Valek has been president of Brazosport College (BC) since 1996. During her tenure, BC has garnered the support of the community for a major facility expansion as well as the legislative authority to offer one of the first bachelor's degrees at a Texas community college. Valek began her community college career at Austin Community College, where she served first as an adjunct instructor and then as the director for faculty development. She left Austin to become the chief academic officer for Arizona Western College, where she served as vice president for 8 years prior to being named president of BC. Valek holds a bachelor's degree from the University of Texas, a master's degree from Southwest Texas State University, and a PhD from The University of Texas at Austin Community College Leadership Program.

Steven R. Wallace became the fourth president of Florida Community College Jacksonville (FCCJ) in 1997, having already served as president of Austin Community College (1990–1992) and Inver Hills Community College (1992–1997). Wallace's career spans 25 years. He began at Chaffey Community College, his alma mater, as an adjunct, then full-time, faculty member. In 1977, he became Chaffey's district director of learning disabilities, and 2 years later he served as director of marketing and legislative affairs for the 20,000-student college. In 1981, Wallace became vice president for administrative services at Lakeland Community College in Ohio, a position he held for 9 years. Since arriving at FCCJ, Wallace has been actively involved in the community, serving on numerous local boards such as the Jacksonville Regional Chamber of Commerce, United Way, Alliance for World Class Education, Communities in Schools, First Coast YMCA, Enterprise North Florida, WorkSource, Jacksonville Symphony Association, Take Stock in Children Leadership Council, WJCT Public Broadcasting, and Schultz Center for Teaching & Leadership. His statewide leadership roles include past chair of the Community College Council of Presidents and appointments to the boards of the North Florida Technology Alliance, Florida Distance Learning Consortium, the Florida Virtual Campus, and the Business & Higher Education Partnership of the Florida Council of 100. He was vice chair of the Community College

Baccalaureate Association and a member of Leadership Florida's Class 18 (2000) and the Leadership Jacksonville Class of 1999. Wallace earned an AA degree in 1972 from Chaffey, followed by bachelor's and master's degrees in psychology from California State University at San Bernardino. He received a doctorate in higher education administration in 1989 from Claremont Graduate University in California.

Accelerated Career Education (ACE) program (Iowa), **84–85**

accountability, **119–120**

ADVANCE (Kirkwood Community College), **87**

Advanced Technology Center (Midland College), **103–104**

AEGON Corporate Data Center, **83**

AEGON USA, **4, 83, 90–91**

AgrowKnowledge, **82**

Allen, Steve, **75**

Allstate Center (St. Petersburg College), **42–44**

Allstate Insurance Company, **42–43**

American Association of Community Colleges, **ix**

American Culinary Federation, **54**

Andrew M. Scibelli Enterprise Center (Springfield Technical Community College), **109**

annexation, **27–28**

Association of Universities and Colleges of Canada, **77**

athletics programs, **54–57**

Aykroyd, Dan, **75**

Ballantyne, Selby A., **81–82, 91**

Ballet Folklorico de Mexico, **105**

Barton, Thomas, Jr., **5, 7, 58–59, 117–121**

Beatts, Anne, **75**

Belleville, Ryan, **76**

Bennis, Warren, **7**

Bensen, Cliff, **99**

Berry, Rick, **28**

Best Educational E-Practices (BEEP), **45**

board of directors, **141**

Branson, Richard, **6**

Brazosport College (BC)
background of, **xiii, 125–126**
Center for Business/Industry Training at, **4, 126, 130–132**
environmental factors affecting, **127**
4-year college partnerships at, **128–130**
fundraising at, **132–133**
leadership direction in, **127–128, 133**

Breslin, Mark, **75, 76**

Brin, Sergey, **1**

British Columbia Open University (BCOU), **77–78**

Brown. Jack E., **107**

Burns, Ken, **105**

Bush, George W., **4, ix–x**

Bush, Jeb, **49**

Business Incubator (Springfield Technical Community College), **115**

Cameron, Donald W., **xii, 7**

Canadian Broadcasting Corporation, **76**

Career Edge Academy programs (Iowa), **85**

Carrey, Jim, **75**

Cedar Rapids/Iowa City Technology Corridor committee, **85**

Center for Building Construction (Seminole Community College), **95–96**

Center for Business and Technology (Springfield Technical Community College), **109, 114**

Center for Business/Industry Training (Brazosport College), **4, 126, 130–132**

Center for Digital Education (Florida

Community College at Jacksonville), 14

Center for Employee Benefits (Humber College Institute of Technology and Advanced Learning), 72–75

Centers for Disease Control and Prevention, 89

Central Florida Auto Dealers Association (CFADA), 96–97

Certificate of Proficiency in Employee Benefits (CEB), 73–75

Chase, Chevy, 75

China, 71–72

Cingular Wireless Company, 104

Cisco Systems, 109

City of Houston Airport System, 29

City of Midland, 103

Clemson University, 118, 122

Cogdell, Bill, 105–106

Cogdell Learning Center (Midland College), 103, 105–106

Comedy College (Humber College), 4, 75–76

Comedy Network, 76

Commission on Colleges of the Southern Association of Colleges and Schools, 118

Community colleges. *See also* Entrepreneurial community colleges; *specific community colleges*

challenges facing, ix–xi

competitive advantages for, 139–140

facility upgrades for, 132–133

4-year degree programs and, 128–130

funding cuts to, 2–3

future outlook for, 8–10, 135–136

status of entrepreneurship at, 136–137

transformation of, xi–xiv, 1–2, 8–9

Community Training and Response Center (Kirkwood Community College), 89

Compaq, 29

competitive advantages, 139–140

construction industry, 95

Cowan, Phyllis, 105

Cowan, Robert, 105

Creative Artists Agency, 76

Culinary technology program, at Guilford Technical Community College, xii, 52–54

Cy-Fair College, xii, 32–35

Cy-Fair Volunteer Fire Department, 33

Cypress-Fairbanks (Cy-Fair) Independent School District, 27–28

DaimlerChrysler, 76–79

Daniel, David E., xiii, 5

Davidson Distinguished Lecture Series (Midland College), 105

De Pree, Max, 25–26

Delco, Wilhelmina, 5

Deliso Videoconferencing Center (Springfield Technical Community College), 114

distance learning

at Humber College Institute of Technology and Advanced Learning, 77

in St. Petersburg College, 44–46

The Dorothy and Todd Aaron Medical Science Building (Midland College), 106

Dow, Alden B., 126

Dow, H. H., 126

Dow Chemical Company, xiii, 126

Drucker, Peter, x, 7, 38

Drug Free Kids (Allstate Center), 43

Duke Power, 53

e-spirit (St. Petersburg College), xii, 38–40, 49

East Central Iowa Regional Fire Service Training Center, 89

East Montgomery County Improvement District (Texas), 29

Edna, Dame, 75

Eliot, T. S., 142

Entrepreneur for a Day (Springfield Technical Community College), 115

Entrepreneurial community colleges. *See also* Community colleges; *specific community colleges*

  approaches for, 140

  business and industry training in, 4

  community relations and, 110, 141

  competitive advantages for, 139–140

  culture in, 67–68, 121

  explanation of, xi, 3

  foundations and, 5, 139, 141

  fundraising and, 5, 94, 97–98, 100, 119

  future outlook for, 8–10, 135–136

  human resources for, 140

  implications and opportunities for, 38–39, 107

  legislative lobbying and, 5–6, 141

  organization of, 140–141

  outsourcing and, 5

  programming and, 4

  risk taking in, 120, 125, 133

  strategic alliances and, 4, 139

  strategies for successful, 137–141

  vision for, 141

Entrepreneurial Institute (Springfield Technical Community College), 109–110

entrepreneurial leaders

  characteristics of, 6–7

  goals of, 7–8

  strategies for, 138–139, 142

entrepreneurship

  changes driving, 2–3

  definitions and descriptions of, 3, 37–38, 68

  innovation and, 13, 22

  move toward, 2

entrepreneurship associate degree (Springfield Technical Community College), 115

entrepreneurship education, 115–116

Entrepreneurship Honors Colloquium (Springfield Technical Community College), 115–116

Environmental Training Center (ETC) (Kirkwood Community College), 88

EpiCenter (St. Petersburg College), 48–49

Equestrian Center (Kirkwood Community College), 82

Excellence in Youth Entrepreneurship (Springfield Technical Community College), 115

fitness centers, 55

Flaherty, Joe, 75

Florida Community College at Jacksonville (FCCJ), 2

  background of, xi, 13–14

  business development via institute model at, 18–22

  Navy alliance at, 16–18

  programming philosophy at, 4

  Xerox alliance at, 14–16

Florida Community Colleges Council of Presidents, 48

Florida Department of Community Affairs, 43

Florida International University, 47

Florida Progress Corporation, 43

Ford Motor Company, 109

foundations, 5, 139, 141

friend raising. *See also* Fundraising

  examples of, 101–103

  explanation of, 5

Frohman, Lorne, 75

fundraising

  methods for, 5, 101–103

  role of presidents in, 100, 119

  training in, 99

Furman University, 122

George Washington Carver High School, 29

Gleazer, Edmund, **xi**

Google, 1

Gordon, Robert A., **xii**, 4

Grazer, Brian, 76

Greenville Higher Education Center, **122**

Greenville Tech Foundation (GTF), **118**, 122–123

Greenville Technical Center, 117

Greenville Technical College (GTC)
  background of, **xiii**, 117–119
  institutional culture at, 121
  job training at, 58–59
  leadership at, 119–121, 124
  McAlister Square project at, 121–123
  University Center at, 5, 121–122

Grow Iowa Values Fund, 85–86

Guilford County, North Carolina, 51–52, 57–58

Guilford County Industrial Education Center, 51

Guilford Technical Community College (GTCC), 7
  background of, **xii**, 51–52, 57
  commercial food service program in, 52–54
  encouragement of entrepreneurial leadership in, 52, 60–61
  job training by, 57–60
  YMCA program at, 54–57

Guilford Technical Institute, 51, 57

Hall-Perrine Foundation, 87

Hamlisch, Marvin, **105**

Harris County Public Library, **xii**, 32

Harvey, Barron, 6

Hash, Bruce, **103**

Hazardous Materials Training and Research Institute (HMTRI), 88–89

Hollings, Ernest F., 117

homeport training, 17–18

Houston Advanced Research Center (HARC), **31–32**

Houston Area Research Center, **30**

Howard, Frank, 7, **119**

Howard, Ron, 76

Humber College Institute of Technology and Advanced Learning, 3
  background of, **xii**, 63–64
  Board of Governors of, 66
  Center for Employee Benefits at, 72–75
  Comedy College at, 4, 75–76
  DaimlerChrysler partnership and, 76–79
  entrepreneurship model for, 68–69, 79
  government policy affecting, 65–66
  international ventures of, 70–72
  labor and economic forces affecting, 64
  leadership continuity at, 66–68
  population shifts affecting, 65
  risk taking at, 69–70

Humble Independent School District (Texas), 29

Industrial Education Center (IEC) (Guilford County), 57

Institute model, at Florida Community College at Jacksonville, **19–22**

Intel Corporation, **109**

Internal Revenue Code, 5

international students, 72

international ventures, 70–72

Iowa Division of Emergency Management, 89

The Jack E. Brown Dining Hall (Midland College), **107**

Johnson, R. A., **x**

Kirkwood Community College, 8
  background of, **xii**, 81–82
  entrepreneurial approach of, **82–83**
  funding for, **84**

initiatives to meet workplace needs by, 84–87

leadership at, 83–84

National Mass Fatalities Institute at, **xii**, 88–90

Resource Center at, 87–88

Training and Outreach Services Center at, 4, 90–91

Kordestani, Omid, **1**

Kuratko, D. F., **39**

Kuttler, Carl M., Jr., **xii**

Lander University, **122**

Larry Gatlin School of Music (Guilford Technical and Community College), **xii**

leaders. *See* Entrepreneurial leaders

League for Innovation in the Community College, **64, 82**

legislative lobbying, 5–6, 141

Leno, Jay, **75**

Levin, Jonathan, **76**

Levy, Eugene, **75**

Linn County Emergency Management Agency, **89**

locus of control, **120**

Louisburg College, **99**

MacDougall, Levi, **76**

Martinez, Bob, **43**

McAlister Limited Liability Corporation (LLC), 122–123

McAlister Square project (Greenville Technical Community College), 121–123

McCullough, David, **105**

McGee, E. Ann, **xii, 7, 48**

McGilvray, David H., **xiii**

McLeod USA, **85**

Medical University of South Carolina, **122**

Merle Watson Festival, **102**

Michaels, Lorne, 75–76

Microsoft Corporation, **109**

MiddleBiz (Springfield Technical Community College), **115**

Midland College

Advanced Technology Center at, **103, 104**

background of, **xiii,** 103–104

Cogdell Learning Center at, **103,** 105–106

friend raising at, **5**

relationships between area professionals and, 106–107

resource development at, **105, 106**

Midland Independent School District, **103**

Midland International Airport, **103**

Midland Police Department, **105**

Military Education Institute (Florida Community College at Jacksonville), **14,** 16–19

Mitchell, George, **28, 30**

Mochrie, Colin, **75**

Moranis, Rick, **75**

Moscow Boys Choir, **105**

Moyers, Bill, **105**

Myers, Mike, **75**

National Association for Community College Entrepreneurship (NACCE), **xiii, 110, 114, 116**

National Association of State Budget Officers, **x**

National Center for Telecommunications Technologies (Springfield Technical Community College), **109**

National Dialogue on Entrepreneurship, **38**

National Mass Fatalities Institute (NMFI) (Kirkwood Community College), **xii, 89**

National Science Foundation, **109**

National Terrorism Preparedness Institute (St. Petersburg College), **44**

Navy College Program Distance Learning Partnership, 17–18

New England Next Step program (Verizon), 109

Nielsen, Norm, xii, 8

Ningbo University, 71–72

Nissan, 29

Nordstrom, 25

North American Free Trade Agreement (NAFTA), 58

North Carolina Community College System, 51, 53–54

North Harris College Carver Center, 29

North Harris Montgomery Community College District (NHMCCD), 5
annexation by, 26–28
background of, xi–xii, 23–24
college-county library partnership in, 32–33
emergency services training center and community fire station partnership in, 33–34
leadership style of, 25, 35
opportunities and challenges for, 28–30
relationship building by, 25–26
services and training center in, 31–32
University Center in, 30–31

Occupational Safety and Health Administration, 88

O'Connor, Sandra Day, 105

O'Hara, Catherine, 75

Ontario Colleges Act of 1965, 65

Outsourcing, 5

Page, Larry, 1

Parnell, D., xiii

Payne, Nikki, 76

Peck, R. D., 8

Pell Grants, 58

Pension Fund Investment Certificate (PFIC), 74

Pension Plan Administration Certificate (PPAC), 74

Perkins Tech Prep federal funds, 85

Phyllis and Bob Cowan Performing Arts Series (Midland College), 105

physical education programs, 54–57

Pickelman, John, xi, 5

Piedmont Natural Gas, 53

Pinellas County, Florida, 37–38, 48

PMX, 89

politics, 5–6, 141

Preservation Hall Jazz Band, 105

presidents. See Entrepreneurial leaders

pricing strategies, 19–20

programming, 4

Project Eagle (St. Petersburg College), 45

Promise Jobs, 87

Pryor, Richard, 75

Quick Jobs With a Future (Guilford Technical Community College), xii, 59–60

Ramis, Harold, 76

Raspberry, William, 38

Reiner, Carl, 75

Reitman, Ivan, 75–76

Resource Center (Kirkwood Community College), 87–88

Rivers, Joan, 75

Rockwell Collins, 85

Roueche, John E., x

Rouse, Jason, 76

S. Prestley Blake Student Venture Center (Springfield Technical Community College), 116

Schumpeter, Joseph, 3

Scibelli, Andrew M., xiii, 2

Seminole Community College (SCC), 7, 48
background of, xii, 93
Central Florida Auto Dealers Association

project and, 96–97
  community connectivity at, 95–96
  construction trades facility at, 3
  fundraising efforts at, 94, 97–98
  leadership in, 94
Servicemembers Opportunity College
  program (Coast Guard), 18
Shapiro, George, 75
Sharron, Harvey, 99
Sheridan College, 65
Short, Martin, 75
Skills 2000 Report (Iowa), 84
Skills 2006 Technology Corridor Report
  (Iowa), 86
South Carolina Commission on Higher
  Education, 122
South Carolina State University, 122
Spalding, Carol, 17
Springfield Armory National Historic
  Site, 109
Springfield Enterprise Center (Springfield
  Technical Community College),
  114–116
Springfield Technical Community College
  Assistance Corporation (STCCAC), 112
Springfield Technical Community College
  (STCC)
  background of, xiii, 109–110
  entrepreneurship education at, 115–116
  leadership at, 2, 110–111, 116
  Springfield Enterprise Center at, 114–116
  Technology Park at, 109, 112–114
St. Luke's Hospital, 29
St. Petersburg College (SPC)
  Allstate Center at, 42–44
  background of, xii, 38, 47–48
  distance learning at, 44–46
  entrepreneurial spirit in, 38–40, 49
  EpiCenter at, 48–49
  objectives accomplished at, 41–42
  university partnership center at, 46–47

Stevenson, H. H., 49
Stewart, Bill F., 81
strategic alliances, 4, 139
Student Business Incubator (Springfield
  Technical Community College), 115
Students
  e-generation, 135
  international, 72
Summers, Michael D., xiii

Tarrant County Junior College, 28
Technology Park (Springfield Technical
  Community College), 109, 112–114
Texas A&M, 31
Texas State University System, 31
Texas Tech University (TTU), 106
Texas Workforce Commission grants, 131
Thomas, Dave, 75
Toffler, A., xiv
Tomball Regional Hospital, 29
Training and Outreach Services Center
  (KTOS) (Kirkwood Community
  College), 4, 90–91
Trustee Development Program (TDP), 74

U.S. Marine Corps, 18
Ullman, Jeff, 1
United Way, 87
University Center of Greenville, 122–123
University of Florida, 47
University of Houston, 128–129
University of North Carolina, 51
University of South Carolina, 122
University of South Carolina-Spartanburg, 122
University of South Florida, 47
University of Texas, 31
University Partnership Center (UPC) (St.
  Petersburg College), 46
The University Center (TUC) (North Harris
  Montgomery Community College
  District), 30–31

U.S. Army, **18**
U.S. Army National Guard, **18**
U.S. Coast Guard, **18**
U.S. Navy, **xi**, **14**, **16–18**
USLA Conference on Establishing Junior
    Colleges, **xi**

Valek, Millicent, **xiii**
Verizon, **109**

Wallace, Steven R., **xi**, **2**
Walter Reed Hospital, **47**
Watson, Arthel "Doc," **102**
wellness centers, **55–57**
Welsh, Jack, **14**
West Facility (Midland College), **103**
The Wildcatter's Club, **107**
Wilkes Community College (WCC),
    101–103

Will, Norm, **15–16**
Wingspread Group on Higher Education, **x**
Woodlands Corporation, **30**
The Woodlands, **28**, **30**
Workforce Investment Act, **58**, **87**
workforce training programs, **84–87**
Workplace Learning Connection (WLC), **87**
Wriston, Walter B., **25**

Xerox Corporation, **15–16**

Yahoo, **1**
YMCA, **55–57**
Young, C. W. Bill, **44**
Youth Entrepreneurship Scholars (Yes!)
    (Springfield Technical Community
    College), **115**